David P. Page, William H. Payne

Theory and Practice of Teaching

The motives and methods of good school-keeping

David P. Page, William H. Payne

Theory and Practice of Teaching

The motives and methods of good school-keeping

ISBN/EAN: 9783337825409

Printed in Europe, USA, Canada, Australia, Japan

Cover: Foto ©Paul-Georg Meister /pixelio.de

More available books at **www.hansebooks.com**

THEORY AND PRACTICE

OF

TEACHING

OR

THE MOTIVES AND METHODS

OF

GOOD SCHOOL-KEEPING

By DAVID P. PAGE, A.M.

FIRST PRINCIPAL OF THE STATE NORMAL SCHOOL, ALBANY, NEW YORK

TO WHICH IS PREFIXED

A BIOGRAPHICAL SKETCH OF THE AUTHOR

A NEW EDITION, EDITED AND ENLARGED

BY

W. H. PAYNE

PROFESSOR OF THE SCIENCE AND THE ART OF TEACHING IN THE UNIVERSITY OF MICHIGAN

NEW YORK ·:· CINCINNATI ·:· CHICAGO

AMERICAN BOOK COMPANY

AUTHOR'S PREFACE.

MANY a meritorious book has failed to find readers by reason of a toilsome preface. If the following volume meets a similar fate, whatever its merits, it shall lack a like excuse.

This work has had its origin in a desire to contribute something toward elevating an important and rising profession. Its matter comprises the substance of a part of the course of lectures addressed to the classes of the Institution under my charge, during the past two years. Those lectures, unwritten at first, were delivered in a familiar, colloquial style,—their main object being the inculcation of such practical views as would best promote the improvement of the teacher. In writing the matter out for the press, the same style, to a considerable extent, has been retained,—as I have written with an aim at usefulness rather than rhetorical effect.

If the term *theory* in the title suggests to any mind the bad sense sometimes conveyed by that word, I would simply say, that I have not been dealing in the speculative dreams of the closet, but in convictions derived from the realities of the school-room during some twenty years of actual service as a teacher. Theory may justly mean the *science* distinguished from the *art* of Teaching,—but as in practice these should never be divorced, so in the following chapters I have endeavored constantly to illustrate the one by the other.

If life should be spared and other circumstances should warrant the undertaking, perhaps a further course comprising the *Details of Teaching* may, at some future time, assume a similar form to complete my original design.

DAVID P. PAGE.

STATE NORMAL SCHOOL,
Albany, N. Y., Jan. 1, 1847.

EDITOR'S PREFACE.

NEARLY forty years have passed since Mr. Page wrote his *Theory and Practice of Teaching*, and within that period some marked changes have taken place in the state of educational thought and practice; and in undertaking the preparation of this new edition, my purpose has been, by making some additions to the text, to carry forward the main lines of thought, so that the book may be as useful to the coming generation of teachers as it has been to the past. Since its first appearance, the *Theory and Practice of Teaching* has held a unique place in our educational literature. Far more than any other book of its kind, it has set before the young teacher, in a clear and attractive manner, the problem of the school, and at the same time has enlisted the feelings as a motive power in attaining the ends thus pointed out. This treatment embodies the highest philosophy; for to know the end is almost to know the way, and to feel a strong impulse to reach the end, is finally to find the way.

My reverence for Mr. Page and his work has forbidden me to make the slightest change in the expression of his thought, and in this new edition the text is essentially untouched. In only a very few places have I made omissions of original matter. The Program of the Albany Normal School, and a few sentences in explanation of it, have been omitted, and a new list of books has been substituted for the one given on page 278 of the original edition. In every respect I have tried to treat this work as I would wish a successor to treat any piece of my own writing that may have survived my professional life.

W. H. PAYNE.

UNIVERSITY OF MICHIGAN,
July 1, 1885.

CONTENTS.

	PAGE
BIOGRAPHICAL SKETCH OF THE AUTHOR	11

CHAPTER I.
FITNESS FOR TEACHING........................... 19

CHAPTER II.
SPIRIT OF THE TEACHER.......................... 25

CHAPTER III.
RESPONSIBILITY OF THE TEACHER 30
    SECTION I.—A Neglected Tree................. 30
    SECTION II.—The Teacher is Responsible......... 35
    SECTION III.—The Auburn State Prison 54

CHAPTER IV.
PERSONAL HABITS OF THE TEACHER................. 60

CHAPTER V.
LITERARY QUALIFICATIONS OF THE TEACHER 71

CHAPTER VI.

RIGHT VIEWS OF EDUCATION 91

CHAPTER VII.

RIGHT MODES OF TEACHING 105
   SECTION I.—Pouring-in Process 107
   SECTION II.—Drawing-out Process 109
   SECTION III.—The more excellent Way 114
   SECTION IV.—Waking up Mind 117
   SECTION V.—Remarks 130

CHAPTER VIII.

CONDUCTING RECITATIONS 137

CHAPTER IX.

EXCITING INTEREST IN STUDY 154
   SECTION I.—Incentives...Emulation 155
   SECTION II.—Prizes 162
   SECTION III.—Proper Incentives 175

CHAPTER X.

SCHOOL GOVERNMENT 186
   SECTION I.—Requisites in the Teacher for Good Government 186
   SECTION II.—Means of Securing Good Order 197
   SECTION III.—Punishments 216
      I. Improper 219
      II. Proper 230

	PAGE
Section IV.—Corporal Punishment	235
Section V.—Limitations and Suggestions	249
Motives	259

CHAPTER XI.

School Arrangements	262
Section I.—Plan of the Day's Work	269
Program	273
Remarks	274
Section II.—Interruptions	279
Section III.—Recesses	283
Section IV.—Assignment of Lessons	286
Section V.—Reviews	288
Section VI.—Public Examinations..Exhibitions..Celebrations	290

CHAPTER XII.

The Teacher's Relation to the Parents of his Pupils	296

CHAPTER XIII.

Teacher's Care of his Health	304
Health..Exercise..Diet	305

CHAPTER XIV.

Teacher's Relation to his Profession	319
Section I.—Self-culture	325
Section II.—Mutual Aid	333

CHAPTER XV.

MISCELLANEOUS SUGGESTIONS. 344
    SECTION I.—Things to be Avoided............. 344
    SECTION II.—Things to be Performed........... 361

CHAPTER XVI.

THE REWARDS OF THE TEACHER.................... 388

CHAPTER XVII.

NOTES ON THE TEACHER'S AUTHORITY AND RIGHTS.... 405

INDEX....................................... 412

BIOGRAPHICAL SKETCH

OF

DAVID PERKINS PAGE.

Taken from Barnard's Journal of Education.

AMONG the self-educated teachers of our time, the men who, as was said of old, of poets, "were born, not made" teachers, and in whom the instinct for knowledge, and for imparting it to others, was sufficiently strong to overpower all obstacles and carry them to the highest eminence in their profession, there are none who have excelled the subject of this brief memoir.

DAVID PERKINS PAGE was born at Epping, New Hampshire, on the 4th of July, 1810. His father was a prosperous, though not an affluent farmer, and his early life was passed as a farmer's boy, with that scant dole of instruction which, forty years ago, fell to the lot of farmers' sons in small country villages in New Hampshire, or, for that matter, anywhere in New England. From his earliest years, however, the love of books was the master-passion of his soul, and in his childhood he plead often and earnestly with his father for the privilege of attending an academy in a neighboring town, but the father was inexorable; he had determined that David should succeed him in the management of the farm, and he did not consider an academical education necessary for this. His refusal doubtless exerted a good influence on his son; for a mind so active as his, if denied the advantages of the school, must find vent in some exercise, and the admirable illustrations he drew from nature, so often, to embellish and enforce his instructions in after years, showed conclusively that at this period of his life, the pages of the wondrous book of nature had been wide open before him, even though his father's fiat had deprived him of other sources of information.

But He who guides the steps of his creatures had provided a way for the gratification of the thirst for knowledge which was consuming the farmer's boy, and that by what seemed an untoward Providence. At the age of sixteen, he was brought to the borders of the grave by a severe illness; for a long time he lingered between life and death; and, while in this condition, his friends despairing of his recovery, and his father, whose heart yearned over him, watching his enfeebled frame, seemingly nigh to dissolution, the apparently dying boy turned his large, full eyes upon his father's face, and, in an almost inaudible whisper, begged that if he recovered, he might be allowed to go to Hampton Academy and prepare to become a teacher. Was not this, indeed, an example of "the ruling passion strong in death"? The father could not refuse the request proffered at such a time; what father could? The boy did recover, and he did go to the academy, a plain farmer's boy: he dressed in plain farmer's clothes, and hence, some self-conceited puppies, whose more fashionable exterior could not hide the meanness of their souls, deemed him fit subject for their gibes and sneers; but his earnest nature and his intense love of study were not to be thwarted by such rebuffs; he pursued the even tenor of his way, and, having spent some months at the academy, he taught a district school for the ensuing winter, and then returned again to the academy. Here his progress in study was rapid; but, the ensuing winter, we find him again teaching in his native town, and his further studies were prosecuted without assistance. The next winter, he had determined to make teaching a profession, and accordingly, having taught a district school at Newbury, Mass., during the winter, at its close he opened a private school: a daring step for a young man but nineteen years of age, and who had enjoyed so few advantages of education. The success which followed fully justified the self-reliance which led him to attempt it. At the beginning he had five pupils, but he persevered, and before the close of the term, the number he had contemplated was full. Here, as every-where else, during his career as a teacher, was manifested that diligence, industry, and careful preparation for his duties, which made him so eminently successful. He studied the lessons he was to teach, thoroughly, that he might impart instruction with that freshness and interest which such study would give; he studied his scholars thoroughly, that he might adapt his teachings to their several capacities, encouraging the diffident and sluggish, restraining the froward, and rousing the listless and careless to unwonted interest and energy; he studied, too, their moral natures, and sought to rouse in their youthful hearts aspirations for goodness and purity; and he studied whatever would enlarge his sphere of thought, intelligence, and usefulness.

Such a teacher was sure to rise in reputation,—slowly, perhaps, but certainly; and hence it need not surprise us to learn that within two years he was associate principal of the Newburyport High School, having charge of the English department. Here, for twelve years, he was associated with Roger S. Howard, Esq., one of the most eminent teachers in Massachusetts, and how well he fulfilled his duties, Mr. Howard, who survived him, testifies. The same intense fondness for study characterized him, leading him to acquire a very competent knowledge of the Latin language, and something of the Greek; that same earnest and conscientious performance of all his school duties, and delight in them, were manifested here as in his humbler position. It was while occupying this post, that he first began to come before the public as a lecturer. He was an active and prominent member of the Essex County Teachers' Association, one of the most efficient educational organizations in Massachusetts, and delivered before that body several lectures which Hon. Horace Mann characterized as the best ever delivered before that or any other body. Of one of these, on "*The Mutual Duties of Parents and Teachers,*" six thousand copies were printed and distributed (3,000 of them at Mr. Mann's expense) throughout the State. Mr. Page's powers as an orator and debater were of a very high order; he possessed, says Mr. Mann (himself an orator of no mean powers), "that rare quality, so indispensable to an orator, *the power to think, standing on his feet, and before folks.*" As a teacher, he exhibited two valuable qualifications: the ability to turn the attention of his pupils to the principles which explain facts, and in such a way that they could see clearly the connection; and the talent for reading the character of his scholars, so accurately, that he could at once discern what were their governing passions and tendencies, what in them needed encouragement, and what repression. Thus, useful, active, and growing in reputation, Mr. Page remained at Newburyport, till December, 1844.

In the winter preceding, the Legislature of New York, wearied with the costly but unsuccessful measures which, year after year, had been adopted for the improvement of her public schools, had appointed a committee of their own body, warm friends of education, to visit the normal schools of Massachusetts, and make a report thereon. The committee attended to their duties and made an elaborate report in favor of the adoption of the normal school system. That report was adopted, and an appropriation of ten thousand dollars outfit and ten thousand dollars per annum, for five years, was voted, to establish a normal school as an experiment. The friends of education in New York felt that, liberal as this appropriation was, every thing depended upon securing the right *man* to take charge of it, and long and carefully did they ponder the question, who that man should be.

Mr. Page's reputation had already outrun the town and the county in which he resided; and, on the recommendation of Hon. Horace Mann, and other friends of education in Massachusetts, Dr. (afterward Bishop) Potter, Col. Young, and other members of the executive committee, entered into correspondence with him on the subject. In reply to the first communication, he addressed numerous inquiries to the committee, concerning the plan proposed for the organization and management of the school.

These questions were so pointed and so well chosen, that Col. Young, on hearing them, at once exclaimed, "That is the man we need", and expressed himself entirely satisfied, without any further evidence. So cautious, however, were the committee, that it was decided that, before closing the negotiation, Dr. Potter should visit Newburyport and have a personal interview with Mr. Page. He accordingly repaired thither, called at Mr. Page's residence, and found him in his every-day dress and engaged in some mechanical work connected with the improvement of his dwelling. An interview of a single half hour so fully prepossessed him with Mr. Page's personal bearing and conversation, that he at once closed the negotiations with him and secured his services as Principal of the New York State Normal School.

Mr. Page closed his connection with the Newburyport High School about the middle of December, 1844, not without numberless demonstrations of regret and affectionate regard on the part of his pupils and friends. While on his way to Albany, he spent a night with Mr. Mann, in Boston, and the new duties he was about to undertake, the obstacles and difficulties, the opposition and misrepresentations he would meet, and the importance and necessity of success, formed themes of converse which occupied them till the early morning hours; in parting, Mr. Mann said to Mr. Page, as a veteran commander might have said to a youthful officer going to lead a forlorn hope, " Succeed or die." The words sank deep into his heart; they were adopted as his motto in the brief but brilliant career which followed, and once, on recovering from a dangerous illness, he reminded his friend of his injunction, and added, "I thought I was about to fulfill your last alternative." He arrived at Albany a few days before the commencement of the "experiment", as the Normal School was designated, and found every thing in a chaotic state; the rooms intended for its accommodation, yet unfinished; there was no organization, no apparatus, and indeed very few of the appliances necessary to a successful beginning; while the few were hoping, though not without fear, for its success, and the many were prophesying its utter failure. From this chaos, the systematic mind of Mr. Page soon evolved order: full of hope and confident of the success of the Normal School system himself, he infused energy and courage into the hearts of its desponding friends, and caused its enemies to falter, as they saw how all obstacles yielded to the fascination of his presence, or the power of his will. The school commenced with twenty-five scholars, but ere the close of its first term, the number had increased to one hundred. At the commencement of the second term, two hundred assembled for instruction. From this time its course was onward; every term increased its popularity; and the accommodations provided for it, large as they were, were soon crowded. For the first three years, it had to contend with numerous and unscrupulous foes, some of whom attacked the system, others its practical workings, others still, who were strangers to his person, attacked the character of the principal of the school. Meantime, Mr. Page labored indefatigably: against the assaults upon the organization, or its practical operations, he interposed able, manly, and courteous defenses; those which were leveled at himself, he bore in silence; but no man, whatever his position in the State, and however bitter might have been his hostility to the school, or to its principal, ever came within the magnetism of his presence and influence without being changed from an enemy into a friend. Among the most decided, as well as the most conscientious opposers of the Normal School, was the Hon. Silas Wright; indeed, in his election as governor, the enemies of the school claimed a triumph and counted largely on his eminent abilities to aid them in putting it down; but a very few months' residence in Albany converted this man, of strong and determined will, into one of its sincerest friends. During the vacations of the school, Mr. Page gave himself no rest; he visited different parts of the State, attended teachers' institutes, lectured day after day, and, wherever he went, removed prejudices, cleared up doubts, and won golden opinions. Every such visit **drew** a large number of pupils to the school, from the section visited, the ensuing term. The State Superintendent was accustomed to say "that he needed only to look at the catalogue of the Normal School, to tell where Mr. Page had spent his vacations."

Before four years had passed, the school had ceased to be an "experiment"; it was too firmly rooted in the hearts of the people to be abandoned, and the opposition, which had at first been so formidable, had dwindled into insignificance. But the toil requisite to accomplish this had been too arduous for any constitution, however vigorous, to endure. The autumnal term of 1847 found him cheerful and hopeful as ever, but with waning physical strength; he sought (an unusual thing for him) the aid of his colleagues in the performance of duties he had usually undertaken alone, and at length consented to take a vacation of a week or two during the Christmas holidays. Alas! the relaxation came too late; the evening before he was to leave, there was a meeting of the faculty at his residence; he was cheerful, but complained of slight indisposition, and retired early. With the night, however, came violent fever and restlessness, and by the morning light the physicians in attendance pronounced the disease pneumonia. At first, the attack excited little alarm, but it soon became evident that his overtasked vital powers had not the ability to resist the violence of the disorder. On the fourth day, he expressed to a friend his conviction that he should not recover. The severity of the disease soon increased, and, on the morning of January 1, 1848, he passed away.

Six months before his death, he had, in company with one of his colleagues, made a brief visit to his former home, at Newburyport; and, while visiting the beautiful cemetery there, he stopped suddenly near a shady spot, and said, "Here is where I desire to be buried." The sad funeral train which bore the clay that once had been his earthly habitation from Albany to Newburyport, laid it sadly, yet hopefully, in that quiet nook, to repose till the archangel's trump shall be heard, and the dead be raised.

His life had been short, as men count time; he lacked six months of completing his thirty-eighth year when he was summoned to the better land; but, if life be reckoned by what is accomplished, then had his life been longer far than that of the antediluvian patriarchs. Of the hundreds of teachers who were under his care at Albany, there was not one who did not look up to him with admiration and love; not one who did not bear, to some extent, at least, the impress of his character and influence. Men who were trained under him at Albany are occupying high positions in the cause of education in several of the Western States; and gifted women, who, under his teachings, were moved to consecrate themselves to the holy duty of training the young, are now at the head of seminaries and female schools of high order, extending his influence in widening circles over the boundless prairies of the West.

Our brief narrative exhibits, we think, clearly what were the marked traits of Mr. Page's character—industry, perseverance, decision, energy, great executive ability, ready tact, and conscientious adherence to what he regarded as duty. But no language can describe the fascination of his manner, the attraction of his presence, his skill in what he was accustomed to call the drawing-out process, or his tact in making all his knowledge available. His familiar lectures to his pupils on subjects connected with the teacher's life and duties, could they be published, would form an invaluable hand-book for teachers. He possessed, beyond most men, the happy talent of *always saying the right thing at the right time.* In personal appearance, Mr. Page was more than ordinarily prepossessing— of good height, and fine form, erect, and dignified in manner, scrupulously neat in person, and easy in address, he was a living model to his pupils of what a teacher should be. Aside from a few lectures, published at different times, to some of which we have already alluded, Mr. Page left but one published work—"*The Theory and Practice of Teaching*," a work which has had a large circulation, and one which no teacher can afford to be without.

THEORY AND PRACTICE OF TEACHING.

CHAPTER I.

FITNESS FOR TEACHING.

THE history of education shows that there have been three well marked and progressive stages of opinion with respect to fitness for teaching. During the earlier and the greater part of the historic period, when learning was monopolized by the few, all scholars were necessarily teachers, and it was an easy step to the inference that all who were learned could teach. At a much later period, when a general diffusion of knowledge had taken place, and the number of schools had greatly increased, it was observed that some scholars had high teaching power, while others had little or none of this gift. As this difference could not be attributed to differences in scholarship, nor wholly to differences in natural ability, it was ascribed to high and low degrees of *skill*, and so the question of *method* was called into prominence. This step necessarily led to a comparison of methods, and finally to a search for some criterion by which they could be tested. This criterion turned out to be some general principle or law of psychology, physiology, or ethics. In this way there began to appear a *science* of teaching. If we arrange these three conceptions of fitness for teaching in the order of their historical sequence, they will stand as follows:

1. Scholarship.
2. Scholarship and Method.
3. Scholarship, Method, and Science.

In which stratum of thought are we living to-day? In all three. The first is represented in the laws regulating the granting of licenses to teach; the second, speaking generally, in normal schools; and the third, in universities where the study of education has been made a part of the curriculum. The conservatism of law is well known, and in prescribing scholarship as the main, if not the only test of fitness to teach, it has preserved the primitive conception of competence for the teaching office. In the main, the distinctive feature of the normal school is that it instructs its pupils in the best methods of doing the various work of the school, at the same time that it carries forward their academic training. This instruction in methods is either given out of books or by lecture, or in observing the work done in model schools, or by doing actual teaching work in practice schools. In this country, the professional instruction of teachers in universities is of recent date, and consists chiefly in communicating the cardinal doctrines of education and

Natural ability.—Study.—Experience.

teaching, on the hypothesis that students who have been liberally trained will be able, on the occasion of experience, to draw a rational art of teaching out of a science of teaching. The current of the educational thought of to-day may be interpreted as follows: True fitness for teaching, so far as it can be gained from instruction, consists first of all in a liberal scholarship, then in a knowledge of the best methods of doing the work of the school, and of the principles that underlie these methods. Many, perhaps the most, of those who are to teach for a long time to come, will fall short of these attainments; but this is a reasonable ideal toward which all should aspire.

The professional education of two teachers may be the very same in kind and amount, and yet their actual teaching power may be very unequal; and this inequality we ascribe to differences in ability. Some are born with a predisposition to this kind of labor, and for others it is more or less unnatural. How are natural ability, study, and experience related to each other? This has never been more forcibly or more truly stated than by Lord Bacon in these terms: "To spend too much Time in *Studies*, is Sloth; To use them too much for Ornament, is Affectation; To make Judgement wholly by their Rules is the Humour of a Scholler. They perfect Nature, and are perfected by Experience: For Naturall Abilities, are like Naturall Plants, that need Proyning by *Study:*

Knowing prepares for doing.

And *Studies* themselves, doe give forth Directions too much at Large, except they be bounded in by experience." The proper sequence, then, is this: NATURAL ABILITY, STUDY, EXPERIENCE. No matter what our natural gifts may be, they should be improved by study; and the purpose of professional study should be (1) to take advantage of the recorded experiences of those who have made high attainments in the vocation which we purpose to follow; (2) to form a proper conception of the work we are to do; and (3) to gain the instrumental knowledge that is needed in the practice of our art. Only when we have done this are we ready to undertake the duties of our chosen profession, for the antecedent to *doing* is *knowing;* it is only the quack who will venture to learn his art by the practice of his art.

Those who are beginning the study of education should be reminded that the field of inquiry is a vast one, and that if they would attain the highest professional standing, they must pursue this subject in its three main phases—the practical, the scientific, and the historical. If the time for preparation is short, a beginning should be made in becoming acquainted with the best current methods of organizing, governing, and instructing a school. Then should follow a study of the science of education, to the end that the teacher may interpret the lessons of daily experience, and thus be helped to grow into higher

Professional study.—Culture.

and higher degrees of competence; and, finally, for giving breadth of view, for taking full advantage of all past experience and experiments, and for gaining that inspiration which comes from retracing the long line of an illustrious professional ancestry, there should be a study of the history of education.

All who propose to teach need to recollect that the very basis of fitness for teaching, so far as it can be gained from study, is a broad and accurate scholarship. To be a teacher, one must first of all be a scholar. So much stress is now placed on method, and the theory of teaching, that there is great danger of forgetting the supreme importance of scholarship and culture. For these there is no substitute; and any scheme of professional study that is pursued at the expense of scholarship and culture, is essentially bad. To be open-minded, magnanimous, and manly; to have a love for the scholarly vocation, and a wide and easy range of intellectual vision, are of infinitely greater worth to the teacher than any authorized set of technical rules and principles. Well would it be for both teachers and taught, if all who read this book were to be inspired by Plato's ideal of the cultured man: "A lover, not of a part of wisdom, but of the whole; who has a taste for every sort of knowledge and is curious to learn, and is never satisfied; who has magnificence of mind, and is the spectator of all time and all existence; who is harmoniously consti-

Plato's idea of culture.

tuted; of a well-proportioned and gracious mind, whose own nature will move spontaneously towards the true being of every thing; who has a good memory, and is quick to learn, noble, gracious, the friend of truth, justice, courage, temperance." *

* Republic, *passim*, 475-487.

CHAPTER II.

SPIRIT OF THE TEACHER.

PERHAPS the very first question that the honest individual will ask himself, as he proposes to assume the teacher's office, or to enter upon a preparation for it, will be—"*What manner of spirit am I of?*" No question can be more important. I would by no means undervalue that degree of natural talent—of mental power, which all justly consider so desirable in the candidate for the teacher's office. But the *true spirit of the teacher*,—a spirit that seeks not alone pecuniary emolument, but desires to be in the highest degree useful to those who are to be taught; a spirit that elevates above every thing else the nature and capabilities of the human soul, and that trembles under the responsibility of attempting to be its educator; a spirit that looks upon gold as the contemptible dross of earth, when compared with that imperishable gem which is to be polished and brought out into heaven's light to shine forever; a spirit that scorns all the rewards of earth, and seeks that highest of all rewards, an approving conscience and an approving God; a spirit that earnestly inquires what is right, and that dreads to do what is wrong; a spirit that can recognize and reverence the handiwork of God in every child, and that burns with the desire to be instrumental in training it to the highest attainment of which it is capable,—*such a spirit* is the first thing to be sought by the teacher, and without it the highest talent can not make him truly excellent in his profession.

The candidate for the office of the teacher should look well to his motives. It is easy to enter upon the duties of the teacher without preparation; it is easy to do it without that lofty purpose which an enlightened conscience would ever demand; but it is not so easy to undo the mischief which a single mistake may produce in the mind of the child, at that tender period when mistakes are most likely to be made.

Too many teachers are found in our schools without the spirit for their work which is here insisted on. They not only have not given attention to any preparation for their work, but resort to it from motives of personal convenience, and in many instances from a consciousness of being unfit for every thing else! In other professions this is not so. The lawyer is not admitted to the bar till he has pursued a course of thorough preparation, and even then but warily employed. The physician goes through his course of reading and his course of lectures, and often almost through a *course of starvation* in the country

Preparation neglected.

village where he first puts up his sign, before he is called in to heal the maladies of the body. It is long before he can inspire confidence enough in the people to be intrusted with their most difficult cases of ailing, and very likely the noon of life is passed before he can consider himself established. But it is not so with the teacher. He gains access to the sanctuary of mind without any difficulty, and the most tender interests for both worlds are intrusted to his guidance, even when he makes pretension to no higher motive than that of filling up a few months of time not otherwise appropriated, and to no qualifications but those attained by accident. A late writer in the Journal of Education hardly overstates this matter:—" Every stripling who has passed four years within the walls of a college; every dissatisfied clerk, who has not ability enough to manage the trifling concerns of a common retail shop; every young farmer who obtains in the winter a short vacation from the toils of summer,—in short, every young person who is conscious of his imbecility in other business, esteems himself fully competent to train the ignorance and weakness of infancy into all the virtue and power and wisdom of maturer years,—to form a creature, the frailest and feeblest that heaven has made, into the intelligent and fearless sovereign of the whole animated creation, the interpreter and adorer and almost the representative of Divinity!"

Teaching a secondary object.—Ignorance does not excuse.

Many there are who enter upon the high employment of teaching a common school as a *secondary* object. Perhaps they are students themselves in some higher institution, and resort to this as a temporary expedient for paying their board, while their chief object is, to pursue their own studies and thus keep pace with their classes. Some make it a stepping-stone to something beyond, and, in their estimation, higher in the scale of respectability,—treating the employment, while in it, as irksome in the extreme, and never manifesting so much delight as when the hour arrives for the dismissal of their schools. Such have not the true spirit of the teacher; and, if their labors are not entirely unprofitable, it only proves that children are sometimes submitted to imminent danger, but are still unaccountably preserved by the hand of Providence.

The teacher should go to his duty full of his work. He should be impressed with its overwhelming importance. He should feel that his mistakes, though they may not speedily ruin him, may permanently injure his pupils. Nor is it enough that he shall say, "I did it ignorantly". He has assumed to fill a place where ignorance itself is sin; and where indifference to the wellbeing of others is equivalent to willful homicide. He might as innocently assume to be the physician, and, without knowing its effects, prescribe arsenic for the colic. Ignorance is not in such cases a valid excuse, because the assumption of

Dangerous to mislead mind.

the place implies a pretension to the requisite skill. Let the teacher, then, well consider what manner of spirit he is of. Let him come to this work only when he has carefully pondered its nature and its responsibilities, and after he has devoted his best powers to a thorough preparation of himself for its high duties. Above all, let him be sure that his motives on entering the school-room are such as will be acceptable in the sight of God, when viewed by the light beaming out from His throne.

> "O! let not then unskillful hands attempt
> To play the harp whose tones, whose living tones
> Are left forever in the strings. Better far
> That heaven's lightnings blast his very soul,
> And sink it back to Chaos' lowest depths,
> Than knowingly, by word or deed, he send
> A blight upon the trusting mind of youth."

CHAPTER III.

RESPONSIBILITY OF THE TEACHER.

SECTION I.—A NEGLECTED PEAR-TREE.

SOME years ago, while residing in the north-eastern part of Massachusetts, I was the owner of a small garden. I had taken much pains to improve the condition and appearance of the place. A woodbine had been carefully trained upon the front of the little homestead; a fragrant honeysuckle, supported by a trellis, adorned the door-way; a moss-rose, a flowering almond, and the lily of the valley, mingled their fragrance in the breath of morn,—and never, in my estimation at least, did the sun shine upon a lovelier, happier spot. The morning hour was spent in "dressing and keeping" the garden. Its vines were daily watched and carefully trained; its borders were free from weeds, and the plants expanded their leaves and opened their buds as if smiling at the approach of the morning sun. There were fruit-trees, too, which had been brought from far, and so carefully nurtured, that they were covered with blossoms, filling the air with their fragrance and awakening the fondest hopes of an abundant harvest.

Neglected pear-tree.—Pruning commenced.

In one corner of this miniature paradise there was a hop-trellis; and, in the midst of a bed of tansy hard by, stood a small, knotty, crooked *pear-tree*. It had stood there I know not how long. It was very diminutive in size; but, like those cedars which one notices high up the mountain, just on the boundary between vegetation and eternal frost, it had every mark of the decrepitude of age.

Why should this tree stand here so unsightly and unfruitful? Why had it escaped notice so long? Its bark had become *bound* and cracked; its leaves were small and curled; and those, small as they were, were ready to be devoured by a host of caterpillars, whose pampered bodies were already grown to the length of an inch. The tendrils of the hop-vine had crept about its thorny limbs, and were weighing down its growth, while the tansy at its roots drank up the refreshing dew and shut out the genial ray. *It was a neglected tree!*

"Why may not this tree be pruned?" No sooner said, than the small saw was taken from its place and the work was commenced. *Commenced?* It was hard to determine where to commence. Its knotty branches had grown thick and crooked, and there was scarcely space to get the saw between them. They all seemed to deserve amputation, but then the tree would have no top. This and that limb were lopped off as the case seemed to demand. The task was nei-

Disagreeable toil.—Grafting of a Bartlet Pear.—Anxiety.

ther easy nor pleasant. Sometimes a violent stroke would bring down upon my own head a shower of the filthy caterpillars; again, the long-cherished garden coat—threadbare and faded as it was—got caught, and, before it could be disengaged, what an unsightly rent had been made! With *pain* I toiled on, for one of the unlucky thorns had pierced my thumb; and I might have been said to be working on the *spur* of the occasion!

The hop-vine, however, was removed from its boughs, the tansy and weeds from its roots, the scales and moss from its bark. The thorns were carefully pared from its limbs, and the caterpillars were all shaken from its leaves. The mold was loosened and enriched—and the sun shone that day upon a long *neglected*, but now a promising tree.

The time for grafting was not yet passed. One reputedly skilled in that art was called to put the new scion upon the old stock. The work was readily undertaken and speedily accomplished, and the assurance was given that the BARTLET PEAR—that prince among the fruits of New England—would one day be gathered from my *neglected tree*.

With what interest I watched the buds of the scion, morning after morning, as the month grew warmer, and vegetation all around was "bursting into birth!" With what delight did I greet the first opening of those buds, and how did I rejoice

The pears ripen.— Chagrin and mortification.— A moral garden.

as the young shoots put forth and grew into a fresh green top! With tender solicitude I cherished this tree for two long summers; and, on the opening of the third, my heart was gladdened with the sight of its first fruit blossoms. With care were the weeds excluded, the caterpillars exterminated, the hop-vine clipped, the bark rubbed and washed, the earth manured and watered. The time of fruit arrived. The Bartlet pear was offered in our market—but my pears were not yet ripe! With anxious care they were watched till the frost bade the green leaves wither, and then they were carefully gathered and placed in the sunbeams within doors. They at length turned yellow, and looked fair to the sight and tempting to the taste; and a few friends who had known their history, were invited to partake of them. They were brought forward, carefully arranged in the best dish the humble domicile afforded, and formally introduced as the first fruits of the "*neglected tree.*" What was my chagrin and mortification, after all my pains and solicitude, after all my hopes and fond anticipations, to find they were miserable, tasteless—*choke pears!*

This pear-tree has set me to thinking. It has suggested that there is such a thing as a *moral garden*, in which there may be fair flowers, indeed, but also some *neglected trees.* The plants in this garden may suffer very much from neglect—from neglect of the gardener. It is deplor-

Many neglected trees.—Infancy.

able to see how many crooked, unseemly branches shoot forth from some of these young trees, which early might have been trained to grow straight and smooth by the hand of cultivation. Many a youth, running on in his own way, indulging in deception and profanity, yielding to temptation and overborne by evil influences, polluting by his example, and wounding the hearts of his best friends as they yearn over him for good, has reminded me of *my neglected tree*, its caterpillars, its roughened bark, its hop-vine, its tansy bed, its cruel piercing thorns. And when I have seen such a youth brought under the influence of the educator, and have witnessed the progress he has made and the intellectual promise he has given, I have also thought of my *neglected tree*. When, too, I have followed him to the years of maturity, and have found, as I have too often found, that he brings not forth "the peaceable fruits of righteousness", but that he disappoints all the fondly-cherished hopes of his friends—perhaps of his own teachers, because the best principles were not engrafted upon him, I again think of my *neglected tree*, and of the unskillful, perhaps dishonest gardener, who acted as its *responsible educator*.

From the above as a text, several inferences might be drawn. 1. Education is necessary to develop the human soul. 2. Education should begin early. We have too many *neglected* trees. 3. It should be right education. And 4. The educator should be a safe and an honest man; else the education may be all wrong—may be worse, even, than the *neglect.*

But especially we may infer that

SECTION II.—THE TEACHER IS RESPONSIBLE.

IT is the object of the following remarks feebly to illustrate the extent of the teacher's responsibility. It must all along be borne in mind that he is not *alone* responsible for the results of education. The parent has an overwhelming responsibility, which he can never part with or transfer to another while he holds the relation of parent.

But the teacher is responsible in a very high degree. An important interest is committed to his charge whenever a human being is placed under his guidance. By taking the position of the teacher, all the responsibility of the relation is voluntarily assumed; and he is fearfully responsible, not only for what he *does,* but also for what he neglects to do. And it is a responsibility from which he can not escape. Even though he may have thoughtlessly entered upon the relation of teacher, without a single glance at its obligations; or though, when reminded of them, he may laugh at the thought, and disclaim all idea of being thus seriously held to a fearful account —yet still *the responsibility is on him.* Just as true as it is a great thing to guide the mind aright,—just as true as it is a deplorable, nay,

Bodily health.

fatal thing to lead it astray, so true is it that he who attempts the work, whether ignorant or skillful, whether thoughtless or serious, incurs all the responsibility of success or failure,—a responsibility he can never shake off as long as the human soul is immortal, and men are accountable for such consequences of their acts as are capable of being foreseen.

I. *The teacher is in a degree responsible for the* BODILY HEALTH *of the child.* It is well established that the foundation of many serious diseases is laid in the school-room. These diseases come sometimes from a neglect of exercise; sometimes from too long confinement in one position, or upon one study; sometimes from over-excitement and over-study; sometimes from breathing bad air; sometimes from being kept too warm or too cold. Now the teacher should be an intelligent physiologist; and from a knowledge of what the human system can bear, and what it can not, he is bound to be ever watchful, to guard against all those abuses from which our children so often suffer. Especially should he be tremblingly alive to avert that excitability of the nervous system, the overaction of which is so fatal to the future happiness of the individual. And should he, by appealing to the most exciting motives, encourage the delicate child to press on to grasp those subjects which are too great for its comprehension, and allow it to neglect exercise in the open air, in

Laws of physical health. — Nervous excitement.

order to task its feverish brain in the crowded and badly ventilated school-room; and then, in a few days, be called to look upon the languishing sufferer upon a bed of exhaustion and pain — perhaps a bed of premature death, could he say, "I am not responsible"? Parents and teachers often err in this. They are so eager to develop a precocious intellect, that they crush the casket in order to gratify a prurient desire to astonish the world with the brilliancy of the gem. Each is responsible for his share of this sin; and the teacher especially, because by his education he should know better.

The growing prevalence of myopia among school children should excite the watchful care of all teachers. Specialists have observed that cases of near-sight rapidly increase from the primary grades upward; and so common has this defect of the eye become, that it is now called a "school disease". The causes acting within the school-room to induce this malformation of the eye are the following: Insufficient light, causing the pupil to bring the book too near the eye; a stooping posture of the body, inducing congestion of the membranes of the eye; typography that is "trying to the eye". In his "School and Industrial Hygiene," Mr. Lincoln states that a child with normal eyes ought to be able to read from a page like this, in a good light, at a distance of forty inches, and at all intervening distances down to four inches; and that a child who can

Care of the eyes.—Order of study.

not read under such conditions as far as fifteen inches off, should have his eyes examined by a competent oculist (p. 49). The best light is that which comes from above, and falls vertically upon the book. Though in most cases this mode of lighting is impracticable, it is a hint that the windows of school-rooms should be placed as high as possible. The worst light is that which falls in the face of the pupil, or that which, coming from the rear, throws a shadow on his book. In rooms of moderate width, the best light is that which falls over the left shoulder.

II. *The teacher is mainly responsible for the* INTELLECTUAL GROWTH *of the child.* This may be referred chiefly to the following heads:—

1. *The order of study.* There is a natural order in the education of the child. The teacher should know this. If he presents the subjects out of this order, he is responsible for the injury. In general, the *elements* should be taught first. Those simple branches which the child first comprehends, should first be presented. *Reading*, of course, must be one of the first; though I think the day is not distant when an enlightened community will not condemn the teacher, if, while teaching reading, he should call the child's attention by oral instructions to such objects about him as he can comprehend, even though in doing this he should somewhat prolong the time of learning to read. It is indeed of little consequence that the child should read *words* simply;

Translation of thought.—Mental Arithmetic.

and that teacher may be viewed as pursuing the order of nature, who so endeavors to develop the powers of observation and comparison, that words when learned shall be the vehicles of ideas. Whether the pupil is merely learning words, or is really gaining ideas, may be tested in a very simple and effective way: *Require him to express the thought of the paragraph in his own words.* If he can do this accurately, it is certain that he has comprehended the thought; for he is able to separate it from the form of words employed by the author, and to embody it in a different form. This *translation of thought* should form an essential part of every reading exercise; expressive reading will then be a very simple thing. Reading proper, or the gaining of thought from the printed page, should be distinguished from elocution, or the *expression* of thought. A rule for good teaching is, first make sure that the thought has been gained, then attend to its proper expression.

Next to Reading and its inseparable companions—*Spelling* and *Defining*—I am inclined to recommend the study of *Mental Arithmetic*. The idea of Number is one of the earliest in the mind of the child. He can be early taught to count, and quite early to perform those operations which we call adding, subtracting, multiplying, and dividing. This study at first *needs no book.* The teacher should be thoroughly versed in "Colburn's Intellectual Arithmetic", or its equivalent, and he

Recite without book.—Geography.

can find enough to interest the child. When the scholar has learned to read, and has attained the age of six or seven, he may be allowed a book in *preparing his lesson,* but never during the recitation. Those who have not tried this kind of mental discipline, will be astonished at the facility which the child acquires, for performing operations that often puzzle the adult. Nor is it an unimportant acquisition. None can tell its value but those who have experienced the advantage it gives them in future school exercises and in business, over those who have never had such training.

Geography may come next to Mental Arithmetic. The child should have an idea of the relations of size, form, and space, as well as number, before commencing Geography. These, however, he acquires naturally at an early age; and very thoroughly, if the teacher has taken a little pains to aid him on these points in the earliest stages of his progress. A map is a picture, and hence a child welcomes it. If it can be a map of some familiar object, as of his school-room, of the school district, of his father's orchard or farm, it becomes an object of great interest. A map of his town is very desirable, also of his county and his own State. Further detail will be deferred here, as it is only intended in this place to hint at the *order* of taking up the subjects.

The purpose of geographical study may be stated to be, *to form an adequate conception of the earth as the dwelling-place of man.*

History. — Literature. — Other studies.

History should go hand in hand with Geography. Perhaps no greater mistake is made than that of deferring History till one of the last things in the child's course.

The purpose of historical study may be thus defined: *To form an adequate conception of the most notable things done by the human race.*

Literature should hold a co-ordinate rank with Geography and History, its purpose being *to give the pupil an adequate conception of the most notable things written by the wisest and the best of the human race.* These three subjects are entitled to be called the *modern culture trivium.*

Writing may be early commenced with the *pencil* upon the slate, because it is a very useful exercise to the child in prosecuting many of his other studies. But writing with a pen may well be deferred till the child is *ten years of age,* when the muscles shall have acquired sufficient strength to grasp and guide it.

Written Arithmetic may succeed the mental; indeed, it may be practiced along with it.

Composition — perhaps by another name, as *Description* — should be early commenced and very frequently practiced. The child can be early interested in this, and in this way he probably acquires a better knowledge of practical grammar than he could in any other.

Grammar, in my opinion, as a study, should be one of the last of the common school branches to be taken up. It requires more maturity of mind to understand its relations and dependencies than any other; and that which is taught of grammar without such an understanding, is a mere smattering of *technical terms*, by which the pupil is injured rather than improved. It may be said, that unless scholars commence this branch early, they never will have the opportunity to learn it. Then let it go unlearned; for, as far as I have seen the world, I am satisfied that this early and superficial teaching of a difficult subject is not only useless, but positively injurious. How many there are who study grammar for years, and then are obliged to confess in after life, because "their speech bewrayeth" them, that they never understood it! How many, by the too early study of an intricate branch, make themselves *think* they understand it, and thus prevent the hope of any further advancement at the proper age! *Grammar, then, should not be studied too early.*

That form of grammatical study known as *Language Lessons*, may be begun at an early age. The purpose of these lessons is to instruct the pupil in the correct use of language, both in speaking and in writing, not by precept and rule, but by *practice*. This is the proper introduction to grammar proper, or the formal study of language. At present, there is such a strong reaction from grammar to Language Lessons, that there is danger of losing sight of the high claims of the formal study of language, based on parsing, or the classification of words. The parsing

How to study.—Not words, but thoughts.

exercise, when properly conducted, is an invaluable means of mental discipline; in the art of classifying, and in reasoning on contingent matters parsing is the logic of the primary school. It is stated in objection to the study of formal grammar, that the rules of syntax so laboriously learned have but little effect in promoting accuracy of speech. It is a fact of common observation that an accurate knowledge of the proper uniformities of speech, is no absolute defense against a violation of these same uniformities; but this merely proves how obstinate ingrained habit is. If the young heard only the authorized forms of speech, they would have no need of the rules of formal grammar for purposes of guidance; but since they are always in imminent danger of copying the incorrect forms of speech which they hear, they need a defense against this danger; and the most available and the most effective is a knowledge of the much decried English Grammar.

Of the manner of teaching all these branches, I shall have more to say in due time. At present, I have only noticed *the order* in which they should be taken up. This is a question of much consequence to the child, and the teacher is generally responsible for it. He should, therefore, carefully consider this matter, that he may be able to decide aright.

2. *The manner of study.* It is of quite as much importance *how* we study, as *what* we study. In-

How to study.—Not words, but thoughts.

deed, I have thought that much of the difference among men could be traced to their different habits of study, formed in youth. A large portion of our scholars study for the sake of preparing to recite the lesson. They seem to have no idea of any object beyond *recitation*. The consequence is, they study mechanically. They endeavor to remember phraseology rather than principles; they study the *book*, not the subject. Let any one enter our schools and see the scholars engaged in preparing their lessons. Scarcely one will be seen who is not repeating over and over again the words of the text, as if there was a saving charm in repetition. Observe the same scholars at recitation, and it is a struggle of the memory to recall the forms of *words*. The vacant countenance too often indicates that they are words without meaning. This difficulty is very much increased, if the teacher is confined to the text-book during recitation; and particularly if he relies mainly upon the *printed questions* so often found at the bottom of the page.

The scholar should be encouraged to *study the subject;* and his book should be held merely as the instrument. "Books are but helps", is a good motto for every student. The teacher should often tell how the lesson should be learned. His precept in this matter will often be of use. Some scholars will learn a lesson in one tenth of the time required by others. Human life is too short to have any of it employed to disadvantage. The

Books but helps.—Study objects.

teacher, then, should inculcate such habits of study as are valuable; and he should be particularly careful to break up, in the recitations, those habits which are so grossly mechanical. A child may almost be said to be educated, who has learned to study aright; while one may have acquired in the mechanical way a great amount of knowledge, and yet have no profitable mental discipline.

For this difference in children, as well as in men, the teacher is more responsible than any other person. Let him carefully consider this matter.

3. *Collateral study.* Books to be sure are to be studied, and studied *chiefly*, in most of our schools. But there is much for the teacher to do toward the growth of the mind, which is not to be found in the school-books; and it is the practical recognition of this fact which constitutes the great difference in teachers. *Truth*, in whatever department, is open to the faithful teacher. And there is such a thing, even in the present generation, as "opening the eyes of the blind", to discover things new and old, in nature, in the arts, in history, in the relation of things. Without diminishing in the least the progress of the young in study, their powers of observation may be cultivated, their perception quickened, their relish for the acquisition of knowledge indefinitely increased, by the instrumentality of the teacher. This must, of course, be done adroitly. There is

such a thing as excessively cramming the mind of a child, till he loathes every thing in the way of acquisition. There is such a thing, too, as exciting an all-pervading interest in a group of children, so that the scholar shall welcome the return of school-hours, and, by his cheerful step and animated eye, as he seeks the school-house, disclaim as false, when applied to him, the language of the poet, who described the school-boy of his darker day,—

> " with his satchel,
> And shining morning face, creeping, *like snail,*
> *Unwillingly* to school."

The teacher, who is responsible for such a result, should take care to store his own mind with the material, and exercise the ingenuity, to do that which is of so much consequence to the scholar.

The desire to interest pupils in the common things about them, to call their observing powers into systematic exercise, and to cultivate their use of language, led to an elaborate system of Object Lessons; but it now seems to be the verdict of experience that this formal study of objects has not proved of high value. The teacher who accepts the lesson on the *ear of corn*, and the *elm-tree*, given in the chapter on "Waking up Mind", as types of this kind of instruction, will stand on safe ground.

III. *The teacher is in a degree responsible for the* MORAL TRAINING *of the child.*

Moral training neglected. — Precept. — Example.

I say *in a degree*, because it is confessed that in this matter very much likewise depends upon parental influence.

This education of the heart is confessedly too much neglected in all our schools. It has often been remarked that "knowledge is power", and as truly that "knowledge without principle to regulate it may make a man a powerful villain"! It is all-important that our youth should early receive such moral training as shall make it safe to give them knowledge. Very much of this work must devolve upon the teacher; or rather, when he undertakes to teach, he *assumes* the responsibility of doing or of neglecting this work.

The *precept* of the teacher may do much toward teaching the child his duty to God, to himself, and to his fellow-beings. But it is not mainly by precept that this is to be done. Sermons and homilies are but little heeded in the school-room; and unless the teacher has some other mode of reaching the feelings and the conscience, he may despair of being successful in moral training.

The teacher should be well versed in human nature. He should know the power of conscience and the means of reaching it. He should himself have deep principle. His *example* in every thing before his school should be pure, flowing out from the purity of his soul. He should ever manifest the tenderest regard to the law of right and of love. He should never violate his own sense of justice, nor outrage that of his pupils. Such a man teaches by his example. He is a "living epistle, known and read of all." He teaches, as he goes in and out before the school, as words can never teach.

The moral feelings of children are capable of systematic and successful cultivation. Our muscles acquire strength by use; it is so with our intellectual and moral faculties. We educate the power of calculation by continued practice, so that the proficient adds the long column of figures almost with the rapidity of sight, and with infallible accuracy. So with the moral feelings. "The more frequently we use our conscience," says Dr. Wayland, "in judging between actions, as right and wrong, the more easily shall we learn to judge correctly concerning them. He who, before every action, will deliberately ask himself, 'Is this right or wrong'? will seldom mistake what is his duty. And children may do this as well as grown persons." Let the teacher appeal as often as may be to the pupil's conscience. In a thousand ways can this be done, and it is a duty the faithful teacher owes to his scholars.

By such methods of cultivating the conscience as the judicious teacher may devise, and by his own pure example, what may he not accomplish? If he loves the truth, and ever speaks the truth; if he is ever frank and sincere; if, in a word, he shows that he has a tender conscience in all things, and that he always refers to it for its

Evil example to be dreaded. — Consequences.

approval in all his acts, — what an influence does he exert upon the impressible minds under his guidance! How those children will observe his consistent course; and, though they may not speak of it, how great will be its silent power upon the formation of their characters! And in future years, when they ripen into maturity, how will they remember and bless the example they shall have found so safe and salutary.

Responsibility in this matter can not be avoided. The teacher by his example *does teach*, for good or for evil, whether he will or not. Indifference will not excuse him; for when most indifferent, he is not less accountable. And if his example be pernicious, as too often, even yet, the example of the teacher is; if he indulges in outbreaks of passion, or wanders in the mazes of deceitfulness; if the blasphemous oath pollutes his tongue, or the obscene jest poisons his breath; if he trifles with the feelings or the rights of others, and habitually violates his own conscience, — what a blighting influence is his for all coming time!

With all the attachment which young pupils will cherish, even toward a bad teacher, and with all the confidence they will respose in him, who can describe the mischief which he can accomplish in one short term? *The school is no place for a man without principle;* I repeat, THE SCHOOL IS NO PLACE FOR A MAN WITHOUT PRINCIPLE. Let such a man seek a livelihood anywhere else; or, failing to gain it by other means, let starvation seize the body, and send the soul back to its Maker as it is, rather than he should incur the fearful guilt of poisoning youthful minds and dragging them down to his own pitiable level. If there can be one sin greater than another, on which heaven frowns with more awful displeasure, it is that of leading the young into principles of error, and the debasing practices of vice.

> "O, woe to those who trample on the mind,
> That deathless thing! They know not what they do,
> Nor what they deal with. Man, perchance, may bind
> The flower his step hath bruised; or light anew
> The torch he quenches; or to music wind
> Again the lyre-string from his touch that flew;—
> But for the soul, O, tremble and beware
> To lay rude hands upon God's mysteries there!"

Let then the teacher study well his motives when he enters this profession, and so let him meet his responsibility in this matter as to secure the approval of his own conscience and his God.

IV. *The teacher is to some extent responsible for the* RELIGIOUS TRAINING *of the young.*

We live in a Christian land. It is our glory, if not our boast, that we have descended from an ancestry that feared God and reverenced his word. Very justly we attribute our superiority as a people, over those who dwell in the darker portions of the world, to our purer faith derived from that precious fountain of truth — the Bible. Very justly, too, does the true patriot and philanthropist rely upon our faith and practice as a

Christian people, for the permanence of our free institutions and our unequaled social privileges.

If we are so much indebted, then, to the Christian religion for what we are, and so much dependent upon its life-giving truths for what we may hope to be, — how important is it that all our youth should be nurtured under its influences!

When I say religious training, I do not mean sectarianism. In our public schools, supported at the public expense, and in which the children of all denominations meet for instruction, I do not think that any man has a right to crowd his own peculiar notions of theology upon all, whether they are acceptable or not. Yet there is common ground which he can occupy, and to which no reasonable man can object. He can teach a reverence for the Supreme Being, a reverence for his Holy Word, for the influences of his Spirit, for the character and teachings of the Savior, and for the momentous concerns of eternity. He can teach the evil of sin in the sight of God, and the awful consequences of it upon the individual. He can teach the duty of repentance, and the privilege of forgiveness. He can teach our duty to worship God, to obey his laws, to seek the guidance of his spirit, and the salvation by his Son. He can illustrate the blessedness of the divine life, the beauty of holiness, and the joyful hope of heaven; — and to all this no reasonable man will be found to object, so long as it is done in a truly Christian spirit.

Sectarianism for the pulpit.—Danger of skepticism.

If not in express words, most certainly his life and example should teach this. Man is a religious being. The religious principle should be early cultivated. It should be safely and carefully cultivated; and as this cultivation is too often entirely neglected by parents, unless it is attempted by the teacher, in many cases, it will never be effected at all.

Of course all those points which separate the community into sects, must be left to the family, the Sabbath-school, and the pulpit. The teacher is responsible for his honesty in this matter. While he has no right to lord it over the private conscience of any one, he is inexcusable, if, believing the great truths of the Bible, he puts them away as if they concerned him not. They should command his faith and govern his conduct; and their claims upon the young should not be disowned.

At any rate, the teacher should be careful that his teaching and his example do not prejudice the youthful mind against these truths. It is a hazardous thing for a man to be skeptical by himself, even when he locks his opinions up in the secrecy of his own bosom : how great then is the responsibility of teaching the young to look lightly upon the only book that holds out to us the faith of immortality, and opens to us the hope of heaven! Let the teacher well consider this matter, and take heed that his teaching shall never lead one child of earth away from his heavenly Father, or from the rest of the righteous in the home of the blest.

Inexcusable indifference.—Who is sufficient?

In view of what has been said, the young candidate for the teacher's office, almost in despair of success, may exclaim, "Who is sufficient for these things?" "Who can meet and sustain such responsibility?" My answer is, the true inquirer after duty will not go astray. He is insufficient for these things, who is self-confident, who has not yet learned his own weakness, who has never found out his own faults, and who rushes to this great work, as the unheeding "horse rusheth into the battle", not knowing whither he goeth. Alas, how many there are who enter this profession without the exercise of a single thought of the responsibleness of the position, or of any of the great questions which must, in their schools, for the first time be presented for their decision! How many there are who never reflect upon the influence of their example before the young, and are scarcely conscious that their example is of any consequence! Such, in the highest sense, will fail of success. How can they be expected to go right, where there is only one right way, but a thousand wrong? Let such persons pause and consider, before they assume responsibilities which they can neither discharge nor evade. Let such ask with deep solicitude, "Who is sufficient for these things?"

But to the young person really desirous of improvement; to him who has taken the first and important step toward knowledge, by making the discovery that every thing is not already known;

to him who sees beforehand that there are real difficulties in this profession, and who is not too proud or self-conceited to feel the need of special preparation to meet them; to him who has some idea of the power of example in the educator, and who desires most of all things that his character shall be so pure as to render his example safe; to him who has discovered that there are some deep mysteries in human nature, and that they are only to be fathomed by careful study; to him who really feels that a great thing is to be done, and who has the sincere desire to prepare himself to do it aright; to him, in short, who has the *true spirit of the teacher*,—I may say, there is nothing to fear. An honest mind, with the requisite industry, *is sufficient for these things.*

SECTION III.—THE AUBURN STATE PRISON.

DURING my visit at Auburn in the autumn of 1845, I was invited by a friend to visit the prison, in which at that time were confined between six and seven hundred convicts. I was first taken through the various workshops, where the utmost neatness and order prevailed. As I passed along, my eye rested upon one after another of the convicts, I confess, with a feeling of surprise. There were many good-looking men. If, instead of their parti-colored dress, they could have been clothed in the citizen's garb, I should have thought them as good in appearance as laboring men in general.

And when, to their good appearance, was added their attention to their work, their ingenuity, and the neatness of their work-rooms, my own mind began to press the inquiry, *Why are these men here?* It was the afternoon of Saturday. Many of them had completed their allotted work for the week, and with happy faces were performing the customary ablutions preparatory to the Sabbath. Passing on, we came to the library, a collection of suitable books for the convicts, which are given out as a reward for diligence to those who have seasonably and faithfully performed their labor. Here were many who had come to take their books. Their faces beamed with delight as they each bore away the desired volume, just as I had seen the faces of the happy and the free do before. *Why are these men here?* was again pressed upon me;—*why are these men here?*

At this time, the famous WYATT, since executed upon the gallows for his crime, was in solitary confinement, awaiting his trial for the murder of Gordon, a fellow-prisoner. I was permitted to enter his room. Chained to the floor, he was reclining upon his mattress in the middle of his apartment. As I approached him, his large black eye met mine. He was a handsome man. His head was well developed, his long black hair hung upon his neck, and his eye was one of the most intelligent I ever beheld. Had I seen him in the Senate among great men,—had I seen him in a school of philosophers, or a brotherhood of poets,

Sabbath morn.—Worship.—Singing.—Prayer.

I should probably have selected him as the most remarkable man among them all, without suspecting his distinction to be a distinction of villainy. Why is that man here? thought I, as I turned away to leave him to his dreadful solitude.

The morrow was the Sabbath. I could not repress my desire to see the convicts brought together for worship. At the hour of nine, I entered their chapel and found them all seated in silence. I was able to see most of the faces of this interesting congregation. It was by no means the worst looking congregation I had ever seen. There were evidently bad men there; but what congregation of *free* men does not present some such?

They awaited in silence the commencement of the service. When the morning hymn was read, they joined in the song, the chorister being a colored man of their own number. They sung as other congregations sing, and my voice joined with theirs. The Scripture was read. They gave a respectful attention. The prayer was begun. Some bowed in apparent reverence at the commencement. Others sat erect, and two or three of these appeared to be the hardened sons of crime. The chaplain's voice was of a deep, perhaps I should say, a *fatherly* tone, and he seemed to have the Father's spirit. He prayed for these "wayward ones", who were deprived of their liberty for their offenses, but whom God would welcome to his throne of mercy. He prayed for their homes, and for their friends who this day

Deep feeling.—Speculation.—Their teachers.

would send their thoughts hither in remembrance of those in bonds. He alluded to the scenes of their childhood, the solicitude of their early friends, and the affection of their parents. When the words *home, friend, childhood,* were heard, several of those sturdy sons of crime and wretchedness instinctively bowed their heads and concealed their faces in their hands; and, as a *father's blessing* and a *mother's love* were alluded to, more than one of these outcasts from society, were observed to dash the scalding tear from the eye. These men *feel* like other men,—*why are they here?* was again the thought which forced itself upon my mind; and while the chaplain proceeded to his sermon, in the midst of the silence that pervaded the room, my mind ran back to their educators. Once these men were children like others. They had feelings like other children, affection, reverence, teachableness, conscience,—why are they here? Some, very likely, on account of their extraordinary perversity; but most because they had a wrong education. More than half, undoubtedly, have violated the laws of their country not from extraordinary viciousness, but from the *weakness* of their moral principle. Tempted just like other and better men, *they fell,* because in early childhood no one had cultivated and strengthened the conscience God had given them. I am not disposed to excuse the vices of men, nor to screen them from merited punishment; neither do I worship a "painted morality", based solely upon education, thus leaving nothing for the religion of the Bible to accomplish by purifying the heart, that fountain of wickedness: yet how many of these men might have been saved to society; how many of them have powers which, under different training, might have adorned and blessed their race; how many of them may date their fall to the evil influence and poisonous example of some guide of their childhood, some recreant teacher of their early days,—God only knows! But what a responsibility still rests upon the head of any such teacher, if he did not know, or did not try to know, the avenue to their hearts; if he did not feel, or try to feel, the worth of moral principle to these very fallen ones! And what would be his feelings if he could look back through the distant days of the past, and count up exactly the measure of his own faithfulness and his own neglect? This, the all-seeing eye alone can do,—this, He who looketh upon the heart ever does!

Teachers, go forth, then, conscious of your responsibility to your pupils, conscious of your accountability to God, go forth and teach this people; and endeavor *so to teach*, that when you meet your pupils, not in the walks of life merely, not, perhaps, in the Auburn Prison, not, indeed, upon the shores of time, but at the final Judgment, where you must meet them all, you may be able to give a good account of the influence which you have exerted over mind.

Study to know and to do.

As it may then be forever too late to correct your errors and efface any injury done, study now to act the part of wisdom and the part of love.

Study the human heart by studying the workings of your own; seek carefully the avenues to the affections; study those higher motives which elevate and ennoble the soul; cultivate that purity which shall allure the wayward, by bright example, from the paths of error; imbue your own souls with the love of teaching and the greatness of your work; rely not alone upon yourselves, as if by your own wisdom and might you could do this great thing; but seek that direction which our heavenly Father never withholds from the honest inquirer after his guidance,—and though the teacher's work is, and ever must be, attended with overwhelming responsibility, YOU WILL BE SUFFICIENT FOR THESE THINGS.

CHAPTER IV.

PERSONAL HABITS OF THE TEACHER.

THE importance of correct habits to any individual can not be overrated. The influence of the teacher is so great upon the children under his care, either for good or evil, that it is of the utmost importance to them, as well as to himself, that his habits should be unexceptionable. It is the teacher's sphere to *improve* the community in which he moves, not only in learning, but in morals and manners; *in every thing* that is "lovely and of good report". This he may do partly by precept,—but very much by example. *He teaches, wherever he is.* His manners, his appearance, his character, are all the subject of observation, and to a great extent, of imitation, by the young in his district. He is observed not only in the school, but in the family, in the social gathering, and in the religious meeting. How desirable, then, that he should be a *model* in all things!

Man has been said to be a "bundle of habits"; and it has been as pithily remarked: "Happy is the man whose habits are his friends". It

Cleanliness. — Ablution.

were well if all persons, before they become teachers, would attend carefully to the formation of their personal habits. This, unhappily, is not always done,—and therefore I shall make no apology for introducing in this place some very plain remarks on what I deem the essentials among the habits of the teacher.

1. NEATNESS. This implies cleanliness of the person. If some who assume to teach were not proverbial for their slovenliness, I would not dwell on this point. On this point, however, I must be allowed great plainness of speech, even at the expense of incurring the charge of excessive nicety; for it is by attending to a *few little things* that one becomes a strictly neat person. The morning ablution, then, should never be omitted; and the comb for the hair, and brush for the clothes should always be called into requisition before the teacher presents himself to the family, or to his school. Every teacher would very much promote his own health by washing the whole surface of the body every morning in cold water. This is now done by very many of the most enlightened teachers, as well as others. When physiology is better understood, this practice will be far more general. To no class of persons is it more essential than to the teacher; for on account of his confinement, often in an unventilated room, with half a hundred children during the day, very much more is demanded of the exhalents in him than

in others. His only safety is in a healthy action of the skin.

The *teeth* should be attended to. A brush and clean water have saved many a set of teeth. It is bad enough to witness the deplorable neglect of these important organs so prevalent in the community; but it is extremely mortifying to see a filthy set of teeth in the mouth of the teacher of our youth. The *nails*, too, I am sorry to say, are often neglected by some of our teachers, till their *ebony tips* are any thing but ornamental. This matter is made worse, when, in the presence of the family or of the school, the penknife is brought into requisition to remove that which should have received attention at the time of washing, in the morning. The *teacher* should remember that it is a *vulgar* habit to pare or clean the nails while in the presence of others, and especially during conversation with them.

The teacher should be neat in his *dress*. I do not urge that his dress should be expensive. His income ordinarily will not admit of this. He may wear a very plain dress; nor should it be any way singular in its fashion. All I ask is, that his clothing should be in good taste, and *always clean*. A slovenly dress, covered with dust, or spotted with grease, is never so much out of its proper place, as when it clothes the teacher.

While upon this subject I may be indulged in

Tobacco.—Order, system.

a word or two upon the use of tobacco by the teacher. It is quite a puzzle to me to tell why any man but a Turk, who may lawfully dream away half his existence over the fumes of this filthy narcotic, should ever use it. Even if there were nothing wrong in the use of unnatural stimulants themselves, the filthiness of tobacco is enough to condemn it among teachers, especially in the form of chewing. It is certainly worth while to ask whether there is not some moral delinquency in teaching this practice to the young, while it is admitted, by nearly all who have fallen into the habit, to be an evil, and one from which they would desire to be delivered. At any rate, I hope the time is coming when the good taste of teachers, and a regard for personal neatness and the comfort of others, shall present motives sufficiently strong to induce them to break away from a practice at once so unreasonable and so disgusting.

2. ORDER. In this place I refer to that *system* and regularity so desirable in every teacher. He should practice it in his room at his boarding-house. Every thing should have its place. His books, his clothing, should all be arranged with regard to this principle. The same habit should go with him to the school-room. His desk there should be a pattern of orderly arrangement. Practicing this himself, he may with propriety insist upon it in his pupils. It is of great moment to the teacher that, when he de-

Courtesy. — Coarseness. — Profanity.

mands order and arrangement among his pupils, they can not appeal to any breach of it in his own practice.

3. COURTESY. The teacher should ever be courteous, both in his language and in his manners. *Courtesy of language* may imply a freedom from all *coarseness*. There is a kind of communication, used among boatmen and hangers-on at bar-rooms, which should find no place in the teacher's vocabulary. All vulgar jesting, all double-entendres, all low allusions, should be forever excluded from his mouth. And profanity — can it be necessary that I should speak of this as among the habits of the teacher? Yes, it is even so. Such is the want of moral sense in the community, that men are still employed in some districts whose ordinary conversation is poisoned with the breath of blasphemy; ay, and even the walls of the school-room resound to undisguised oaths! I can not find words to express my astonishment at the indifference of parents, or at the recklessness of teachers, wherever I know such cases to exist.

Speaking of the *language* of the teacher, I might urge also that it should be both *pure* and *accurate*. Pure as distinguished from all those cant phrases and provincialisms which amuse the vulgar in certain localities; and accurate as to the terms used to express his meaning. As the *teacher teaches* in this, as in every thing, by example as well as by precept, he should be very careful to

Courtesy of manner. — Politeness.

acquire an unexceptionable use of our language, and never deviate from it in the hearing of his pupils or elsewhere.

There is a *courtesy of manner*, also, which should characterize the teacher. This is not that ridiculous obsequiousness which some persons assume, when they would gain the good opinion of others. It is true politeness. By politeness I do not mean any particular form of words, nor any prescribed or prescribable mode of action. It does not consist in *bowing* according to any approved plan, nor in a compliance simply with the formulas of etiquette in the fashionable world. True politeness is founded in benevolence. Its law is embodied in the golden rule of the Savior: — "Whatsoever ye would that men should do to you, do ye even so to them." It is the exercise of real kindness. It entertains a just regard for the feelings of others, and seeks to do for them what would make them really happy.

The teacher should possess this quality. Whenever he meets a child, it should be with the looks and words of kindness. Whenever he receives any token of regard from a pupil, he should acknowledge it in the true spirit of politeness. Whenever he meets a pupil in the street, or in a public place, he should cordially recognize him. In this way and a thousand others, which, if he have the right spirit, will cost him nothing, he will cultivate true courtesy in his pupils. He can do it in this way more effectually than he can

---
Good manners may be inculcated.
---

by formally lecturing upon the subject. True politeness will always win its true reciprocation. Two teachers were once walking together in the streets of a large town in New England. Several lads whom they met on the sidewalk, raised their caps as they exchanged the common salutations with one of the teachers. "What boys are these that pay you such attention as they pass?" inquired the other. "They are my scholars," answered his friend. "Your scholars! Why, how do you teach them to be so very polite? Mine are pretty sure never to look at me; and generally they take care to be on the other side of the street." "I am unable to tell," said his friend; "I never say any thing about it. I usually bow to them, and they are as ready to bow to me." The whole secret consisted in this teacher's meeting his pupils in the spirit of kindness.

I would not, however, discourage a teacher from actually inculcating good manners by precept. It should indeed be done. The manners of pupils are too much neglected in most of our schools, and, I am sorry to say, in most of our families. Our youth are growing up with all the independence of sturdy young republicans,—and, in their pride of freedom from governmental restraint, they sometimes show a want of respect for their seniors and superiors, which is quite mortifying to all lovers of propriety. It is the teacher's province to counteract this; and in order to do it well, he should possess the

The commercial value of politeness.

virtue of true courtesy, both in theory and practice.

The law of good manners and politeness is the duty of being kind and agreeable to others. By means of this test, pupils may be made to discriminate between rudeness and politeness, and so to form an ideal of conduct. Cases in illustration may be cited by the teacher and discussed by the pupils, such as boisterous conversation in public places, smoking in cars where ladies are sitting, whispering and giggling during concerts or lectures, etc.

The young should be shown the commercial value of politeness, and taught that nothing pays better in the conduct of business than uniform courtesy to all with whom we have dealings. I once reached a town at night, and made my way to a hotel for refreshment and rest. It was with no little difficulty that I finally gained the ear of the clerk, who graciously permitted me to register my name. The next night I sought the hospitalities of another hotel. The clerk spied me from afar, took my hand-baggage, promptly ordered a supper, and conducted me to one of his best rooms. He seemed to have been awaiting my arrival! I would go many miles to shun the first place, and as many to gain the second. The difference in the two cases was that between rudeness and courtesy. We patronize the tradesman who treats us kindly and courteously; and we instinctively shun one who is rude and ill-natured.

Punctuality.—Dismiss punctually.

PUNCTUALITY. This, as a *habit*, is essential to the teacher. He should be punctual in every thing. He should always be present at or before the time for opening the school. A teacher who goes late to school once a week, or even once a month, can not very well enforce the punctual attendance of his pupils. I once knew a man who, for seven long years, was never late at school a single minute, and seldom did he fail to reach his place more than five minutes before the time. I never knew but one such. I have known scores who were frequently tardy, and sometimes by the *space of a whole hour!*

A teacher should be as punctual in dismissing as in opening his school. I know that some make a virtue of keeping their schools beyond the regular hours. I have always considered this a very questionable virtue. If a teacher wishes to stay beyond his time, it should be either with delinquents, who have some lessons to make up, or with those who voluntarily remain. But, after all, if he has been strictly punctual to the hours assigned for his various duties in school, there will scarcely be the necessity for him, or any of his pupils, to remain beyond the time for dismission; and, as a general rule, a regard both for his own health and theirs should forbid this. It is better to work diligently while one does work, and not to protract the time of labor, so as to destroy one's energy for to-morrow.

This habit of punctuality should run through

every thing. He should be punctual at all engagements; he should be studiously so in all the detail of school exercises; he should be so at his meals, at his private studies, at his hour of retiring at night and of rising in the morning, and also at his exercise and recreation. This is necessary to a truly exemplary character, and it is equally as necessary to good health.

5. HABITS OF STUDY. Unless the teacher takes care to furnish his own mind. he will soon find his present stock of knowledge, however liberal that may be, fading from his memory and becoming unavailable. To prevent this, and to keep along with every improvement, he should regularly pursue a course of study. I say *regularly;* for in order to accomplish any thing really desirable, he must do something every day. By strict system in all his arrangements, he may find time to do it; and whenever I am told by a teacher that he *can not find time* to study, I always infer that there is a want of order in his arrangements, or a want of punctuality in the observance of that order. Human life, indeed, is short; but most men still further abridge the period allotted to them, by a disregard of system.

What has now been said, upon the *teacher's spirit*, the *teacher's responsibility*, and the *teacher's personal habits*, will embody, perhaps, my views upon the *character of the individual*, who

A high standard.—Excelsior!

may be encouraged to engage in the work of teaching. Nor do I think the requirements in this department have been overstated. I know, indeed, that too many exercise the teacher's functions without the teacher's spirit as here described, and without the sense of responsibility here insisted on, and with habits entirely inconsistent with those here required. But this does not prove that such teachers have chosen the right calling, or that the children under their care are under safe and proper guidance. It proves, rather, that parents and school officers have too often neglected to be vigilant, or that suitable teachers could not be had.

Let none think of lowering the standard to what has been, or what may even now be, that of a majority of those who are engaged in this profession. Every young teacher's eye should be directed to the very best model in this work; and he should never be satisfied with bare mediocrity. EXCELSIOR, the motto of the Empire State, may well be the motto of the young teacher.

CHAPTER V.

LITERARY QUALIFICATIONS OF THE TEACHER.

I AM now about to enter an extensive field. Since the teacher is to be the life of the school, it is of great consequence that he have within him the means of sustaining life.

As the statutes in many of the states prescribe the *minimum* of attainment for the teacher, I might, perhaps, spare myself the labor of writing on this point. Yet in a thorough work on the Theory and Practice of Teaching, this very properly comes under consideration.

The profession of teaching is advancing. The present standard of acquirement demanded of the teacher, excludes many who were considered quite respectable in their vocation ten years ago. This may well be so; for within that time quite an advance has been made in the compensation offered to teachers. It is but reasonable that acquirement should keep pace with the reward of it. Indeed, the talent and attainment brought into the field must always be in advance of the rate of compensation. The people must be first convinced that teachers are better than they were years ago, and then they will be ready to reward them. In Massachusetts, according to statistics in the possession of the Hon. Horace Mann, Secretary of the Board of Education, the compensation of teachers has advanced thirty-three per cent. within ten years; nor is it reasonable to suppose that this advance has been made independent of any improvement among the teachers. Their system of supervision has increased in strictness, during this time, in an equal ratio; and many teachers, who were entirely incompetent for their places, have thus been driven to other employments. The course is still onward; and the time is not far distant when the people will demand still more thorough teachers for the common schools, and they will find it to their interest to pay for them.

Under these circumstances, it will not be my design to give the very lowest qualifications for a teacher at present. I shall aim to describe those which a teacher *ought to possess*, in order to command, for some time to come, the respect of the enlightened part of the community. I will not say that a man, with less attainment than I shall describe, may not keep a good school; I have no doubt that many do. Yet if our profession is to be really respectable, and truly deserving of the regard of an enlightened people, we must have a still higher standard of qualification than I shall now insist on. The following is a list of the studies of which every teacher *should have* a competent knowledge. I add also

Orthography.—Our alphabet.

to each such word of comment as appears to be necessary.

1. ORTHOGRAPHY. This implies something more than mere *spelling*. Spelling is certainly indispensable. No person should ever think of teaching who is not an accurate speller. But the *nature* and *powers* of letters should also be mastered. We have in our language about forty elementary sounds; yet we have but twenty-six characters to represent them. Our alphabet is therefore imperfect. This imperfection is augmented by the fact that several of the letters are employed each to represent several different sounds. In other cases, two letters combined represent the element. There are also letters, as *c*, *q*, and *x*, which have no sound that is not fully represented by other letters. Then a very large number of our letters are silent in certain positions, while they are fully sounded in others. It were much to be desired that we might have a *perfect* alphabet—that is, as many characters as we have elementary sounds—and that each letter should have but one sound. For the present this can not be; and the present generation of teachers, at least, will have to teach our present orthography. Those systems of orthography are much to be preferred which begin with the *elementary sounds*, and then present the letters as their representatives, together with the practice of analyzing words into their elements, thus showing at once the silent letters and the *equiv-*

alents. These systems may be taught in half the time that the old systems can be; and when acquired, they are of much greater practical utility to the learner. As my views have been more fully presented in the "NORMAL CHART OF ELEMENTARY SOUNDS," prepared for the use of schools, I will only refer the reader to that work.

2. READING. Every teacher should be a good reader. Not more than one in every hundred among teachers, can now be called a good reader. To be able to read well implies a quick perception of the meaning as well as a proper enunciation of the words. It is a branch but poorly taught in most of our schools. Many of the older pupils get *above* reading before they have learned to read well; and, unfortunately, many of our teachers can not awaken an interest in the subject, because, very likely, they can not read any better than their scholars.

It would be interesting to ascertain how large a proportion of our youth leave the schools without acquiring the power readily to *take the sense* of any common paragraph which they may attempt to read. I am inclined to think the number is not small.* In this way, I account for the

---

* Since writing the above, my eye has fallen upon the following, from the Second Annual Report of the Secretary of the Massachusetts Board of Education. "I have devoted," says Mr. Mann, "especial pains to learn, with some degree of numerical accuracy, how far the reading in our schools is an exercise of the mind in thinking and feeling, and how far it is a barren action of the organs of speech upon

Hard labor.—Analysis of words.

fact that so many cease to read as soon as they leave school. It costs them so much *effort* to decipher the meaning of a book, that it counteracts the desire for the gratification and improvement it might otherwise afford. It should not be so. The teacher should be a model of good reading; he should be enthusiastic in this branch, and never rest till he has excited the proper interest in it among the pupils, from the oldest to the youngest, in the school.

It would be well if our teachers could be somewhat acquainted with the Latin and Greek languages, as this would afford them great facilities in comprehending and defining many of our own words. As this can not be expected for the present, a substitute may be sought in some analysis of our derivative words. Several works on word-analysis have been prepared, to supply, as far as may be, the wants of those who have not studied the classics. I should advise

the atmosphere. My information is derived principally from the written statements of the school committees of the different towns,—gentlemen who are certainly exempt from all temptation to disparage the schools they superintend. The result is that more than eleven twelfths of all the children in the reading classes in our schools do not understand the meaning of the words they read; that they do not master the sense of their reading lessons; and that the ideas and feelings intended by the author to be conveyed to and excited in the reader's mind, still rest in the author's intention, never having yet reached the place of their destination. It would hardly seem that the combined efforts of all persons engaged, could have accomplished more in defeating the true objects of reading. How the cause of this deficiency is to be apportioned among the legal supervisors of the schools, parents, teachers, and authors of text-books, it is impossible to say; but surely it is an evil gratuitous, widely-prevalent, and threatening the most alarming consequences."

every teacher, for his own benefit, to master some one of these.

3. WRITING. It is not respectable for the teacher of the young to be a bad writer; nor can it ever become so, even should the majority of bad writers continue to increase. The teacher should take great pains to write a plain, legible hand. This is an essential qualification.

4. GEOGRAPHY. A knowledge of the principles of geography is essential. This implies an acquaintance with the use of the globes, and the art of map-drawing. The teacher should be so well versed in geography, that, with an outline map of any country before him, he could give an intelligent account of its surface, people, resources, history, etc.; and if the outline map were not at hand, he ought to be able to draw one from memory,—at least of each of the grand divisions of the earth, and of the United States.

Nothing is more necessary for giving interest and charm to geographical instruction than a fund of anecdote and illustration, that may be found in books of travel; and such literature should be regarded as a part of the necessary outfit of the teacher.

5. HISTORY. The teacher should be acquainted with history,—at least, the history of the United States. He can hardly teach geography successfully without a competent knowledge of both ancient and modern history. It should, in the

Literature.—Mental Arithmetic.

main, be taught in our common schools in connection with geography.

6. LITERATURE. If the teacher aims to be a man of culture, he must have an acquaintance with general literature. Not to know what the better spirits of the world have written, and not to have gained some appreciation of their masterpieces, is to have missed one of the prime conditions of high teaching power. A defense against the many narrowing tendencies in the teacher's life, may be found in the three catholic studies just named,—Geography, History, and Literature.

7. MENTAL ARITHMETIC. Let every teacher be thoroughly versed in some good work on this subject. Colburn's was the first, and it is probably the best that has been prepared. That little book has done more than any other for the improvement of teaching in this country. It is not enough that the teacher is able in some way to *obtain the answers* to the questions proposed. He should be able to give the reason for every step in the process he takes to obtain them, and to do it in a clear and concise manner. It is this which constitutes the value of this branch as a discipline for the mind.

I may never forget my first introduction to this work. On entering an academy as a student, in 1827, after I had "ciphered through" some four or five arithmetics on the old plan, my teacher asked me if I had ever studied Mental Arithmetic, extending to me the little book above

Written Arithmetic.

named. "No, sir." "Perhaps you would like to do so." I opened to the first page, and saw this question: "How many thumbs have you on your right hand?" This was enough; the color came into my face, and I pettishly replied, "I think I can find out the number of my thumbs without studying a *book* for it." "But," said the teacher, "many of our young men have studied it, and they think they have been profited. If you will take it, and turn over till you find a little exercise for your mind, I think you will like it." His manner was open and sincere, and I took the little book. In three weeks, I had mastered it; and I had gained, in that time, more knowledge of the principles of arithmetic than I had ever acquired in all my life before. I no longer "saw through a glass darkly."

8. WRITTEN ARITHMETIC. This everybody demands of the teacher; and he is scarcely in danger of being without fair pretensions in this branch. He should, however, know it by its *principles*, rather than by its rules and facts. He should so understand it, that if every arithmetic in the world should be burned, he could still make another, constructing its rules and explaining their principles. He should understand arithmetic so well, that he could teach it thoroughly though all text-books should be excluded from his school-room. This is not demanding too much. Arithmetic is a *certain science*, and used every day of one's life,—the teacher should be an entire master of it.

English Grammar.—Algebra.

9. ENGLISH GRAMMAR. It is rare that a teacher is found without some pretensions to English Grammar; yet it is deplorable to observe how very few have any liberal or philosophical acquaintance with it. In many cases, it is little else than a system of barren technicalities. The teacher studies *one* book, and too often takes that as his creed. In no science, is it more necessary to be acquainted with several authors. The person who has studied but one text-book on grammar, even if that be the best one extant, is but poorly qualified to teach this branch. There is a philosophy of language which the teacher should carefully study; and if within his power, he should have some acquaintance with the peculiar structure of other languages besides his own. It can hardly be expected that the common teacher should acquire an accurate knowledge of other languages by actually studying them. As a substitute for this, I would recommend that the teacher should very carefully read the little work of De Sacy on General Grammar, also the article "Grammar" in the Edinburgh and other encyclopedias. In this science, the mind naturally runs to *bigotry;* and there is no science where the learner is apt to be so *conceited* upon small acquirements, as in grammar. Let the teacher spare no pains to master this subject.

10. ALGEBRA. This branch is not yet required to be taught in all our schools; yet the teacher should have a thorough acquaintance with it.

Geometry.—Trigonometry.—Surveying.—Natural Philosophy.

Even if he is never called upon to teach it (and it never should be introduced into our common schools till very thorough attainments are more common in the other branches), still it so much improves the mind of the teacher, that he should not be without a knowledge of it. He will teach simple arithmetic much better for knowing algebra. I consider an acquaintance with it indispensable to the thorough teacher, even of the common school.

11. GEOMETRY. The same may be said of this branch that has been said of algebra. Probably nothing disciplines the mind more effectually than the study of geometry. The teacher should pursue it for this reason. He will teach other things the better for having had this discipline, to say nothing of the advantage which a knowledge of the principles of geometry will give him, in understanding and explaining the branches of mathematics.

12. PLANE TRIGONOMETRY and SURVEYING. In many of our schools, these branches are required to be taught. They are important branches in themselves, and they also afford good exercise for the mind in their acquisition. The young teacher, especially the male teacher, should make the acquirement.

13. NATURAL PHILOSOPHY. This branch is not taught in most of our district schools. The teacher, however, should understand it better than it is presented in many of the simple text-books on

Chemistry.—Human Physiology.

this subject. He should have studied the *philosophy* of its principles, and be fully acquainted with their demonstration. If possible, he should have had an opportunity also of seeing the principles illustrated by experiment. This is a great field; let not the teacher be satisfied with cropping a little of the herbage about its borders.

14. CHEMISTRY. As a matter of intelligence, the teacher should have acquaintance with this branch. It is comparatively a new science, but it is almost a science of miracles. It is beginning to be taught in our common schools; and that department of it which relates to agriculture, is destined to be of vast importance to the agricultural interests of our country. "Instead of conjecture, and hazard, and doubt, and experiment, as heretofore, a knowledge of the composition of soils, the food of plants, and the processes of nature in the culture and growth of crops, would elevate agriculture to a conspicuous rank among the exact sciences."* The teacher should not be behind the age in this department.

15. HUMAN PHYSIOLOGY. The teacher should well understand this subject. There is an unpardonable ignorance in the community as to the structure of the human body, and the laws of health, the observance of which is, in general, a condition of longevity, not to say of exemption from disease. By reference to statistics, it has been ascertained that almost a fourth part of all

* Col. Young.

Importance of a knowledge of the laws of health.

the children that are born, die before they are one year old. More than one third die before they are five years of age; and before the age of eight, more than *one half* of all that are born return again to the earth! Of those who survive, how many suffer the miseries of lingering disease, almost sighing for death to deliver them from the pangs of life! There is something deplorably wrong in our philosophy of living, else the condition of man would not so commonly appear an exception to the truth that God does all things well.* Dr. Woodward, late of the Massachusetts State Lunatic Hospital, says: "From the cradle to the grave, we suffer punishment for the violation of the laws of health and life. I have no doubt that *half* the evils of life, and *half* the deaths that occur among mankind, arise from ignorance of these natural laws; and that a thorough knowledge of them would diminish the sufferings incident to our present state of being in very nearly the same proportion." I know not how an acquaintance with these laws can be in any way so readily extended as through the agency of our

---

* "It is the vast field of ignorance pertaining to these subjects, in which *quackery* thrives and fattens. No one who knows any thing of the organs and functions of the human system, and of the properties of those objects in nature to which that system is related, can hear a quack descant upon the miraculous virtues of his nostrums, or can read his advertisements in the newspapers,—wherein, fraudulently toward man and impiously toward God, he promises to sell an 'Elixir of Life', or 'The Balm of Immortality', or 'Resurrection Pills',—without contempt for his ignorance or detestation of his guilt. Could the quack administer his nostrums to the great enemy, Death, then indeed *we* might expect to live forever!"—HORACE MANN.

Intellectual Philosophy.

teachers of the young. At any rate, the teacher himself should understand them, both for his own profit and the means thus afforded him of being directly useful in the discharge of his duties to others. I have already shown that he is responsible to a great extent for the bodily health of his pupils. A thorough knowledge of physiology will enable him to meet this responsibility. In several States, legislation now enjoins on teachers the duty of giving instruction on the physiological effects of alcohol; and to do this discreetly and effectively, requires exact knowledge of the subject. Text-books on Physiology have been expressly prepared to meet this new requirement.

16. INTELLECTUAL PHILOSOPHY. This is necessary for the teacher. His business is with the mind. He, of all men, should know something of its laws and its nature. He can know something, indeed, by observation and introspection; but he should also learn by careful study. His own improvement demands it, and his usefulness depends upon it.

For the teacher, Psychology may have all the concrete interest of Botany or Geology. The study of mental phenomena is almost forced on his notice; and, with enough knowledge of mental science to enable him to interpret the phenomena of hourly appearance, he would soon feel a new zeal in his work and might make needed contributions to educational science.

Moral Philosophy.—Rhetoric.—Book-keeping.

17. MORAL PHILOSOPHY. A knowledge of this may be insisted on for the same reasons which apply to intellectual philosophy. It is so important that the moral nature of the child be rightly dealt with, that he is a presumptuous man who attempts the work without the most careful attention to this subject.

18. RHETORIC AND LOGIC. These are of great service to the teacher personally, as means of mental discipline and the cultivation of his own taste. Even if he is never to teach them, they will afford him much assistance in other departments of instruction. He certainly should have the advantage of them.

19. BOOK-KEEPING. Every teacher should know something of book-keeping, at least by single entry; and also be conversant with the ordinary forms of business. The profound ignorance on this subject among teachers is truly astonishing.* Book-keeping should be a common-school study. In looking over the able Report of the Superintendent of Common Schools in New York, I notice in fifty-three counties, during the winter of 1845-6, that among 225,540 pupils in the common schools, only 922 studied book-keeping!

---

* A teacher, who kept a private school, was met in a country store one day by one of his patrons, who paid him for the tuition of his child, asking at the same time for a receipt. The teacher stared vacantly at his patron. "Just give me a bit of paper," said the patron, "to show you've got the money." "O, yes, sir," said the teacher; and taking a pen and paper, wrote the following:

☞ I have got the money.
J— D—.

Science of Government.

That is, a study, which in practical life comes home to the interest not only of every merchant, but of every farmer, every mechanic, in short, every business man, is almost entirely neglected in the schools,—while it is yet true that our courts of justice display evidences of the most deplorable ignorance in this important art. Some still keep their accounts on bits of paper; others use books, but without any system, order, or intelligibility; and others still, mark their scores in chalk, or charcoal, upon the panel of the cellar-door!

The teacher should qualify himself, not only to understand this subject, but to teach it in such a way that it can be easily comprehended by the classes in our common schools.

20. SCIENCE OF GOVERNMENT. The teacher should, at least, be well acquainted with the history and genius of our own government, the constitution of the United States, and of his own State. In a republican government, it is of great importance that the young, who are to take an active part in public measures as soon as they arrive at the age of twenty-one, should before that time be made acquainted with some of their duties and relations as citizens. This subject has been introduced successfully into many of our common schools; but whether it is to be matter of formal teaching or not, it is a disgrace* to a teacher and

---

* Not long since a teacher of a public school afforded lasting amusement for the hangers-on at a country grocery. He was jeered for belonging to the whig party by which Mr. Tyler was brought into power.

Drawing.—Vocal Music.

to his profession, to be ignorant of the provisions of the constitution for the mode of choosing our rulers.*

21. DRAWING. The good teacher should understand the principles of drawing. He should also be able to practice this art. It is of great consequence to him. Without neglect of other things, children can be very profitably taught this art in the common schools. In the absence of apparatus, it is the teacher's only way of addressing the eye of his pupils, in illustrating his teaching. Every teacher should take pains, not only to draw, but to draw well.

22. VOCAL MUSIC. It is not absolutely essential, though very desirable, to the good teacher, that he should understand music, theoretically and practically. Music is becoming an exercise in our best schools; and wherever introduced and judiciously conducted, it has been attended with pleasing results. It promotes good reading and speaking, by disciplining the ear to distinguish sounds; and it also facilitates the cultivation of the finer feelings of our nature. It aids very much in the government of the school, as its exercise gives vent to that restlessness which otherwise would find an *escapement* in boisterous noise and whis-

---

"No, no," said he, "I voted for Gen. Harrison, but *I never voted for John Tyler.*" "How did you do that?" inquired a by-stander. "*Why, I cut Tyler's name off of the ticket,* to be sure!"

* "That which contributes most to preserve the state, is to educate children with reference to the state; for the most useful laws will be of no service, if the citizens are not accustomed to and brought up in the principles of the constitution."—*Aristotle.*

pering,—and thus it often proves a *safety-valve*, through which a love of vociferation and activity may pass off in a more harmless and a more pleasing way. "The school-master that can not sing," says Martin Luther, "I would not look upon." Perhaps this language is too strong; but it is usually more pleasant to look upon a school where the school-master can sing.

I have thus gone through with a list of studies which, it seems to me, every one who means to be a good teacher, even of a common school, should make himself acquainted with. I would not condemn a teacher who, having other good qualities, and a thorough scholarship as far as he has gone, might lack several of the branches above named. There have been many good teachers without all this attainment; but how much better they might have been with it!

I have made this course of study as limited as I possibly could, taking into view the present condition and wants of our schools. No doubt even more will be demanded in a few years. I would have the present race of teachers so good, that they shall be looked upon by those who succeed them, as their "*worthy and efficient predecessors.*"

I ought in this place to add that the teacher increases his influence and, consequently, his use-

General knowledge desirable.—A suggestion.

fulness, in proportion as he makes himself conversant with general knowledge. This is too much neglected. The teacher, by the fatigue of his employment and the circumstances of his life, is strongly tempted to content himself with what he already knows, or, at best, to confine himself to the study of those branches which he is called upon to teach. He should stoutly resist this temptation. He should always have some course of study marked out, which he will systematically pursue. He should, as soon as possible, make himself acquainted generally with the subject of astronomy, the principles of geology, in short, the various branches of natural history. He will find one field after another open before him; and if he will but have the perseverance to press forward, even in the laborious occupation of teaching, he may make himself a well-informed man.

I will venture one other suggestion. I have found it a most profitable thing in the promotion of my own improvement, to take up annually, or oftener, some particular subject to be pursued with reference to writing an extended lecture upon it. This gives point to the course of reading, and keeps the interest fixed. When the thorough investigation has been made, let the lecture be written from memory, embodying all the prominent points, and presenting them in the most striking and systematic manner. It should be done, too, with reference to accuracy and even elegance of style, so that the composition may be

A point gained.—Self-improvement.

yearly improved. In this way, certain subjects are forever *fixed* in the mind. One who carefully reads for a definite object, and afterward writes the results from memory, never loses his hold upon the facts thus *appropriated*.

No matter what a teacher's opportunities for professional training may have been, he should ever feel himself under obligations to work in the line of self-improvement. As education is a matter of life, activity, and growth, these qualities should manifest themselves in the teacher in a pre-eminent degree. A teacher who has ceased to be an active student, has lost the secret of his greatest power.* In the presence of a cultured man or woman who is animated by the zeal of a scholar, the young imbibe the scholarly spirit by a sort of *induction*. Taking the teaching class as it is, it must be confessed that active scholarship is not one of its marks. There is more than one cause for this. In most cases, teaching is an avocation, and so professional improvement is not a matter of self-interest; in many cases, an imperfect academic training has left behind it the bane of complacent self-satisfaction; and in all cases, generally speaking, there is lacking the stimulus to progress which comes from an exacting auditory. As our pupils are satisfied with less than we have, we do not feel obliged to strive after more than we have.

* "How shall he give kindling in whose inward man there is no live coal, but all is burnt out to a dead grammatical cinder?"—*Carlyle.*

Public opinion.—Reading Circles.

Public opinion, acting through school officers, is now stimulating the teaching class to higher literary and professional qualifications, and there is every-where manifest a sincere desire on the part of teachers to meet these reasonable requirements. The difficulty consists in not knowing what definite things to do, or how to do them, and in not having the hope of a tangible reward. In response to these needs, State organizations, known as "Reading Circles", are now in process of formation.* The general plan is to prescribe a course of reading in two main lines,—PROFESSIONAL, including the art, the science, and the history of education, and in GENERAL LITERATURE, comprising *History* and *Belles-lettres*. Examinations and certificates of proficiency are provided for, and it is expected that examining boards will credit candidates with the work done in these Circles. This is a movement in the right line, and deserves hearty encouragement.

* Such organizations have now been made in Ohio, Indiana, Illinois, Iowa, Michigan, Minnesota, and New York.

CHAPTER VI.

RIGHT VIEWS OF EDUCATION.

EVERY teacher, before he begins the work of instruction, should have some definite idea of what constitutes an education; otherwise, he may work to very little purpose. The painter, who would execute a beautiful picture, must have beforehand a true and clear conception of beauty in his own mind. The same may be said of the sculptor. That rude block of marble, unsightly to the eyes of other men, contains the godlike form, the symmetrical proportion, the life-like attitude of the finished and polished statue; and the whole is as clear to his mental eye before the chisel is applied, as it is to his bodily vision when the work is completed. With this perfect *ideal* in the mind at the outset, every stroke of the chisel has its object. Not a blow is struck, but it is guided by consummate skill; not a chip is removed, but to develop the ideal of the artist. And when the late unsightly marble, as if by miraculous power, stands out before the astonished spectator in all the perfection of beauty,— when it almost breathes and speaks,— it is to the artist but the realization of his own conception.

Now let the same astonished and delighted spec-

A spectator's efforts.—The difference.

tator, with the same instruments, attempt to produce another statue from a similar block. On this side, he scores too deep; on the other, he leaves a protuberance; here, by carelessness, he encroaches upon the rounded limb; there, by accident, he hews a chip from off the nose; by want of skill, one eye ill-mates the other; one hand is distorted as if racked by pangs of the gout; the other is paralyzed and deathlike. Such would be his signal failure. Thus he might fail a thousand times. Indeed, it would be matter of strange surprise, if, in a thousand efforts, he should once succeed.

Now the difference between the artist and the spectator lies chiefly in this: the one knows beforehand what he means to do,—the other works without any plan. The one has studied beauty till he can see it in the rugged block; the other only knows it when it is presented to him. The former, having an ideal, produces it with unerring skill; the latter, having no conception to guide him, brings out deformity.

"What sculpture is to the block of marble," says Addison, "education is to the human soul;" and may I not add, that the sculptor is a type of the true educator,—while the spectator, of whom I have been speaking, may aptly represent too many false teachers, who, without study or forethought, enter upon the delicate business of fashioning the human soul, blindly experimenting amidst the wreck of their heaven-descended material, maiming and marring, with scarcely the

Blindness of employers.—Illustrated.

possibility of final success,—almost with the certainty of a melancholy failure!

In other things besides education, men are wiser. They follow more the teachings of nature and of common sense. But in education, where a child has but one opportunity for mental training, as he can be a child but once,—where success, unerring success, is every thing to him for time and eternity, and where a mistake may be most ruinous to him,—in education, men often forget their ordinary wisdom and providence, and commit the most important concerns to the most incompetent hands. "The prevailing opinions," says Geo. B. Emerson, "in regard to this art are such as the common sense of mankind and the experience of centuries have shown to be absurd as to every other art and pursuit of civilized life. To be qualified to discourse upon our moral and religious duties, a man must be educated by years of study; to be able to minister to the body in disease, he must be educated by a careful examination of the body in health and in disease, and of the effects produced on it by external agents; to be able to make out a conveyance of property, or to draw a writ, he must be educated; to navigate a ship, he must be educated by years of service before the mast or on the quarter-deck; to transfer the products of the earth or of art from the producer to the consumer, he must be educated; to make a hat or a coat, he must be educated by years of apprenticeship; to make a plow, he must be educated; to make a nail, or a shoe for a horse or an ox, he must be educated. But to prepare a man to do all these things,—to train the body in its most tender years, according to the laws of health so that it should be strong to resist disease—to fill the mind with useful knowledge, to educate it to comprehend all the relations of society, to bring out all its powers into full and harmonious action—to educate the moral nature, in which the very sentiment of duty resides, that it may be fitted for an honorable and worthy fulfillment of the public and private offices of life,—to do all this is supposed to require no study, no apprenticeship, no preparation!"

Many teachers, therefore, encouraged by this unaccountable indifference in the community, have entered the teacher's profession without any idea of the responsibilities assumed, or of the end to be secured by their labors, aside from receiving, at the close of their term, the compensation for their service in dollars and cents. And even many who have entered this profession with good intentions, have made the most deplorable mistakes from a want of an adequate idea of what constitutes an education. Too often has educating a child been considered simply the act of imparting to it a certain amount of knowledge, or of "carrying it through" a certain number of studies, more or less. Education has too frequently been held to be a cultivation of the intellectual to the neglect of the moral powers; and the poor body, too, except among savages, has had but little share in its privileges or benefits. In a very large number of our schools, the physical and the moral have both been sacrificed to the intellectual. Even some of our public speakers have dwelt upon the necessity of *intelligence* to the perpetuity of our free institutions, scarcely seeming to be aware that intelligence, without moral principle to direct and regulate it, might become the very engine through which evil men might effect our overthrow. Who has not seen that an educated man, without virtue, is but the more capable of doing evil? Who does not know that knowledge misdirected, becomes, instead of a boon to be desired, a bane to be deprecated?

From what has been said, I place it among the highest qualifications of the teacher that he should have *just views of education*. I consider it all-important that he should have a well-defined object at which to aim, whenever he meets a young mind in the transition state. He should have an *ideal* of a well-educated human soul, tenanting a healthy, well-developed human body; an ideal which he at once and systematically labors to reach, as does the sculptor when he commences his work upon the quarried marble. "What is it to educate a human being aright?" should be one of the first questions the candidate for the teacher's office should ask himself with the deepest seriousness. I say the *candidate;* for this question should be settled, if possible, *before* he begins his work. It is a great question, and he may not be able to answer it in a day. Let him consult the dictates of his own mind, — let him consult the teachings of experience and of wisdom, as they are to be found in the writings of Milton, Locke, Wyse, Cousin, Brougham, and others of the eastern continent, and of Wayland, Potter, Mann, G. B. Emerson, Dwight, and many others of our own countrymen. Let him, enlightened by all this, carefully observe human nature around him; consider its tendencies, its wants, and its capabilities; and after a patient survey of all the truth he can discover upon the subject, let him come to an honest conclusion as to what is a correct answer to the query with which he started — "What is it to educate a human being aright?"

The conclusions of the honest and intelligent inquirer after the truth in this matter, will be something like the following: — That education (from *e* and *duco*, to lead forth) is development; that it is not instruction merely — knowledge, facts, rules — communicated by the teacher, but it is discipline, it is a waking up of the mind, a growth of the mind, — growth by a healthy assimilation of wholesome aliment. It is an inspiring of the mind with a thirst for knowledge, growth, enlargement, — and then a disciplining of its powers so far that it can go on to educate itself.

Discipline the primary purpose.

It is the arousing of the child's mind to think, without thinking for it; it is the awakening of its powers to observe, to remember, to reflect, to combine. It is not a cultivation of the memory to the neglect of every thing else; but it is a calling forth of all the faculties into harmonious action. If to possess facts simply is education, then an encyclopedia is better educated than a man.

It should be remarked that though knowledge is not education, yet there will be no education without knowledge. Knowledge is ever an incident of true education. No man can be properly educated without the acquisition of knowledge; the mistake is in considering knowledge the *end* when it is either the *incident* or the *means* of education. The discipline of the mind, then, is the great thing in intellectual training; and the question is not, how much have I acquired?—but, how have my powers been strengthened in the act of acquisition?

Nor should the intellectual be earlier cultivated than the moral powers of the mind. The love of moral truth should be as early addressed as the love of knowledge. The conscience should be early exercised in judging of the character of the pupil's own acts, and every opportunity afforded to strengthen it by legitimate use. Nor should the powers of the mind be earlier cultivated than those of the body. It is the theory of some, indeed, that the body should engross most of the attention for several of the first years of childhood. This, I think, is not nature's plan. She cultivates all the powers at once,—the body, mind, and heart. So should the teacher do. "Education," in the pertinent language of Mr. Fox,* "has reference to the *whole man*, the body, the mind, and the heart; its object, and, when rightly conducted, its effect is, to make him a complete creature after his kind. To his frame it would give vigor, activity, and beauty; to his senses, correctness and acuteness; to his intellect, power and truthfulness; to his heart, virtue. The educated man is not the gladiator, nor the scholar, nor the upright man, alone; but a just and well-balanced combination of all three. Just as the educated tree is neither the large root, nor the giant branches, nor the rich foliage, but all of them together. If you would mark the perfect man, you must not look for him in the circus, the university, or the church, exclusively; but you must look for one who has '*mens sana* in *corpore sano*'—a healthful mind in a healthful body. The being in whom you find this union, is the only one worthy to be called educated. To make all men such, is the object of education."

I have dwelt thus fully on this subject, because it is so obvious that egregious mistakes are made in education. How many there are who are called "good scholars" in our schools, of whom we hear nothing after they go forth into

* Lecture before the Am. Institute, 1835.

Errors in education.

the world. Their good scholarship consists in that which gives them no impulse to go on to greater attainments by themselves. Their learning is either that of *reception*—as the sponge takes in water—or that of mere memory. Their education is not discipline; it kindles none of those desires which nothing but further progress can satisfy; it imparts none of that self-reliance which nothing but impossibilities can ever subdue. While these are pointed out by their teachers as the ornaments of their schools, there are others, known as the heavy, dull, "poor scholars", in no way distinguished but by their stupidity,— of whom no hopes are entertained, because of them nothing is expected,—who in after-life fairly outstrip their fellows and strangely astonish their teachers. Almost every teacher of fifteen years' experience has noticed this. Now, why is it so? There must have been somehow in such cases a gross misjudgment of character. Either those pupils who promised so much by their quickness, were educated wrong, and perhaps educated too much, while their teachers unwittingly and unintentionally educated their less distinguished companions far more judiciously; or else, nature in such cases must be said to have been playing such odd pranks that legitimate causes could not produce their legitimate effects. We must charge nature as being extremely capricious, or we must allege that the teachers entirely misunderstood their work, failing where they expected most, and succeeding, as if by chance—almost against their will—where they expected least. I incline to the latter alternative; and hence I infer that there is such a thing as teaching a mind naturally active too much—exciting it too much,—so that it will prematurely exhaust its energies and gladly settle back into almost imbecility; and that there is such a thing as leaving the mind so much to its own resources, that without dazzling the beholder like the flash of the meteor when it glares upon the startled vision, it may be silently gathering materials to support the more enduring light of the morning-star which anon will rise in majesty and glory.

It will be well for our youth when our teachers shall so understand human nature, and so comprehend the science and the art of education, that these mistakes shall seldom occur; and when he who tills the nobler soil of the mind, shall, with as much faith and as much certainty as he who tills the literal field, rely upon the fulfillment of heaven's unchangeable law: "Whatsoever a man soweth that shall he also reap."

Education, in its absolute sense, is a process that aims at realizing the typical man.

Among trees, we observe various degrees of perfection as to form and structure; and in estimating the degree of perfection, we compare the given specimen with a typical tree of its kind. We conceive that each tree of a species is fashioned after an ideal—a perfect and invariable

Education as an ideal.

pattern; and the ideal cultivation of a tree would consist in causing it to grow into its typical form.

Every animal of a given species, as a horse, approaches its type in a greater or less degree; and the ideal training of an animal would consist in having it grow into the type of its kind.

In man, there are numberless degrees of physical perfection. At one extreme, there is unsightly deformity, at the other divine beauty, and between, an ascending scale of infinite gradations. In mind, the range is from imbecility to inspired genius, with countless gradations between. In morals, the slow ascent is from the monster to the saint. In each of these three orders of growth, the ascent is toward an ideal type; and the sphere of education, as a conscious art, is to lead man up to the typical perfection of his physical, mental, and moral being.

The type toward which education aspires is a mental creation. The best specimens that come under our notice are imperfect; and to the ideal that is formed from the aggregate of the highest observed excellences, the mind adds something of its own to complete the type.

All human beings are under the law of ascent toward a typical form. This is their law of growth. The natural education of man takes place through the unassisted action of this law; just as a plant, when abandoned to itself, will undergo a fortuitous growth. This natural education is the typical education in only one respect: *an upward tendency in the line of growth.*

Education in the absolute sense above illustrated, has been thus defined: "The harmonious and equable evolution of the human powers."

This conception of education is subject to the following limitations in practice:

1. It comprehends the whole period of life, from the cradle to the grave, while in practice, the period of education is limited to a few years.

2. It involves physical, mental, moral, and religious training, while the efforts of the actual educator can scarcely extend beyond the training of the intellect.

3. It aims at the perfection of the human being as a whole, while the exigencies of life require men to be trained for specific duties.

Under these limitations, education becomes nearly synonymous with instruction, and may be defined as a process having three purposes:

1. To develop the intellectual faculties, so as to produce robustness of mind and habits of ready and accurate thinking.

2. To furnish the mind with knowledge for use.

3. To impart skill in the use of instrumental knowledge.

The difference between education in its absolute sense, and education under its practical limitations, may be illustrated as follows:

If a tree or a shrub is needed for a special

Special training, and its results.

use, as for a hedge, the cultivator abandons the typical form and determines the growth into a modified form. Whenever one part of a vegetable, as the root, the flower, or the seed, becomes especially valuable, the idea of symmetrical growth is abandoned, and this part is given an abnormal (unnatural) growth.

In training a horse, instead of aiming at the most perfect specimen of his kind, the horseman may train him for the race-course, or the plow, or the saddle. A modified form is found more useful, and so the typical form is abandoned.

There is an antagonism between man as an ideal of his kind, and man as an instrument of service; and education is forced to depart from her ideal in order to fit man for the limitations under which he lives. To make a lawyer, or a carpenter, there must be some departure from the course of training that would lead up to the typical man.

By reason of the limitations of time, education, as a practical art, must abandon formal physical and moral training. Physical soundness must be a postulate, and direct moral and religious training must be relegated to the family and the church.

A liberal education aims at the ideal perfection of the mind. Its purpose is to give it all possible perfection as the instrument of thought, to furnish it with knowledge the most fit for

A professional education.

the man, and to train it to a dexterous use of all its energies.

A professional or technical education either supplants or supplements a liberal education. It is either the instrument alone, or the man first and then the instrument.*

* "The end desired must be known before the way. All means or arts of education will be, in the first instance, determined by the ideal we entertain of it."—RICHTER, *Levana*, p. 29.

CHAPTER VII.

RIGHT MODES OF TEACHING.

FROM what has been said of Education, it is very obvious that it is no small thing to be a successful teacher. It is admitted by all that the teacher should be APT TO TEACH. He can not be useful without this. He may have an unimpeachable character; he may have the most liberal and thorough literary acquirements; he may deeply feel his responsibility, and yet after all he may fail to teach successfully.

Aptness to teach has been said to be a native endowment, a sort of instinct, and therefore incapable of being improved by experience or instruction,—an instinct such as that which guides the robin, though hatched in an oven, to build a perfect nest like that of its parent, without ever having seen one. I am of opinion that such instincts in men are rare; but that aptness to teach, like aptness to do any thing else, is usually an acquired power, based upon a correct knowledge of what is to be done, and some accurate estimate of the fitness of the means used for the end. If there are exceptions to this, they are very uncommon; and the safer way, therefore, for the majority of teachers, is, to study carefully the

| A mistake.—The way literary nurselings are made. |

rationale of their processes, and to rely rather upon sound and philosophical principles in their teaching, than upon a very doubtful intuition.

One of the most common errors into which young teachers fall (and some old ones too), is that of misjudging of the degree of assistance which the young scholar needs in the pursuit of learning. There are a few who forget the difficulties which impeded their own perception of new truths when learners, and therefore have no sympathy with the perplexities which surround the children under their charge, when they encounter like difficulties. They refuse to lend a helping hand, even where it is needed, and by making light of the child's doubts, perhaps sneering at his unsuccessful struggles, they dishearten him so far that imaginary obstacles become insurmountable, and he gives up in despair. But a far more numerous class tend toward the other extreme. From a mistaken kindness, or a mistaken estimate of the child's ability, or both, they are disposed to do quite too much for him, and thus they diminish his power to help himself. The child that is constantly dandled upon the lap of its nurse and borne in her arms to whatever point it may desire to go, does not soon learn to walk; and when it at length makes the attempt, it moves not with the firm tread of him who was early taught to use his own limbs. There is a great deal of literary dandling practiced in our schools; and as a consequence, a

Anecdote of folly.—Pouring-in.—The "oral hobby."

great many of our children are mere sickly nurselings, relying upon leading-strings while in the school and falling, for very weakness, just as soon as the supporting hand is withdrawn. This evil is so common and in some instances so monstrous,* that I shall be pardoned if I dwell upon it a little more fully.

In illustrating this subject, I must mention two processes of teaching, not, indeed, exactly opposite to each other, though widely different,— into one or both of which many of our teachers are very liable to fall. I shall, for the sake of a name, designate the former as the

SECTION I.—POURING-IN PROCESS.

This consists in *lecturing* to a class of children upon every subject which occurs to the teacher, it being his chief aim to bring before them, in a limited time, as many facts as possible. It is as if he should provide himself with a basket of sweetmeats, and every time he should come within reach of a child, should seize him and compel him to swallow—regardless of the condition of his stomach—whatever trash he should

---

* Not long since I visited a school, where the teacher with much self-complacency requested me to examine the *writing* of the children. It was indeed very fair. But when I drew from him the fact that he first wrote each page himself with a lead pencil and only required his scholars to *black his marks over with ink*, and that with unremitting labor he did this week after week for all the writers in his school, I knew not which most to wonder at, the docility of the children or the weakness of the teacher. The writing ceased to be wonderful.

Victims of kindness.—Passive recipient.—A jug.

happen first to force into his mouth. Children are indeed fond of sweetmeats, but they do not like to have them *administered*,—and every physiologist knows there is such a thing as eating enough even of an agreeable thing to make one sick and thus produce loathing forever after. Now many teachers are just such misguided caterers for the mind. They are ready to seize upon the *victims* of their kindness, force open their mental gullets, and pour in, without mercy and without discretion, whatever sweet thing they may have at hand, even though they surfeit and nauseate the poor sufferer. The mind, by this process, becomes a mere *passive recipient*, taking in, without much resistance, whatever is presented till it is full.

"A passive recipient!" said one to his friend, "what is a *passive recipient?*" "A passive recipient," replied his friend, "is a *two-gallon jug*. It holds just two gallons, and as it is made of potter's ware, it can never hold but just two gallons." This is not an unfit illustration of what I mean by making the mind a passive recipient. Whenever the teacher does not first excite inquiry, first prepare the mind by *waking it up* to a desire to know, and if possible to find out by itself, but proceeds to think *for* the child, and to give him the results, before they are desired or before they have been sought for,—he makes the mind of the child a *two-gallon jug*, into which he may pour just *two gallons*, but no more. And if, day after day, he should continue to pour in, day after day he may expect that what he pours in will *all run over*. The mind, so far as retention is concerned, will act like the jug; that is, a part of what is poured in to-day, will be diluted by a part of that which is forced in to-morrow, and that again will be partially displaced and partially mingled with the next day's pouring, till at length there will be nothing characteristic left. But aside from retention, there is a great difference between the jug and the mind. The former is inert material and may be as good a jug after such use as before; but the mind suffers by every unsuccessful effort to retain.

This process of lecturing children into imbecility is altogether too frequently practiced; and it is to be hoped that intelligent teachers will pause and inquire before they pursue it further.

The other process to which I wish to call attention, is that which, for the sake of distinguishing it from the first, I shall denominate the

SECTION II.—DRAWING-OUT PROCESS.

This consists in asking what the lawyers call *leading questions*. It is practiced, usually, whenever the teacher desires to help along the pupil. "John," says the teacher when conducting a recitation in Long Division, "what is the number to be divided called?" John hesitates. "Is it the dividend?" says the teacher. "Yes, sir—

An example.—A spectator astonished.—Teaching History!

the dividend." "Well, John, what is that which is left after dividing called?—the remainder—is it?" "Yes, sir." A visitor now enters the room, and the teacher desires to show off John's talents. "Well, John, of what denomination is the remainder?"

John looks upon the floor.

"Isn't it always the same as the dividend, John?"

"Yes, sir."

"Very well, John," says the teacher, soothingly, "what denomination is this dividend?" pointing to the work upon the board. "Dollars, is it not?"

"Yes, sir; dollars."

"Very well; now what is this remainder?"

John hesitates.

"Why, *dollars*, too, isn't it?" says the teacher.

"O, yes, sir, *dollars!*" says John, energetically, while the teacher complacently looks at the visitor to see if he has noticed how *correctly* John has answered!

A class is called to be examined in History. They have committed the text-book to memory—that is, they have learned the *words*. They go on finely for a time. At length one hesitates. The teacher adroitly asks a question in the language of the text. Thus: "*Early in the morning, on the* 11*th of September*, what did *the whole British army* do?" The pupil, thus timely reassured, proceeds: "*Early in the morning, on the*

A further example.

11th of September, the whole British army, drawn up in two divisions, commenced the expected assault." Here again she pauses. The teacher proceeds to inquire: "Well,—'Agreeably to the plan of Howe, the right wing' did what?"

Pupil. "*Agreeably to the plan of Howe, the right wing——*"

Teacher. "The right wing, commanded by whom?"

Pupil. "O! '*Agreeably to the plan of Howe, the right wing, commanded by* Knyphausen, made a feint of crossing the Brandywine at Chad's Ford,'" etc.

This is a very common way of helping a dull pupil out of a difficulty; and I have seen it done so adroitly, that a company of visitors would agree that it was wonderful to see how thoroughly the children had been instructed!

I may further illustrate this *drawing-out* process, by describing an occurrence, which, in company with a friend and fellow-laborer, I once witnessed. A teacher, whose school we visited, called upon the class in Colburn's First Lessons. They rose, and in single file marched to the usual place, with their books in hand, and stood erect. It was a very good-looking class.

"Where do you begin?" said the teacher, taking the book.

Pupils. On the 80th page, 3d question.

Teacher. Read it, Charles.

Charles. (*Reads.*) "A man being asked how

Yes, sir.—Hard mental labor.

many sheep he had, said that he had them in two pastures; in one pasture he had eight; that three fourths of these were just one third of what he had in the other. How many were there in the other?"

Teacher. Well, Charles, you must first get one fourth of eight, must you not?

Charles. Yes, sir.

Teacher. Well, one fourth of eight is two, isn't it?

Charles. Yes, sir; one fourth of eight is two.

Teacher. Well, then, three fourths will be three times two, won't it?

Charles. Yes, sir.

Teacher. Well, three times two are six, eh?

Charles. Yes, sir.

Teacher. Very well. (A pause.) Now the book says that this six is just one third of what he had in the other pasture, don't it?

Charles. Yes, sir.

Teacher. Then if six is one third, three thirds will be—three times six, won't it?

Charles. Yes, sir.

Teacher. And three times six are—eighteen, ain't it?

Charles. Yes, sir.

Teacher. Then he had eighteen sheep in the other pasture, had he?

Charles. Yes, sir.

Teacher. Next, take the next one.

At this point I interposed, and asked the

An interposition.—Process of Extraction.

teacher if he would request Charles to go through it alone. "O, yes," said the teacher; "Charles, you may do it again." Charles again read the question, and — looked up. "Well," said the teacher, "you must first get one fourth of eight, mustn't you?" "Yes, sir." "And one fourth of eight is two, isn't it?" "Yes, sir." And so the process went on as before till the final eighteen sheep were *drawn out* as before. The teacher now looked round, with an air which seemed to say, "Now I suppose you are satisfied."

"Shall *I* ask Charles to do it again?" said I. The teacher assented. Charles again read the question, and again—looked up. I waited, and he waited; but the teacher could *not* wait. "Why, Charles," said he, impatiently, "you want one fourth of eight, don't you?" "Yes, sir," said Charles, promptly; and I thought best not to insist further at this time upon a repetition of "*yes, sir*", and the class were allowed to proceed in their own way.

This is, indeed, an extreme case, and yet it is but a fair sample of that teacher's method of stupefying mind. This habit of assisting the pupil to some extent, is, however, a very common one, and as deleterious to mind as it is common. The teacher should at once abandon this practice and require the scholar *to do the talking* at recitation. I need hardly suggest that such a course of *extraction* at recitation, aside from the waste of time by both parties, and the waste of strength by the teacher, has a direct tendency to make the scholar miserably superficial. For why should he study, if he knows from constant experience that the teacher, by a leading question, will relieve him from all embarrassment? It has often been remarked, that "the teacher makes the school". Perhaps in no way can he more effectually make an inefficient school, than by this *drawing-out process*.

I look upon the two processes just described, as very prominent and prevalent faults in our modern teaching; and if by describing them thus fully, I shall induce any to set a guard upon their practice in this particular, I shall feel amply rewarded.

SECTION III.—THE MORE EXCELLENT WAY.

It is always a very difficult question for the teacher to settle, "How far shall I help the pupil, and how far shall the pupil be required to help himself?" The teaching of nature would seem to indicate that the pupil should be taught mainly to depend on his own resources. This, too, I think, is the teaching of common sense. Whatever is learned, should be so thoroughly learned, that the next and higher step may be comparatively easy. And the teacher should always inquire, when he is about to dismiss one subject, whether the class understand it so well that they can go on to the next. He may, indeed, some-

Dangerous when excessive.—The true medium.

times give a word of suggestion during the preparation of a lesson, and, by a seasonable hint, save the scholar the needless loss of much time But it is a very great evil if the pupils acquire the habit of running to the teacher as soon as a slight difficulty presents itself, to request him to remove it. Some teachers, when this happens, will send the scholar to his seat with a reproof perhaps, while others, with a mistaken kindness, will answer the question or solve the problem themselves, as the shortest way to get rid of it. Both these courses are, in general, wrong. The inquirer should never be frowned upon; this may discourage him. He should not be relieved from labor, as this will diminish his self-reliance without enlightening him; for whatever is done *for* a scholar without his having studied closely upon it himself, makes but a feeble impression upon him, and is soon forgotten. The true way is, neither to discourage inquiry nor answer the question. Converse with the scholar a little as to the principles involved in the question; refer him to principles which he has before learned, or has now lost sight of; perhaps call his attention to some rule or explanation before given to the class; go just so far as to enlighten him a little and *put him on the scent*, then leave him to achieve the victory himself. There is a great satisfaction in discovering a difficult thing for one's self,—and the teacher does the scholar a lasting injury who takes this pleasure from him.

"Not to-day, sir."—"I've got it!"

The teacher should be simply suggestive, but should never take the glory of a victory from the scholar by doing his work for him, at least, not until he has given it a thorough trial himself.

The skill of the teacher, then, will be best manifested, if he can contrive to awaken such a spirit in the pupil, that he shall be very unwilling to be assisted; if he can kindle up such a zeal, that the pupil will prefer to try again and again before he will consent that the teacher shall interpose. I shall never forget a class of boys, some fourteen or fifteen years of age, who in the study of algebra had imbibed this spirit. A difficult question had been before the class a day or two, when I suggested giving them some assistance. "*Not to-day, sir,*" was the spontaneous exclamation of nearly every one. Nor shall I forget the expression that beamed from the countenance of one of them, when, elated with his success, he forgot the proprieties of the school and audibly exclaimed, "*I've got it! I've got it!*" It was a great day for him; he felt, as he never before had felt, his own might. Nor was it less gratifying to me to find that his fellows were still unwilling to know his method of solution. The next day, a large number brought a solution of their own, each showing evidence of originality. A class that has once attained to a feeling like this, will go on to educate themselves, when they shall have left the school and the living teacher.

Other than book-studies.

As to the communication of knowledge, aside from that immediately connected with school-studies, there is a more excellent way than that of *pouring it in* by the process already described. It is but just that I should give a specimen of the method of doing this. I shall now proceed to do so, under the head of

SECTION IV.—WAKING UP MIND.

The teacher of any experience knows, that if he will excite a deep and profitable interest in his school, he must teach many things besides *book-studies*. In our common schools, there will always be a company of small children, who, not yet having learned to read understandingly, will have no means of interesting themselves and must depend mainly upon the teacher for the interest they take in the school. This to them is perhaps the most critical period of their lives. Whatever impression is now made upon them will be enduring. If there they become disgusted with the dullness and confinement of school, and associate the idea of pain and repulsiveness with that of learning, who can describe the injury done to their minds? If, on the other hand, the teacher is really skillful, and excites in them a spirit of inquiry and leads them in suitable ways to observe, to think, and to feel that the school is a happy place even for children, it is one great point gained.

General exercise.—A specimen.

I may suggest, here, then, that it would be well to set apart a few minutes once a day for a *general exercise* in the school, when it should be required of all to lay by their studies, assume an erect attitude, and give their undivided attention to whatever the teacher may bring before them. Such a course would have its physiological advantages. It would relieve the minds of all for a few minutes. The erect attitude is a healthful one. It would also serve as a short respite from duty and thus refresh the older scholars for study. I may further add, that, for the benefit of these small children, every general exercise should be conducted with reference to *them*, and such topics should be introduced as they can understand.

It is the purpose of the following remarks to give a *specimen* of the manner of conducting such exercises, for a few days, with reference to *waking up mind* in the school and also in the district.

Let us suppose that the teacher has promised that on the next day, at ten minutes past ten o'clock, he shall request the whole school to give their attention five minutes, while he shall bring something there to which he shall call the attention, especially of the little boys and girls under seven years of age. This very announcement will excite an interest both in school and at home; and when the children come in the morning, they will be more wakeful than usual till the

A fixed time.—Preparation.—Ear of corn.

fixed time arrives. It is very important that this time should be fixed, and that the utmost punctuality should be observed, both as to the beginning and ending of the exercise at the precise time.

The teacher, it should be supposed, has not made such an announcement without considering what he can do when the time arrives. He should have a well-digested plan of operation, and one which he knows beforehand that he can successfully execute.

Let us suppose that in preparing for this exercise he looks about him to find some object which he can make his *text;* and that he finds upon his study-table an *ear of corn.* He thinks carefully what he can do with it, and then with a smile of satisfaction he puts it in his pocket for the "general exercise."

In the morning, he goes through the accustomed duties of the first hour, perhaps more cheerfully than usual, because he finds there is more of animation and wakefulness in the school. At the precise time, he gives the signal agreed upon, and all the pupils drop their studies and sit erect. When there is perfect silence and strict attention by all, he takes from his pocket the ear of corn and in silence holds it up before the school. The children smile, for it is a familiar object; and they probably did not suspect they were to be *fed* with corn.

Teacher. "Now, children," addressing himself

Teacher's address to the children.—Their answers.

to the youngest, "I am going to ask you only one question to-day about this ear of corn. If you can answer it I shall be very glad; if the little boys and girls upon the front seat can not give the answer, I will let those in the next seat try; and so on till all have tried, unless our time should expire before the right answer is given. I shall not be surprised if none of you give the answer I am thinking of. As soon as I ask the question, those who are under seven years old, and think they can give an answer, may raise their hand. WHAT IS THIS EAR OF CORN FOR?"

Several of the children raise their hands, and the teacher points to one after another in order, and they rise and give their answers.

Mary. It is to feed the geese with.

John. Yes, and the hens too, and the pigs.

Sarah. My father gives corn to the cows.

By this time the hands of the youngest scholars are all down; for having been taken a little by surprise, their knowledge is exhausted. So the teacher says that those between seven and ten years of age may raise their hands. Several instantly appear. The teacher again indicates, by pointing, those who may give the answer.

Charles. My father gives corn to the horses when the oats are all gone.

Daniel. We give it to the oxen and cows, and we fat the hogs upon corn.

Laura. It is good to eat. They shell it from the cobs and send it to mill, and it is ground

Closing at the time.—Hear no more till to-morrow.

into meal. They make bread of the meal, and we eat it.

This last pupil has looked a little further into domestic economy than those who answered before her. But by this time, perhaps before, the five minutes have been nearly expended, and yet several hands are up, and the faces of several are beaming with eagerness to tell their thoughts. Let the teacher then say, "We will have no more answers to-day. You may think of this matter till to-morrow, and then I will let you try again. I am sorry to tell you that none of you have mentioned the use I was thinking of, though I confess I expected it every minute. I shall not be surprised if no one of you give this answer to-morrow. I shall now put the ear of corn in my desk, and no one of you must speak to me about it till to-morrow. You may now take your studies."

The children now breathe more freely, while the older ones take their studies, and the next class is called. In order to success, it is absolutely necessary that the teacher should positively refuse to hold any conversation with the children on the subject till the next time for "general exercise".

During the remainder of the forenoon, the teacher will very likely observe some signs of thoughtfulness on the part of those little children who have been habitually dull before. And perhaps some child, eager to impart a new discovery, will seek an opportunity to make it known during the forenoon. "Wait till to-morrow" should be the teacher's only reply.

Now let us follow these children as they are dismissed, while they bend their steps toward home. They cluster together in groups as they go down the hill, and they seem to be earnestly engaged in conversation.

"I don't believe it has any other use," says John.

"O, yes, it has," says Susan; "our teacher would not say so if it had not. Besides, did you not see what a knowing look he had, when he drew up his brow and said he guessed we couldn't find it out?"

"Well, I mean to ask my mother," says little Mary; "I guess she can tell."

By and by, as they pass a field of corn, Samuel sees a squirrel running across the street, with both his cheeks distended with "*plunder*".

At home, too, the ear of corn is made the subject of conversation. "What is an ear of corn for, mother?" said little Mary, as soon as they have taken a seat at the dinner-table.

Mother. An ear of corn, child? why, don't you know? It is to feed the fowls, and the pigs, and the cattle; and we make bread of it, too——

Mary. Yes, we told all that, but the teacher says that is not all.

Mother. The *teacher?*

Mary. Yes, ma'am, the teacher had an ear of

corn at school, and he asked us what it was for; and after we had told him every thing we could think of, he said there was another thing still. Now, I want to find out, so that *I* can tell him.

The consequence of this would be that the family, father, mother, and older brothers and sisters, would resolve themselves into a committee of the whole on the ear of corn. The same, or something like this, would be true in other families in the district; and by the next morning, several children would have something further to communicate on the subject. The hour would this day be awaited with great interest, and the first signal would produce perfect silence.

The teacher now takes the ear of corn from the desk and displays it before the school; and quite a number of hands are instantly raised as if eager to be the first to tell what other use they have discovered for it.

The teacher now says pleasantly, "The use I am thinking of, you have all observed, I have no doubt; it is a very important use indeed; but as it is a little out of the common course, I shall not be surprised if you can not give it. However, you may try."

"It is good to boil!"* says little Susan, almost springing from the floor as she speaks.

---

* The children themselves will be sure to find some new answers to such questions as the above. In giving in substance this lecture to a gathering of teachers in the autumn of 1845, in one of the busy villages of New York, where also the pupils of one of the district schools

"And it is for squirrels to eat," says little Samuel. "I saw one carry away a whole mouthful yesterday from the corn-field."

Others still mention other uses, which they have observed. They mention other animals which feed upon it, or other modes of cooking it. The older pupils begin to be interested, and they add to the list of uses named. Perhaps, however, none will name the one the teacher has in his own mind; he should cordially welcome the answer if perchance it is given; if none should give it, he may do as he thinks best about giving it himself on this occasion. Perhaps, if there is time he may do so,—after the following manner.

"I have told you that the answer I was seeking was a very simple one; it is something you have all observed, and you may be a little disappointed when I tell you. The use I have been thinking of for the ear of corn is this:—*It is to plant. It is for seed*, to propagate that species of plant called corn." Here the children may look

---

were present by invitation, I had described a process similar to that which has been dwelt upon above. I had given the supposed answers for the first day, and had described the children as pressing the question at home. When I had proceeded as far as to take up the ear of corn the second day, and had spoken of the possibility that the true answer to the question might not be given, I turned almost instinctively to the class of children at my right, saying, "*Now what is the ear of corn for?*" A little boy, some six years of age, who had swallowed every word, and whose face glowed as if there was not room enough for his soul within him, bounded upon his feet, and forgetting the publicity of the place and the gravity of the chairman of the meeting, clapping his hands forcibly together, "*It's to pop!*" he exclaimed emphatically, very much to the amusement of the audience. His mind had been *waked up*.

disappointed, as much as to say, "we knew that before."

The teacher continues: "And this is a very important use for the corn; for if for one year none should be planted, and all the ears that grew the year before should be consumed, we should have no more corn. This, then, was the great primary design of the corn; the other uses you have named were merely secondary. But I mean to make something more of my ear of corn. My next question is:—Do OTHER PLANTS HAVE SEEDS?"*

Here is a new field of inquiry. Many hands are instantly raised; but as the five minutes by this time have passed, leave them to answer at the next time.

"*Have other plants seeds?*" the children begin to inquire in their own minds, and each begins to think over a list of such plants as he is familiar with. When they are dismissed, they look on the way home at the plants by the roadside, and when they reach home they run to the garden. At the table they inquire of their parents, or their brothers and sisters.

At the next exercise, they will have more than they can tell in five minutes, as the results of their own observation and research. When enough has been said by the children as to the plants which have seeds, the next question may be:—Do ALL PLANTS HAVE SEEDS? This question

---
* *Plant* is here used in the popular sense.

will lead to much inquiry at home wherever botany is not well understood. There are many who are not aware that all plants have seeds. Very likely the ferns (common brakes) will be noticed by the children themselves. They may also name several other plants which do not exhibit their apparatus for seed-bearing very conspicuously. This will prepare the way for the teacher to impart a little information. Nor is there any harm in his doing so, whenever he is satisfied that the mind has been suitably exercised. The mind is no longer a "passive recipient"; and he may be sure that by inquiry it has increased its *capacity to contain*, and any fact which now answers inquiry, will be most carefully stored up.

The next question may be:—Do TREES HAVE SEEDS? As the children next go out, their eyes are directed to the trees above them. The fruit-trees, the walnut, the oak, and perhaps the pine, will be selected as those which have seeds. They will, however, mention quite a number which do not, or which, they think, do not have seeds. Among these may be the elm, the birch, and the Lombardy poplar. After hearing their opinions, and the results of their observations, take one of their exceptions as the subject of the next question :—*Does the Elm have seeds?* * This will narrow their inquiries down to a specific

---

* It is a very common opinion in the country that the elm has no seeds. I once knew a man who grew gray under the shade of a large elm, and who insisted that it never bore any seeds.

A promise.—A caution.—Example of teaching.

case, and every elm in the district will be inquired of as to its testimony on this point.

If the children can any of them collect and give the truth in the matter, so much the better; but if they, after inquiring of their parents and their grandparents, as I have known a whole school to do, come back insisting that the elm has no seeds; after hearing their reasons for their belief, and perhaps the opinions of their parents, you may promise to tell them something about it at the next exercise. This will again awaken expectation, not only among the children, but among the parents. All will wish to know what you have to bring out.

Great care should be taken not to throw any disparagement upon the opinions of parents. Perhaps, after giving the signal for attention, you may proceed as follows:—

"*Has the elm-tree any seeds?* Perhaps, children, you may recollect after the cold winter has passed away, that, along in the latter part of March, or the first of April, we sometimes have a warm, sunny day. The birds, perhaps, appear and begin to sing a little, and as you look up to the elm, you notice that its buds seem to swell, and you think it is going to put out its leaves. Everybody says we are going to have an early spring. But after this the cold frosty nights and windy days come on again, and then you think the leaves can not come out so early. Now, if you observe carefully, the leaves do not come out till about the 20th of May, or perhaps the first of June. Did you ever see any thing like what I have described?"

"Yes, sir, we remember that."

"Well, the next time you see the buds begin to open, just break off a twig of a good large tree, and you will find they are *not the leaf-buds*. But if you will watch them carefully for two or three weeks, you will find that each bud will put out some beautiful little flowers, brightly colored, and slightly fragrant. If you will still continue to watch them, you will find, as the flowers fall off, that seed vessels are formed, shaped very much like the parsnip seed. These will grow larger and larger every day, and by and by they will turn brown and look as if they were ripe. Just about this time the leaves will come out; and soon after these seeds, during some windy day or night, will all fall off. The ground will be covered with thousands of them. Perhaps you have seen this."

"Yes, sir," says John, "Grandpa calls that *elm-dust*."

"Perhaps next year you can watch this and ask your parents to examine it with you. But the five minutes are ended."

Now, information thus communicated will never be forgotten. The mind, having been put upon the stretch, is no longer a *passive recipient*.

The next question:—How ARE SEEDS DISSEMI-

NATED?—(of course explaining the term "*disseminated*".)

This will bring in a fund of information from the pupils. They will mention that the thistle seed *flies*, and so does the seed of the milkweed; that the burs of the burdock, and some other seeds are provided with hooks, by which they attach themselves to the hair of animals or the clothing of men, and *ride* away to their resting-place, which may be a hundred miles off. Some fall into the water and *sail* away to another shore. Some, like the seed of the Touch-me-not, are thrown at a distance by the bursting of the elastic pericarp; others, as nuts and acorns, are carried by squirrels and buried beneath the leaves. These facts would mostly be noticed by children, when once put upon observation.

Next question:—*Are plants propagated in any other way than by seeds?*

This question would call their attention to the various means of natural and artificial propagation—by layers, by offsets, by suckers, by grafting, by inoculation or budding, etc., etc.

Again:—*Have any plants more ways than one of natural propagation?* Some have one way only,—by seeds, as the annual plants; some have two,—by seeds and by roots, as the potato; some have three,—as the tiger lily, by side-bulbs from the roots, by *stalk-bulbs*, and by the seeds. This can be extended indefinitely.

SECTION V.—REMARKS.

Let it be remembered that the above has been given *simply as a specimen* of what could easily be done by an ingenious teacher, with as common a thing as an ear of corn for the text. Any other thing would answer as well. A chip, a tooth or a bone of an animal, a piece of iron, a feather, or any other object, could be made the text for adroitly bringing in the *uses of wood*, the *food and habits of animals*, the *use and comparative value of metals*, the *covering of birds*, their *migration*, the *covering of animals*, etc., etc. Let the teacher but think what department he will dwell upon, and then he can easily select his *text;* and if he has any tact, he can keep the children constantly upon inquiry and observation.

The advantages of the above course over simply lecturing to them on certain subjects, that is, over the *pouring-in process*, are many and great. Some of the most obvious I will briefly state.

1. *It immediately puts the minds of the children into a state of vigorous activity.* They feel that they are no longer *passive recipients.* They are incited to discover and ascertain for themselves. They are, therefore, profitably employed both in and out of school, and as a consequence are more easily governed. A habit of observation is cultivated in them; and what an advantage is this for a child! It is almost unnecessary to remark that many people go through the

Children should be taught to think.—Parents benefited.

world without seeing half the objects which are brought within their reach. It would be the same to them if their eyes were half the time closed. If they travel through a country presenting the most beautiful scenery or the most interesting geological features, they see nothing. They grow up among all the wonders of God's works, amid all the displays of his wisdom, of his design, to no purpose. They study none of the plans of nature; and by all the millions of arrangements which God has made, to delight the eye, to gratify the taste, to excite the emotions of pleasure instead of pain, they are neither the happier nor the wiser. What a blessing, then, it is to a child, to put his mind upon inquiry; to open his eyes to observe what his Creator intended his intelligent creatures should behold, of his goodness, his wisdom, his power. And how far superior is he who teaches a child to see for himself and to think for himself, to him who sees and thinks *for* the child, and thus practically invites the pupil to close his own eyes and grope in darkness through the instructive journey of life.

2. *It is of great service to the parents in the district to have this waking-up process in operation.* Our children are sometimes our best teachers. Parents are apt to grow rusty in their acquirements, and it is no doubt one of the designs of providence that the inquisitiveness of childhood should preserve them from sinking into

mental inactivity. Who can hear the inquiries of his own child after knowledge, without a desire to supply his wants. Now it is right for the teacher to use this instrumentality to *wake up mind* in his district. Parents, by the course I have recommended, very soon become interested in these daily questions of the teacher; and they are often as eager to know what is the *next question* as the children are to report it. This course, then, will supply profitable topics of conversation at the fireside, and very likely will encourage also the pursuit of useful reading. It will, moreover, soon awaken a deeper interest in the school on the part of the parents. They will begin to inquire of one another as to this new measure; and when they find by conference that the feeling in this matter is becoming general, they will desire to visit the school to witness this as well as the other operations of the teacher. This will secure parental co-operation, and thus in every way the influence of the school will be heightened. It is no small thing for a teacher to enlist the interest of his patrons in the success of his school; and this is the most happily done, when it is achieved through the medium of the pupils themselves.

3. *It wakes up the teacher's own mind.* This is by no means the least important point to be gained. The teacher, by the very nature of his employment, by daily confinement in an unhealthy atmosphere, by teaching over and over

The teacher's temptations.—He must improve his own mind.

again that with which he is quite familiar, by boarding with people who are inclined to be social, and by the fatigue and languor with which he finds himself oppressed every night, is strongly tempted to neglect his own improvement. There are but few who rise above this accumulation of impediments and go on in spite of them to eminence in the profession. A large proportion of all who teach rely upon the attainments with which they commence; and in the course of two or three years, finding themselves behind the age, they abandon the employment. This is very natural. Any man who treads in a beaten track, like a horse in a mill, must become weary, however valuable the product may be which he *grinds out*. It is essential that he should keep his own interest awake by some exercise of his ingenuity, and that he should compel himself to be industrious by undertaking that which will absolutely demand study. The above process will do this; and while he may have the exquisite pleasure of *seeing* the growth of his pupils' minds, he may also have the higher satisfaction of *feeling* the growth of his own.

I must here add, that it has not been my intention, in what I have said, to inculcate the idea that the study of books should in the least degree be abated to make room for this process of *waking up mind*. The various branches are to be pursued, and as diligently pursued, as ever before. The time to be set apart for this exercise should be short,—never probably to exceed five minutes. It is to come in when the scholars need rest for a moment, and when, if not employed about this, they would probably be doing nothing, or, perhaps, worse than nothing. It should be managed with care and should never be made a *hobby* by teachers, as if it were of more importance than any thing else. One secret of success in this—as, indeed, in every thing—is, that it should not be continued too long at once. The pupils should be left "longing—not loathing".

Let me again remind the reader that I have given the above *as a specimen*. The choice of the ear of corn was merely accidental; it happened to lie on my table when I wanted a text. The teacher should look upon this simply as a specimen, and then choose his own subjects. The main point aimed at is this:—Never ask leading questions, which your scholars can hardly fail to answer; and never *lecture* to your pupils till you have somehow first kindled in them a living desire to know; that is, avoid alike the "drawing-out" and the "pouring-in" process. Rather let it be your object to excite inquiry by a question they can not answer without thought and observation,—and such a question as they would deem it disgraceful not to be able to answer. This, adroitly done, is *"waking up mind"*.

Within the last few years, a great extension has been given to oral instruction, as distinguished from text-book instruction; and this reaction has now gone to such an extreme that there is a marked tendency to regard the use of books as an evidence of a poor quality of teaching. It has been assumed that the ideal teaching is that which causes the pupil to discover, or at least to rediscover, every thing for himself. It seems to be forgotten by some that there is knowledge, the reproduction of which, without the aid of books, is even inconceivable; and that there is other knowledge, the reproduction of which, without the aid of books, though conceivable, is practically impossible; and that in all cases, capitalized knowledge is accessible only through books. "Language," says J. S. Mill, "is the depository of the accumulated body of experience to which all former ages have contributed their part, and which is the inheritance of all yet to come." (*Logic*, p. 413.) The misuse of books should not be taken as an argument for their disuse. An intelligent instructor will not allow a pupil to confound words with ideas, but will teach the art of interpreting language. "Words," says Hobbes, "are wise men's counters; they do but reckon by them: but they are the money of fools." (*Leviathan*, Chap. IV.)

The assumption, sometimes made, that instruction by word of mouth is necessarily better than the same instruction given in the written form, is thus disposed of by Mr. Bain: "The suggestion is often made and is probably acted on

The preparation of an improved book.

by some teachers, to teach grammar without books, on the assumption that the difficulties are not inherent in the subject, but come into being when it is reduced to form and put into the pupil's hand in print. There must be some fallacy here. What is printed is only what is proper to to be said by word of mouth; and if the teacher can express himself more clearly than the best existing book, his words should be written down and take the place of the book. No matter what may be the peculiar felicity of the teacher's method, it may be given in print, to be imitated by others, and so introduce a better class of books; the reform that proposes to do away with books entirely, thus ending in the preparation of another book."

CHAPTER VIII.

CONDUCTING RECITATIONS.

IN considering a teacher's qualifications, the power of exciting an interest in the *recitations* of his school may not be overlooked. No man can be successful for any length of time without this. This comprises what is usually implied by APTNESS TO TEACH. All men have not this faculty by nature in an equal degree. Some may talk for an hour upon an interesting topic in the presence of children without commanding their attention; while there are others who can take even a commonplace subject and secure for any length of time an all-absorbing interest in every word. This difference is seen in every grade of public speakers and in all descriptions of writers; but perhaps more strikingly than anywhere else, it is observable among teachers. Enter one school, and you may notice that the scholars are dull and listless; indifference sits undisturbed upon their brows; or perhaps they are driven by the activity of their own natures to some expedient to interest themselves, while the teacher is, with very commendable spirit, laboriously—perhaps learnedly—explaining some principle or fact designed for their edification.

| A contrast.—Not always a natural gift. |

The secret is, he has not yet learned to awaken their attention; he fails to excite their interest.

Pass to another school. A breathless silence pervades the room; the countenances of the children, upturned toward the teacher, beam with delight. As he kindles into earnestness and eloquence, they kindle into responsive enthusiasm. Whenever his eye meets theirs, he sees—he *feels* the glow radiated by the fire he is lighting in their souls, and his own gathers new warmth and enthusiasm in return. Such a man is *apt to teach;* and you could scarcely break the spell by which he holds his class, "though you should give them for playthings, shining fragments broken from off the sun".

He who possesses this gift naturally, has very great advantage as a teacher to begin with. The ability to *tell well* what he knows, is of more consequence to the teacher, than the greatest attainments without the power to communicate them. Combine high attainments with the ability to tell, and you have the accomplished teacher.

But this power to communicate is not necessarily a *natural gift;* it comes not always by intuition. It can be acquired. It is founded in philosophy; and he who can understand any thing of the workings of his own mind, who can revert to the mental processes he went through in order to comprehend a principle, who can go back to that state of mind he was in before he comprehended it, and then, by one step more, can

How acquired.—Natural order.

put himself in the place of the child he is teaching, realizing exactly his perplexities and feeling his precise wants, can become the *apt teacher*. Those who fail in this are usually those who have forgotten the steps they took to acquire their own knowledge, or perhaps who never noticed what steps they did take.

To acquire this rare qualification should be the constant study of the teacher. To this end he should recall, as far as possible, the operations of his own mind in childhood. By studying his own mind, he learns, often most effectually, what he needs to know of others. Whenever he is preparing to teach any principle or fact to others, let him ask himself questions like the following:— What was the dark point in this, when I studied it? Where did my mind labor most? What point did my teacher fail to explain? Such questions will frequently suggest the very difficulty which perplexes every mind in the same process. Again, . the following inquiries may be very useful :—In studying this, what was the first point which appeared clear to me? After this, what was the second step, and *how* did that follow the first? The next in order? And the next? Was this the *natural order?* If not, what is the natural order? The right answers to these questions will suggest the course to be pursued in the instruction of a class.

The teacher can scarcely ask a more important question than this:—*What is the natural*

Science of teaching.—Thorough knowledge.

order of presenting a given subject? The ability to determine this, is what constitutes in a great degree the *science* of teaching. This inquiry should occupy much thought, because a mistake here is disastrous, and ever will be as long as divine wisdom is superior to human. He who can ascertain the order of nature, will be most sure of exciting an interest in the subject he is endeavoring to teach.

Some further suggestions as to conducting school recitations are contained in the following paragraphs.

1. *The teacher should thoroughly understand what he attempts to teach.* It is destructive of all life in the exercise, if the teacher is constantly chained down to the text-book. I have no objection, indeed, that he should take his text-book with him to the class, and that he should occasionally refer to it to refresh his own memory or to settle a doubt. But who does not know that a teacher who is perfectly familiar with what is to be taught, has ten times the vivacity of one who is obliged to follow the very letter of the book? His own enthusiasm glows in his countenance, sparkles in his eye, and leaps from his tongue. He watches the halting of the pupil, perceives his difficulty, devises his expedient for illustrating the dark point in some new way, and, at the proper moment, renders just the amount of assistance which the pupil needs. Not confined to the text, he has the use of his *eyes;* and

Printed questions—Special preparation.

when he speaks or explains, he can accompany his remark with a quickening look of intelligence. In this way his class is enlivened. They respect him for his ready attainment, and they are fired with a desire to be his equal.

How different is it with a teacher who knows nothing of the subject but what is contained in the text before him, and who knows *that* only as he reads it during the intervals occasioned by the hesitations of the class. Every question he proposes is printed at the bottom of the page; and as soon as he reads the question, without a glance at the pupil, his eye sets out on a chase after the answer in the text. If the scholar has not already been stupefied by such teaching, and happens to give an intelligent answer, yet not in the precise language of the book, he is *set right* by the teacher's reading the very words,—just so much detached from the sentence, as he fancies was intended to answer that one question! In this way he discourages thought in his pupils, and sets a bounty on mechanical study. In this way, too, he congeals whatever of interest they bring with them to the recitation, and they sink into indifference,—or, following the instincts of their nature, they seek occupation in play or mischief, even under the sound of his voice!

2. *The teacher should specially prepare himself for each lesson he assigns.* This is naturally suggested by what has just been said. The teacher's memory needs to be refreshed. We all

The tables turned.—Commonplace-book.—Its use.

know how difficult it would be to *recite* a lesson, in geometry for instance, weeks after studying it. It is so in other things. Now, the teacher should be so familiar with the lesson which he proposes to hear recited, that he *could* recite it himself as perfectly as he would desire his scholars to do it. This is seldom the case. I have heard a teacher, with the text-book in his hands, complain of the dullness or inaccuracy of his classes, when, if the tables had been turned, and the pupils allowed to ask the questions, the teacher would scarcely have recited as well. And I may add, *this is no very uncommon thing!* If any one is startled at this assertion, let him request a friend, in whom he can confide, to ask him the questions of a particular lesson in geography, or history, or grammar. The teacher should daily study his class lessons. This will enable him the better to assign his lessons judiciously. In this daily study, he should *master the text-book* upon the subject; and, more than this, he should consider what collateral matter he can bring in to illustrate the lesson. He should draw upon the resources of his own mind,—upon the treasures of his *commonplace-book*,*—upon the contents of

---

* It is an excellent plan for every teacher to keep a commonplace book of considerable size, different portions of it being set apart for the different subjects upon which he is to give instruction. On the first twenty pages, "Geography" may be the *head*,—the next twenty pages may be set apart for "History,"—twenty more may be assigned to "Reading,"—and a like number to "Arithmetic," "Grammar," "Spelling," "Writing," etc., reserving quite a space for "Miscellaneous Matter." This would make a large book; but when it is remembered that it is to

Improvement in teaching power.—Use of the eye.

some encyclopedia,—upon *any* source, from whence he can obtain a supply of knowledge for his purpose. This will improve his own mind, and he will be encouraged, as from time to time he teaches the same branch, to find that he is able to do better than ever before, and that, instead of becoming weary with repetition, he is more and more enthusiastic over the subject.

Going thus to his class—so full of the subject, that were the text-book annihilated, he could make another and better one—he will have no difficulty to secure attention. As he speaks, his eye accompanies his word, and as his pupils answer, he sees the expression of their countenances; and what a world of meaning there is in this expression! It betrays, better than words can do, the clearness or obscurity of the mind's perception, when a truth is presented. How different the beaming of the eye when the soul *apprehends*, from that almost idiotic stare at vacuity when words are used without import. And how necessary it is that the teacher should be free to observe the inward workings of the soul as indicated upon the countenance.

be used for several years, it is well to have it large enough to contain a large amount of matter. Now, whenever the teacher hears a lecture on a peculiar method of teaching either of these branches, let him note the prominent parts of it under the proper head, and *especially the illustrations.* When he reads or hears an anecdote illustrating Geography, History, or Grammar, let it be copied under the proper head. If it illustrates Geography, let the *name of the place* stand at its head. When he visits a school, and listens to a new explanation or a new process, let him note it under its head. In this way he may collect a thousand valuable things to be used with judgment in his school.

Correct language.—"Sums."—"Question."—Anecdote.

3. *The teacher should be able to use our language fluently and correctly.* In this many are deficient. They hesitate and stammer, and after all, express their ideas in vague terms, and perhaps by the use of inaccurate or inelegant language. A teacher in no way gives so effectual instruction in grammar as by his own *use* of our language; and there can be no sight more mortifying than that of a teacher laboring to fix in the minds of his class some rule of syntax, when his own language at the very moment shows an entire disregard of the rule. It is very common to hear teachers talk of "*sums*" to their classes in arithmetic, and even to ask them to do "sums" in subtraction or division! The term "*question*" is often as improperly applied, when no question is asked. The teacher should be accurate in the use of terms. "Question" is sometimes the proper word; sometimes, "problem"; and sometimes, "exercise" or "example", may with more propriety be used: but "*sum*" means the *amount* of several numbers when added, and it should not be applied as the *name of an exercise*. Some teachers use the terms *ratio* and *proportion** interchangeably, as if they were synonyms. Such inaccuracies in the teacher will be sure to be repro-

---

* We are reminded by this of the college student who was examined rather closely by his tutor. "What is ratio?" inquired the tutor. 'Ratio?" said the young man; "ratio is proportion." "Well, what is proportion?" "Proportion? proportion is ratio." "Well, then," said the tutor, looking perplexed, "what are both together?" "Excuse me," aid the pupil. "*I can define but one at a time!*"

Animation.—Children imitative.—Attitude.

duced in the school, and it is a great evil for the scholar to acquire a careless habit in the use of terms.

4. *He should have proper animation himself.* Horace Mann describes some of the Scotch teachers as working themselves up into a feverish excitement in the presence of their classes, and the classes in turn as literally bounding from the floor when they answer their hasty questions. Now, while I think these Scotch teachers go quite too far, I do think that many of our own teachers come short of a proper standard of animation. A teacher should be ready, without being rapid; animated, without being boisterous. Children are imitative beings; and it is astonishing to observe how very soon they catch the manners of the teacher. If he is heavy and plodding in his movements, they will very soon be dull and drowsy in theirs; then, if he speaks in a sprightly tone, and moves about with an elastic step, they almost realize a resurrection from the dead. If he appears absent-minded, taking but little interest in the lesson which is recited, they will be as inattentive, at least, as he; while, if all his looks and actions indicate that the subject is of some importance, he will gain their attention. Nor can I refrain in this place from suggesting to the teacher the importance of regarding his manners, while engaged in conducting a recitation. His *attitude* should not be one of indolence or coarseness,—and when he moves from his seat.

and appears at the blackboard to illustrate any point, it should be done gracefully, and with a constant regard to the fact, that every look and every motion *teaches*.

5. *He should never proceed without the attention of the class.* A loss of interest is sure to follow a want of attention. Besides, a habit of inattention, while it is very common, is also a great calamity to the person who falls into it during life. Many a sermon is lost upon a portion of the audience in our churches every Sabbath from this cause. When the attention is aroused, the impression made is enduring; and one idea then communicated is worth a hundred at any other time.

6. *Avoid a formal routine in teaching.* Children are very apt to imbibe the notion that they *study* in order *to recite*. They have but little idea of any purpose of acquirement beyond recitation; hence they study their text-book as mere words. The teacher should, as soon as possible, lead them to study the *subject*, using the book simply as an *instrument*. "Books are but helps"—should become their motto. In order to bring this about, the instructor would do well occasionally to leave entirely the order of the book, and question them on the *topic* they have studied. If they are pursuing arithmetic, for instance, and they have carefully prepared a definite number of problems, it might be well to test their ability by giving them at the recitation, others of the teacher's

own preparing, involving an application of what they have learned to the business of life. This will lead them to study intelligently. Besides, as soon as they begin to see how their knowledge is to be *useful* to them, they have a new motive to exertion. They should be so taught as to discover that grammar will improve their understanding and use of language; that writing will prepare them for business, and by enabling them to communicate with their friends, will add to their enjoyment; and so of reading and the other branches.

7. *Be careful to use language which is intelligible to children, whenever an explanation is given.* The object of an explanation is to elucidate, to make clearer. How is this object accomplished when the explanation is less intelligible than the thing explained? Suppose a child should ask her teacher to explain the cause of cold in winter and heat in summer; in other words, the cause of the change of seasons. "O, yes," says he, pleasantly. "The annual revolution of the earth round the sun in connection with the obliquity of the ecliptic, occasions the succession of the four seasons."* The child listens to these "words of learned length" and is astonished at the learning of her teacher; but she has no clearer idea, than before, of the point she inquired about.

Mr. S. R. Hall, in his lectures, gives the follow-

* Worcester's Geography.

ing forcible illustration of the same point. "Will you please tell me why I carry one for every ten?" said little Laura to her instructor. "Yes, my dear," said he, kindly. "It is because numbers increase from right to left in a decimal ratio." Laura sat and repeated it to herself two or three times, and then looked very sad. The master, as soon as he had answered, pursued his other business and did not notice her. But she was disappointed. She understood him no better than if he had used words of another language. "Decimal" and "ratio" were words that might have fallen on her ear before; but if so, she understood them none the better for it. She looked in the dictionary and was disappointed again, and after some time, put away her arithmetic. When asked by her teacher why she did so, she replied, 'I don't like to study it; I can't understand it.'

"Now, the injury to little Laura was very great. She had commenced the study with interest; she had learned to answer a great many questions in arithmetic, and had been pleased. She was now using a slate and writing her figures on it, and had found the direction to carry one for every ten. This she might have been made to understand. The master loved his scholars and wished to benefit them, but *forgot that terms perfectly plain to him would be unintelligible to the child.* From that moment, Laura disliked arithmetic, and every effort that could be used with her could not efface the impression that it was a hard study, and she could not understand it."

While upon this subject, I might urge that teachers should not resort to *evasion* when they are *not able* to explain. It is a much more honorable, and far more satisfactory course, for the teacher frankly to confess his inability to explain, than to indulge in some ridiculous mysticism to keep up the show of knowledge. I may never forget the passage I first made through the *Rule of Three*, and the manner in which my manifold perplexities respecting "direct and inverse" proportion were solved. "Sir," said I, after puzzling a long time over "more requiring more and less requiring less"—"will you tell me why I sometimes multiply the second and third terms together and divide by the first—and at other times multiply the *first* and *second* and divide by the third?" "Why, because more requires more sometimes, and sometimes it requires less—to be sure. Haven't you read the rule, my boy?" "Yes, sir, I can repeat the rule, but I don't *understand* it." "Why, it is because 'more requires more and less requires less'!" "But *why*, sir, do I multiply as the rule says?" "Why, because 'more requires more and less requires less'—see, the *rule says so*." "I know the rule says so, but I wished to understand *why*." "Why? *why?*" looking at me as if idiocy itself trembled before him—"why?—why, because the *rule says so; don't you see it?*—☞ *More requires more and less requires less!*"—and in the midst of this inexplicable combination of more and less, I shrunk away to my seat, blindly to follow the rule because *it said so*. Such teaching as this is enough to stultify the most inquiring mind; and it is to secure the *blessing of relief from such influence* to the children of any particular district, that we come to consider an occasional change of teachers a *mitigated* evil.

8. *Require prompt and accurate recitation.* I know of nothing that will abate the interest of a class sooner than dull and dragging recitations. The temptation in such cases is very strong for the teacher to help the class by the "drawing-out process" before described. This, however, only makes the matter worse. The dull recitation calls for the teacher's aid; and his aid reproduces the dull recitation. The only way is to stop at once, and refuse to proceed till the recitation can *go alone*. It is just as easy to have good lessons as poor; and the teacher should have the energy to insist upon them. Mark the countenances of a class as they go to their seats after a good recitation. They feel that they have done something, and they look as if they valued their teacher's approbation and their own so highly, that they will learn the next lesson still better.

It is, moreover, a great saving of time, to have the lessons promptly recited. This saving will afford the opportunity to introduce those additional illustrations I have before suggested, in

Simultaneous recitation.—Its evils.—Sometimes allowable.

order to excite a still deeper interest. It may sometimes, though not always, be well to make a prompt and perfect recitation the *condition* of introducing the additional matter.

9. *Rely not too much upon simultaneous recitation.* This has become quite too fashionable of late. It had its origin in the large schools established some years since, known as Lancasterian schools, and perhaps was well enough adapted to schools kept upon that plan in large cities. But when this mode of reciting is adopted in our district and country schools, where the circumstances of large numbers and extreme backwardness are wanting, it is entirely uncalled for, and, like other city fashions transferred to the country, is *really out of place.*

Seriously, I look upon this as one of the prominent faults in many of our schools. It destroys all independence in the pupil by taking away his individuality. He moves with the phalanx. Learning to rely on others, he becomes superficial in his lessons. He is tempted to indolence by a knowledge that his deficiencies will not stand out by themselves; and he comforts himself after a miserable recitation with the consoling reflection that he has been able to conceal his want of thoroughness from his teacher.

It may *sometimes* be useful. A few questions thus answered may serve to give animation to a class when their interest begins to flag; but that which may serve as a *stimulant* must not be relied on for *nutrition*. As an example of its usefulness, I have known a rapid reader tamed into due moderation by being put in companionship with others of slower speech, just as we tame a friskful colt by harnessing him into a team of grave old horses. But aside from some such definite purpose, I have seen no good come of this innovation. I am satisfied its prevalence is an evil, and worthy of the careful consideration of teachers.

By the foregoing means, and others which will suggest themselves to the thoughtful teacher's mind, he can arouse the interest of his classes so that study will be more attractive than play. For this object every teacher should labor. It is of course impossible to give specific rules to meet every case; it is not desirable to do it. The teacher, put upon the track, will easily devise his own expedients; and *his own*, be it remembered, *will usually be found the best for him.*

As a motive for every teacher to study carefully the art of teaching well at the recitation, it should be borne in mind that then and there he comes before his pupils in a peculiar and prominent manner; it is there his mind comes specially in contact with theirs, and there that he lays in them, for good or for evil, the foundations of their mental habits. It is at the recitation in a peculiar manner, that he makes *his mark* upon their minds; and as the seal upon the wax, so

Attitude of attention important.—How secured.

his mental character upon theirs leaves its impress behind!

During the recitation, pupils should be kept in an attitude of constant attention, and this end may usually be secured as follows: Much is gained by massing pupils. There is always a great dissipation of nervous force in attempting to teach pupils who are scattered over a large area, for inattention is sure to result from such isolation. A long line should be broken up into two or three shorter lines, the shortest pupils in front, the tallest in the rear. In carrying forward the work of the recitation, the questions should always be asked before pupils are summoned to answer them; and in calling up pupils to recite, there should be no fixed order, or no order that can be foreseen; and where there is a strong tendency to inattention, one call should not exempt a pupil from further service. There are decided advantages in calling up pupils by means of cards on which their names are written.

CHAPTER IX.

EXCITING INTEREST IN STUDY.

IT is ever an interesting question to the teacher, and one which he should consider with great care—"How can I excite among my pupils an interest in their studies?" The intelligent teacher feels that this is *the* great question; for he foresees that, if he fails here, his difficulty in governing his school will be very much increased. He therefore turns his attention with deep solicitude to the *motives* he may present, and the methods he may employ to awaken and keep alive the interest of the school.

If he has reflected at all upon the subject, he has already arrived .at the conviction, that it is necessary for the good of all concerned that the interest awakened should be an abiding one; that it should not only not abate during the term of school, but continue—nay, grow stronger and stronger—even after school-days have passed away. There is probably no greater mistake in education, than that of raising in school an artificial excitement, which may aid perhaps in securing better recitations, but which will do nothing toward putting the mind into such a state, that it will press on in the pursuit of knowledge even after the living teacher has closed his labors.

The higher principles of our nature being aroused with difficulty, are too apt to be neglected by the teacher, and thus they remain in their original feebleness; while he contents himself with appealing to our lower characteristics,—thus doing a lasting injury by unduly cultivating and strengthening them, at the same time that he awakens, after all, but a temporary interest.

In view of the importance of the subject, and the difficulty of judging aright upon it, I shall make no apology for devoting a few pages to the consideration of

SECTION I.—INCENTIVES TO STUDY—EMULATION.

The teacher will find, in a greater or less degree, in the mind of every child, the principle of EMULATION. It is a question very much debated of late, *What shall he do with it?* Much has been said and written on this question, and the ablest minds, both of past ages and the present, have given us their conclusions respecting it; and it often increases the perplexity of the young teacher to find the widest difference of opinion on this subject among men upon whom in other things he would confidingly rely for guidance. Why, asks he, why is this? Is there no such thing as truth in this matter? or have these men misunderstood each other? When they have writ-

Experimenting.—Its evil consequences.

ten with so much ability and so much earnestness,—some zealously recommending emulation as a safe and desirable principle to be encouraged in the young, and others as warmly denouncing it as altogether unworthy and improper,—have they been thinking of the *same thing?* Thus perplexed with conflicting opinions, he is thrown back upon his own reflection for a decision; or what is more common, he endeavors to find the truth by *experimenting* upon his pupils. He tries one course for one term, and a different one the next; repeats both during the third, and still finds himself unsettled as he commences the fourth. Meantime, some of his experiments have wrought out a lasting injury upon the minds of his pupils; for, if every teacher must settle every doubt by new experiments upon his classes, the progress that is made in the science and art of teaching must be at the untold expense of each new set of children;—just as if the young doctor could take nothing as settled by the experience of his predecessors, but must try over again for himself the effect of all the various medical agents, in order to decide whether arsenic does corrode the stomach and produce death,—whether cantharides can be best applied inwardly or outwardly,—whether mercury is most salutary when administered in ounces or grains, or whether repletion or abstinence is preferable in a fever! When such is the course of a young *practitioner* in a community, who does not confidently expect the church-yard soon to become the most populous district, and the sexton to be the most thrifty personage in the village, unless indeed he too should become the subject of experiment?

But is there not a good sense and a bad sense, associated with the term Emulation;—and have not these eager disputants fallen into the same error, in this matter, that the two knights committed, when they immolated each other in a contest about the question whether a shield was gold or silver, when each had seen *but one side of it?* I incline to the opinion that this is the case,—and that those who wax so warm in this contest, would do well to give us at the outset a careful *definition of the term* EMULATION, as they intend to use it. This would perhaps save themselves a great deal of toil, and their readers a great deal of perplexity.

Now, it seems to me the truth of this question lies within a nutshell. 1. If emulation means a *desire for improvement, progress, growth,*—an ardent wish to rise above one's present condition or attainments,—or even an aspiration to attain to eminence in the school or in the world, it is a laudable motive. *This is self-emulation.* It presses the individual on to surpass himself. It compares his present condition with what he would be—with what he ought to be; and, "forgetting those things which are behind, and reaching forth unto those which are before, he presses toward the mark for the prize." "An ardor kindled by the praiseworthy examples of others, inciting to imitate them, or to equal, or even excel them, without the desire of depressing them ",* is the sense in which the apostle uses the term [Romans, xi. 14] when he says: "If by any means I may provoke to *emulation* them which are my flesh, and might save some of them." If this be the meaning of emulation, it is every way a worthy principle to be appealed to in school. This principle exists to a greater or less extent in the mind of every child, and may very safely be strengthened by being called by the teacher into lively exercise; provided always, that the eminence is sought from a desire to be useful, and not from a desire of self-glorification.

2. But if emulation, on the other hand, means a *desire of surpassing others*, for the *sake of surpassing them;* if it be a disposition that will cause an individual to be as well satisfied with the highest place, whether he has risen above his fellows by his intrinsic well-doing, or they have fallen below him by their neglect; if it puts him in such a relation to others that *their failures* will be as gratifying to him as *his own success;* if it be a principle that prompts the secret wish in the child that others may miss their lessons, in order to give him an opportunity to gain applause by a contrast with their abasement,—then, without doubt, it is an unworthy and unholy

* Dr. Webster.

principle, and should never be encouraged or appealed to by the teacher. It has no similitude to that spirit which prompts a man to "love his neighbor as himself". It has none of that generosity which rejoices in the success of others. Carried out in after-life, it becomes *ambition*, such as fired the breast of a Napoleon, who sought a throne for himself, though he waded through the blood of millions to obtain it.

It is to this principle that the apostle, before quoted, alludes, when he classes *emulation* with the "works of the flesh", which are these: "adultery, fornication, uncleanness, lasciviousness, idolatry, witchcraft, hatred, variance, EMULATION, wrath, strife, seditions, etc.,—of the which things, I tell you before, as I have told you in times past, that they which do such things shall not inherit the kingdom of God." It is of this principle that the commentator, Scott, remarks:—"This thirst for human applause has caused more horrible violations of the law of love, and done more to desolate the earth, than even the grossest sensuality ever did."

Thus, *Emulation* is a term which indicates a very good or a very bad thing, according to the definition we give it. In one view of it, the warmest aspirings to rise are consistent with a generous wish that others may rise also. It is even compatible with a heartfelt satisfaction in its possessor at the progress of others, though they should outstrip him in his upward course.

It is the spirit which actuates all true Christians, as they wend their way heavenward, rejoicing the more as they find the way is thronged with those who hope to gain an immortal crown.

In the other view of it, we see men actuated by selfishness mingled with pride, inquiring, in the spirit of those mentioned in the Scripture, "Who among us shall be the greatest?" We every-where see men violating these sacred injunctions of divine wisdom: "Let no man seek his own, but every man another's wealth." "Let nothing be done through strife or vain-glory; but in lowliness of mind, let each esteem other better than themselves."—"In honor preferring one another."

If such be the true picture of emulation, in both the good and the bad sense, certainly teachers can not hesitate a moment as to their duty. They may appeal to the principle first described,— cultivate and strengthen it; and in so doing, they may be sure they are doing a good work. But unless they intend to violate the teachings of common sense, and the higher teachings of Christianity, *I know not how they can appeal to the principle of emulation as defined in the second case.*

But it may be urged that the teacher will find emulation, even in this latter sense, existing in human nature; that he can not get rid of it if he will; that it will be one of the most active principles to which he can resort in arousing the the mind to exertion; and, furthermore, that it has been appealed to by many of the most eminent teachers time out of mind.

To this it is replied, that it is not disputed that children are selfish; and that this selfishness may indeed be made a powerful instrumentality in urging them forward to the attainment of a temporary end. But does the existence of selfishness prove that it needs cultivation in the human character? And will the end, when attained, justify the means? Is the end, whatever it may be, if attained at such a cost, a blessing to be desired? Will not the heart suffer more than the head will gain?

It may be further urged, that the child will find the *world* full of this principle when he leaves the school; and why, it is asked, should he at school be thrown into an unnatural position? I answer that evil is not to be overcome by making evil more prevalent,—and though there may be too much of self-seeking in the world, that is the very reason why the teacher should not encourage its growth. The more true Christianity prevails in the world, the less there will be of that spirit which rejoices at another's halting; hence I am convinced the teacher should do nothing to make that spirit more prevalent.

Nor is it essential to the progress of the pupil even temporarily, since there are other and worthier principles which can be as successfully called into action. If we look carefully at the *expediency* of thus stimulating the mind, we find that after the first trial of strength, many become disheartened and fall behind in despair. It will soon be obvious, in a class of twenty, who are the *few* that will be likely to surpass all others; and therefore all the others, as a matter of course, fall back into envy, perhaps into hopeless indifference. Who has not seen this in a class in spelling, for instance, where the strife was for the "*head*" of the class, but where all but two or three were quite as well satisfied with being at the "*foot?*" It does not, then, accomplish the purpose for which it is employed; and since those who are aroused by it, are even more injured than those who are indifferent, their undesirable qualities being thus strengthened, the opinion is entertained that those teachers are the most wise, who bend their ingenuity to find some other means to awaken the minds of the children under their charge.

From what has been said, then, *Emulation* is to be recognised or repudiated among the incentives of the school-room, according to the signification we assign to the term.

SECTION II.—PRIZES.

It has for a long time been the custom of teachers to offer some *prize* as an incentive to exertion in school; a prize of some pecuniary

Honest investigation.—Experience.—Its result.

value, a book, or a medal. In some places beneficent individuals have bestowed by legacy the means to purchase annually the prizes thus to be used. Every young teacher is called upon, therefore, to inquire whether such an incentive is a proper one to be employed in the school-room. If there is any good to be expected from such incentive, will it counterbalance the evils that spring from the practice? Will the good of the whole school be promoted by such a measure,—and will this be a permanent or a temporary good? These are questions which press for an honest answer; and the faithful teacher should not shrink from a careful investigation of the whole matter; and if he finds good reason to differ from time-honored authority, he should abide by the truth rather than by prescriptive usage.

In my own case, I may be allowed to say, my mind was early turned to this point; though, I confess, with a strong bias in favor of the use of prizes. Pretty thoroughly for a series of years did I test their efficacy, but with a growing conviction that the prize was *not* the proper instrumentality to create a healthy interest in the school. This conviction acquired additional strength by three or four years' trial of other incentives; and it was fully confirmed afterward by a trial made for the purpose of testing again the efficiency of a prize, at an age when I could more carefully watch the workings of the human mind, and better appreciate the benefits or evils resulting from such a measure. I am now free to say that I am satisfied that *prizes offered to a school in such a way that all may compete for them, and only two or three obtain them, will always be productive of evil consequences, far overbalancing any temporary or partial good that may arise from them, and therefore they ought not to be used as incitements in our schools.*

Having expressed an opinion so decidedly upon a measure which claims among its friends and advocates some of the best minds in the country, I shall be expected to assign some reasons for the faith I entertain. From this I shall not shrink. I proceed therefore to express such objections to the use of prizes, as have been suggested to my mind by my own experience, and confirmed by the experience and observation of others in whom I have great confidence.

I. *The offer of a prize gives undue prominence to a comparatively unworthy object.* It practically teaches the child to undervalue the higher reward of a good conscience, and a love of learning for its own sake. The dazzling medal is placed in the foreground of his field of vision; and it is very likely to eclipse those less showy

---

* It may be well to remind the reader that I have used the term *Prizes* here in contradistinction from a system of *Rewards*, by which the teacher proposes to give some token of his regard to *every one* who does well,—and the more brilliant success of a few does not necessarily preclude others from participating in the favor according to their merit. Of such a system of Rewards I shall have something to say presently.

Engenders rivalry.—The few only are stimulated.

but more abiding rewards found in a sense of duty and a desire to be qualified for usefulness. In studying his lesson he thinks of the *prize*. He studies that he may merely *recite* well; for it is a good recitation that wins the prize. He thinks not of duty, or of future usefulness; the *prize* outshines all other objects.

II. *The pursuit of a prize engenders a spirit of rivalry among the pupils.* Rivalry in pursuit of an object which only *one* can attain, and which *all others* must lose, must end in exultation on the part of the winner, and disappointment and envy on the part of the losers. It may be said, this *ought not to be so;* but seldom can it be said, that *it is not so.* Such is human nature, and such it ever will be. Unpleasant feelings—sometimes concealed, to be sure, but generally expressed in unequivocal terms—grow out of the award of almost every school prize, and sometimes continue to exert their baleful influence through life. Now, as long as human nature brings forth unlovely traits almost spontaneously, such direct efforts to cultivate them surely are not called for. It is the part of wisdom, then, to omit such culture and avoid such results, especially when safer means are so accessible.

III. *The hope of gaining the prize stimulates only the few, while the many become indifferent.* This is admitted to be true, even by the advocates of the prize system. Let a prize be offered in any class as a reward for the best scholarship,

Exceptions.—In spite of the system.

and in a very few days it becomes perfectly obvious to all, who the *two or three* are that will be likely to outstrip all the others. These two or three will be stimulated to exertion; but the strife is left entirely to them. All others, despairing of success, resolve at once to "let their moderation be known to all men"; and since the prize has been made so prominent an object, they can not be expected now to look at any thing above and beyond it. Feeling that they are not likely to participate in the honors of the class, they have but little disposition to share in its toils.

This, to be sure, is not always so. There are some, who, ceasing to strive for the prize, toil for the more substantial blessing—a good education,—and in the end come out the best scholars. This is the way indeed most of our strong men are made; for it has long been remarked that the *prize* scholars in our schools, and even in our colleges, do not usually become the most distinguished men. On the other hand, many of them are never heard of after receiving their honors. But, though some of the slower scholars do thus hit upon the true path to eminence, it is not to be set down to the credit of the system; they rise in *spite* of the system, rather than by virtue of it; while the ultimate failure of the prize scholars is usually directly attributable to the defect of the system; for having been unduly stimulated to study solely with reference to *reci-*

Why prize scholars finally fail.—The teacher should reach all.

tation, and not with regard to future usefulness, their memories have been developed out of all proportion to the other faculties of their minds; and, though they may have been very good *reciters*, they have no power to become independent *thinkers*. Under different training, they might have become strong men.

But to look no further than the school, the remark holds true in general, that prizes *stimulate the few,* and *the many become indifferent,* not only to prizes, but to other and better motives. That system of incentives only can be approved, which reaches and influences successfully *all the mind* subjected to its operation.

Nor is this an unimportant consideration. It is not sufficient praise for a teacher that he has a *few* good scholars in his school. Almost any teacher can call out the talent of the active scholars and make them brilliant reciters. The highest merit, however, lies in reaching *all the pupils,* the dull as well as the active, and in making the most of them, or rather in leading them to make the most of themselves. It should be remembered of *every* child, that the present is his *only* opportunity of being a child, and of receiving the training appropriate to childhood; and that teacher who rests satisfied with a system that does not reach the many, while he amuses himself and his visitors with the precocity of a few of his most active scholars, is *recreant to his responsible trust.*

Difficulty in awarding the prize.—Judges disagree.—A fact.

IV. *There is much difficulty in awarding the prize so as to do strict justice to all.* So many things are to be taken into the account in order to determine the excellence of a performance compared with others, that some particulars are very likely to be overlooked. Those who are called to judge of the results often disagree among themselves. The following anecdote will illustrate this: Three literary gentlemen were appointed to select the best from several compositions, presented by a class who had written them in competition for a gold medal. Each of the gentlemen carefully read the whole number in private, and conscientiously selected the *best* according to his judgment. When they came together to compare results, it was found that each man had selected *the best*, but that no two had selected the same! They carefully read and compared the three, and still each insisted that his original choice was the best. After much debate and considerable delay, one of the parties being obliged to go to his business, relieved himself from a painful detention, and his friends from a perplexing doubt, by saying he believed the composition he had selected *was the best;* but as he could not stop to claim its rights, he would yield them in favor of the *second best* in the hands of one of his associates. This ended the dispute, and the action in favor of the successful one, was declared to be *unanimous!*

This only proves how difficult it is to decide;

The parties dissatisfied.—Various external aids: exemplified.

and in the case just cited, it might well be asked, why should one of these competitors be held up to the multitude to be applauded and admired, and the others sent back to their classes covered with the shame of a failure? What principle of *justice* sanctioned this decision?

Nor is this a solitary instance. It rarely happens that the case is perfectly clear. There is usually much perplexity about it; and hence one reason why the decision seldom satisfies the friends of the parties, either in the school or at home. But other considerations besides the intrinsic merits of the performance, are to be taken into account in awarding a prize; as,

1. *A difference in the external facilities which the competitors enjoy for getting the lessons.* One pupil may be the son of poverty, and be compelled to labor during all the hours out of school; another may be in easy circumstances and have nothing to prevent giving undivided attention to study during the whole day. One may be the child of parents who have no power to render assistance by way of explaining a difficult point; while the other may have all his doubts removed at once by parental aid. One may never even be encouraged by a kind word at home; another is constantly urged to effort, and perhaps not allowed to be idle. One may have access to no books but his school-manuals; the other may have at his command a large library. This difference in circumstances should be taken into the account;

but it never can be fully understood by those who are called to decide.

2. *The improper means which may have been employed to secure the prize.* Ambition, when aroused, is not always scrupulous of its means. One competitor may be high-minded; may enter the arena determined to succeed by an honorable strife; may resolve to succeed by his own exertions, or to fail rather than bring in any thing which is not the fruit of his own study. Another, regardless of honor or principle, resolves only to *succeed*, whatever it may cost; hesitates not to copy from others if possible, or to apply to a brother in college or some friend in the High School to furnish the difficult solution, prepared to order. One young lady spends days and nights in arranging the glowing thoughts for her composition, determined, if industry, study, good taste, and a careful application of the rules of rhetoric can effect any thing, that her production shall be *worthy* of a prize. Another, in no way distinguished for scholarship, industry, or honor, writes a careless letter to a married sister in a distant city, invoking her aid. In due time the mail brings an elegant essay. It is copied with sufficient accuracy to be read, and at the examination takes the prize! The fair "*authoress*" stands forth and is flattered before the multitude,—is perhaps made to believe that she is *worthy* of praise; she grasps the golden bauble, and, covered with the blushes of modesty, receives the con-

Abuses.—System unsafe.

gratulations and caresses of friends, and is afterward reputed a good scholar. Her competitors meantime become convinced that effort can not rival *genius;* they are mortified to think they have presumed to enter the arena with native talent, and become disheartened as to any future attempt.

Now, where is the justice in all this proceeding? Yet this is not fiction; *it is history!* If such abuses—abuses that might well make an angel weep, revealing, as they do, that woman's heart can be thus sold to deception—are the accompaniments of a prize system, may we not well doubt the utility of that system?

Yet who can know either the different facilities enjoyed by the competitors, or the want of principle in some of them? Who can enter the secret chambers of the mind or the heart, and estimate with any accuracy the just amount of merit in any action? This is God's prerogative; while "man looketh only on the outward appearance". My inference then is: *A system can hardly be safe which is so uncertain.*

V. *The prize rewards* SUCCESS, *not* EFFORT: TALENT, *not* WORTH. Every one knows that in estimating the value and virtue of an action, the motive which prompted it, and the effort it necessarily cost, should be taken into the account. Every one knows, too, that success in study is by no means a criterion by which to judge of the merits of the scholar. Some learn their lessons with great facility and with but little effort; others study long and patiently without any brilliant results. One competitor for a prize may bring results which have cost him midnight toil and the most unremitting perseverance; another with brighter parts, and with but little labor, is able to surpass him, and takes the medal. Now, the former *deserves* in a far higher degree the encouragement of the reward; yet it is given to him who has the talent, but who lacks the industry. The rule of Scripture which announces that "to whom much is given, of him *shall much be required*", is violated, and he is rewarded for producing but little more than the one to whom *little is given.*

It is often urged by those who advocate a system of prizes and rewards, that *God rewards;* and therefore it is at least justifiable that we should imitate his example. I admit that God, in his government, does reward; but he rewards *effort* rather than *success;* he "looketh upon the heart" as man can not do, and rewards *worth*, not *talent.* We might, indeed, imitate his example, if we had less frailty, and were not so liable to be imposed upon by the outward appearance. God indeed rewards men; but he estimates the secret intention, seeing the inward springs of thought before they find expression in words or actions. He regards the motive, and holds out for the encouragement of the humblest child of earth, who does the best he can, as rich a crown

Studying for a prize only.—Argument perverted.

of glory, as he does for those whose outward circumstances, in the eyes of mortals, are more auspicious. When man can as wisely and as righteously bestow his prizes and rewards, there will be far less objection to their use.

VI. *The pupil who studies for a prize as his chief motive, will seldom continue to study when the prize is withdrawn.* This is so obvious as scarcely to need illustration. If it be necessary to add any thing to the mere statement of the fact, an appeal to almost universal experience would confirm it. A teacher who has depended upon prizes in a school, finds it very difficult to awaken an interest there, when he withdraws the prize. Hence many have, on trying the experiment of abandoning the prize system, become discouraged, and have returned again to the use of prizes, believing them essential to their success. Thus the very argument which shows most clearly their pernicious tendency, is made a reason for continuing them. As before hinted, the prize scholars in our academies, and even our colleges, are seldom distinguished men in after-life,—a fact that speaks conclusively on this point. But it can scarcely be necessary to spend words to prove a truth almost self-evident.

VII. *By the prize system, the influence of the good example of some of the best pupils, is lost upon the school.* All who have taught, know how important this influence is to the success of the school. It tells with resistless power upon the other scholars, wherever it exists, unless some unworthy motive can be assigned for it. But under the prize system, let a teacher appeal to the example of his best scholars, and the reply is, "O, yes, he behaves well, or he studies diligently, but *he is trying to get the prize.*" With this understanding, his example becomes powerless, unless, indeed, there may be a disposition to be *unlike* him in every thing. It is believed this is a consideration of considerable importance.

I have thus assigned, at some length, the reasons why I should discountenance, among the incentives of the school, the use of Prizes. As to the use of "*Rewards*", when they are made so numerous that every one who is really deserving may receive one,—and when the basis of their distribution is not talent, not success merely, but good intention and praiseworthy effort,—I have much less to say. As expressions of the teacher's interest in the children, and of his approval of their well-doing, they may serve a good end. Perhaps there is no very strong objection to them in principle; though if the teacher subjects himself to the necessary outlay in the purchase of them, it may become burdensome to him. I may add, however, that *I do not think rewards are necessary to the teacher's success.* I should prefer to do without them. It is possible to produce such a feeling in the school-room, that the approving conscience of the child, and the commendatory smile of the teacher, shall be the richest of all rewards. These come without money and without price, and may always be freely and safely bestowed, wherever there is a good intention exhibited by the child. That is the most healthy state of things where these are most prized. As children whose parents begin early to hire them to do their duty, are seldom ready afterward to render their cheerful service as an act of filial obligation, whenever the pay is withheld,—so children at school, who have been accustomed to expect a reward, seldom pursue their studies as cheerfully when that expectation is cut off.

SECTION III.—PROPER INCENTIVES.

In what has already been said, it has. been more than hinted that there are higher attributes than emulation, which the teacher should address, and which, if he is successful in calling them into exercise, will be quite sufficient to insure the proper application of his pupils to their studies. They have the merit, moreover, of being safe. They do not unduly stimulate the intellectual, at the expense of the moral faculties. Their very exercise constitutes a healthy growth of the moral nature. Some of these I may briefly allude to.

I. A DESIRE TO GAIN THE APPROBATION OF THEIR PARENTS AND TEACHER. The love of approbation is as universal in the human mind as emulation. Not one in a thousand can be found who does not possess it. Within proper limits, it is a desirable trait in human character. It is, to be sure, one of the selfish propensities; but among them all, it is the most innocent. Carried to an extreme, it would lead its possessor to crave the good opinion of the bad as well as of the good, and to become an obsequious seeker after popularity. This, of course, is to be deprecated. But there can be no danger of this extreme, as long as the approbation of *parents* and *teachers* is the object aimed at. It implies in the child a respect for the opinions and a confidence in the justice of his parents and teachers; and hence it implies in him a generous desire to please, as a condition of being commended by them.

In this sense, the love of approbation may be appealed to by the teacher. He perhaps need not frequently use the language of praise. It will generally be sufficient, if the smile of approval beams forth in his countenance. If he is judicious as well as just, this boon soon becomes a precious one to the child. It is a reward, moreover, which

"is twice blest;
It blesseth him who gives and him who takes."

II. A DESIRE OF ADVANCEMENT. This is emulation in its *good* sense. It leads the child, as before remarked, to compare his present standing and attainments with what they should be, and to desire to surpass himself. This is ever commendable. Man was made for progress; and it is no

Desire to be useful.—Desire to do right.

unworthy aspiration, when this desire fires the youthful breast. The teacher, then, may appeal to this desire, may kindle it into a flame even, with safety,—because it is a flame that warms without consuming that on which it feeds.

III. A DESIRE TO BE USEFUL. The good teacher should never fail to impress upon the child that the object of his being placed on earth, was that he might be of some use to the world by which he is surrounded. "No man liveth to himself, and no man dieth to himself." He can be thus useful by storing the mind with knowledge and the heart with right affections. He may be reminded of the connection between his present studies and the pursuits of life to which they may be applied. Some judicious hint at the future application of any branch is always a good preparation of the mind to pursue it. If there is a definite object in view, there will always be more alacrity in the labor of study; and this may be made to influence the young pupil as well as the more advanced. It is no small thing for the child if he can be early made to feel that he is living to some purpose.

IV. A DESIRE TO DO RIGHT. This, in other words, is a disposition to obey conscience by conforming to the will of God. This indeed is the highest and holiest of all the motives to human action. In its fullest sense it constitutes the fundamental principle of a religious character. The teacher should most assiduously cultivate in

Conscience active in childhood.

the child a regard for this principle. God has implanted the conscience in every child of earth, that it should early be made use of to regulate the conduct. That teacher is either grossly ignorant or madly perverse, who disregards the conscience, while he appeals alone to the selfishness of the young, and thus practically teaches that moral obligation is a nullity; that the law of God — so beautifully expounded by the Saviour — "Thou shalt love the Lord thy God with all thy heart, and with all thy soul, and with all thy mind," and "Thou shalt love thy neighbor as thyself" — is of little consequence; and that the injunction of the apostle — "Whether ye eat or drink, or whatsoever ye do, do all to the glory of God," is as good as obsolete.

In early childhood, the conscience is most active. It needs, to be sure, at that period, to be enlightened; but if the teachings of Revelation are made plain to the child, he seldom disregards them. The teacher has at this period very much to do, as I have before said in the chapter on Responsibility of Teachers; and he can not neglect his duty without the most aggravated culpability. The point I urge here, is, that he should use these motives as *incentives to study*. The child can be made to feel that he owes the most diligent efforts for improvement to his teacher, who daily labors for his improvement; to his parents, who have kindly supplied his wants, and have provided the means for his cultivation; to

Sense of obligation.

society, whose privileges he may enjoy, and to which he is bound to make a return by becoming an intelligent and useful member of it; to himself, as a rational and immortal being, capable of unbounded enjoyment or untold misery, just in proportion as he prepares himself for either; and, above all, to his CREATOR, by whose bounty he lives, surrounded with friends and blessed with opportunities, which are denied to millions of his fellow-beings,—by whose gracious providence he has been endowed with faculties and capabilities making him but little lower than the angels, and which he is bound to cultivate for usefulness and for heaven,—by whose mercy he has been supplied, as millions have not, with the word of God, to guide his mind to things above, and with the influences of Christian society, to cheer him in his path to heaven;—above all, I repeat, should the child be taught to feel that he owes to God his best efforts to make the most of all his powers for time and eternity. If this can be done (and I believe to a great extent it can be done), there will be no need of a resort to those questionable incentives found in exciting children to outstrip their fellows by prizes and rewards; while in this very process, the foundation of a good moral training will be laid, without which the perfect structure of a noble character can never be reared in later life.

To the motives already alluded to, if it be necessary to add another, I would urge,

V. THE PLEASURE OF ACQUISITION. This is often underrated by teachers. Our Creator has not more universally bestowed a natural appetite for the food which is necessary for the growth of the body, than he has a mental longing for the food of the mind; and as he has superadded a sensation of pleasure to the necessary act of eating, so he has made it a law of the mind, to experience its highest delight while in the act of receiving the mental aliment. Whoever has observed childhood with an attentive eye, must have been impressed with the wisdom of God in this arrangement. How much the child acquires within the first three years after its birth! He learns a difficult language with more precision than a well-educated adult foreigner could learn it in the same time; yet language is not his only or his chief study. During these same three years, he makes surprising advances in general knowledge. He seeks an intimate acquaintance with all the physical objects by which he is surrounded. The size, form, color, weight, temperature, and use of each are investigated by the test of his own senses, or ascertained by innumerable inquiries. His ideas of height and distance, of light and heat, of motion and velocity, of cause and effect, are all well defined. He has made no mean attainments in morals. He comprehends the law of right and wrong, so that his decisions may well put to the blush his superiors in age; and, unless grossly neglected, he has learned the duty of obedience to parents and reverence toward God. Now, all this amazing progress has been made, because of the irrepressible curiosity with which God has endowed him, and the unspeakable delight he experiences in acquiring the knowledge which gratifies it.

All must have noticed the delight with which the child grasps a new idea; but few have been able so eloquently to describe it, as it is done by Mr. Mann. "Mark a child," says he, "when a clear, well-defined, vivid conception seizes it. The whole nervous tissue vibrates. Every muscle leaps. Every joint plays. The face becomes auroral. The spirit flashes through the body like lightning through a cloud."

"Observe, too, the blind, the deaf, and the dumb. So strong is their inborn desire for knowledge,—such are the amazing attractive forces of their minds for it, that although the natural inlets, the eye and the ear, are closed, yet they will draw it inward, through the solid walls and encasements of the body. If the eye be curtained with darkness, it will enter through the ear. If the ear be closed in silence, it will ascend along the nerves of touch. Every new idea that enters into the presence of the sovereign mind, carries offerings of delight with it, to make its coming welcome. Indeed, our Maker created us in blank ignorance, for the very purpose of giving us the boundless, endless pleasure of learning new things."

The pleasure abates in after life.—Mind may be surfeited.

It is, of course, not to be expected that the same degree of pleasure will attend the learner in every acquisition, as the novelty diminishes and as he advances in age. The bodily appetite is less keen in after life than in childhood, so that the adult may never realize again to the full extent, the delicious flavors which regaled him in his earliest years. Still there will ever be a delight in acquisition. And to carry our illustration a little further,—as the child is soonest cloyed whose stomach is surfeited with dainties and stimulated with condiments and pampered with sweetmeats, till his taste has lost its acumen, and digestion becomes a burden—so the mental appetite is soonest destroyed, when, under the unskillful teacher, it is overloaded with what it can neither digest nor disgorge. The mind may be surfeited; and then no wonder if it loathes even the wholesome aliment. Artificial stimulants, in the shape of prizes, and honors, and flattery, and fear, and shame, may have impaired its functions, so that it ceases to act except under their excitement. But all must see that these are unnatural conditions, superinduced by erroneous treatment. *There is still a delight in acquisition,* just as soon as the faculties are aroused to the effort; and the skillful teacher will strive to *wake up the mind* to find this delight,—and if he understands his work, he will scarcely need a stronger incentive. If he understands the secret of giving just so much instruc-

A desire to know.—Instance of God's wisdom and goodness.

tion as to excite the learner's curiosity, and then to leave him to discover and acquire for himself, he will have no necessity to use any other means as stimulants to exertion.

To this might be added that *irrepressible curiosity*, that all-pervading *desire to know*, which is found in the mind of every child. The mind, as if conscious of its high destiny, instinctively spreads its unfledged wings in pursuit of knowledge. This, with some children, is an all-sufficient stimulant to the most vigorous exertion. To this the teacher may safely appeal. Indeed, it is a convincing proof of the wisdom as well as the goodness of God, that this *desire to know*, as well as the *delight of acquisition*, are the most active at that early period of childhood, when a just appreciation of the utility of knowledge, and the higher motives already detailed, could scarcely find a lodgment in the tender mind. It seems to be, therefore, an indisputable dictate of our very nature, that both these principles should be early employed as incentives.

If, then, *the desire of the approval of parents and teachers,—the desire of advancement,—the desire to be useful,—and the desire to do right*, can be superadded to the *natural love in the child for acquisition, and a natural desire to know*, there will, as I believe, be but little occasion to look further for incentives to exertion in the pupil; and I may venture to add, as a *scholium* to what has already been said, that the teacher who was

Wise instruction will aim at making learning pleasurable.

not yet learned to call into exercise these higher motives, and to rely for success mainly upon them, and who dares not abandon the system of exciting stimulants, for fear of a failure, *has yet much to learn as a true educator of the young.*

Wise instruction will certainly aim at making the process of learning pleasurable; but it is easy to apply this test too rigorously. When pupils manifest a distaste for any kind of learning, it is usual to assume either that the instruction is unskillful, or that the knowledge presented is not adapted to the pupil's present needs; but there is often a deeper and more significant indication. The pupil may have a predisposition to certain modes of mental activity, and the exercise of these will always be pleasurable; but there may be other modes of mental activity that have not yet been established, and the exercise of these will at first be painful. As one dominant aim of education should be symmetry, these dormant modes of activity should be stimulated, and though this stimulation may be unpleasant, it should be kept up till habit has made the exercise agreeable. Under the same conditions of age, sex, and quality of instruction, some pupils will find a delight in mathematical study, while to others it is a repulsive drudgery, the difference being due to the cause just assigned. That a certain study is agreeable, is no reason in itself why it should be pursued; nor is the fact that another study is disagreeable, a reason in itself why it should not

The best teachers sometimes miss their ideal.

be pursued. But in all cases the aim of the teacher should doubtless be to make study pleasurable, to inspire what Mr. Bain has happily called "intrinsic charm"; but the best of teachers will sometimes fall short of this ideal through no fault of their own.

CHAPTER X.

SCHOOL GOVERNMENT.

IT is not necessary that any space in this work should be occupied in speaking of the importance of order in our schools. Every body who has written or spoken on this subject, has conceded the necessity of obedience on the part of the pupil. "ORDER IS HEAVEN'S FIRST LAW"; and it is scarcely more essential to the harmony of heaven, than it is to the happiness and success of the school.

If such be the necessity of order in the school, then the ability to secure and maintain it, is no mean part of the *qualification* of the good teacher. It is lamentable that so many fail in this particular; and yet this frequent failure can in most cases be traced to some defect in the constitutional temperament, or some deficiency in the mental or moral culture of the teacher himself. It shall be my first object, then, to point out some of the

SECTION I.—REQUISITES IN THE TEACHER FOR GOOD GOVERNMENT.

I. SELF-GOVERNMENT. It has frequently been said that no man can govern others till he has

> Angry passions.—Manner.—Levity and moroseness.

learned to govern himself. I have no doubt of the truth of this. If an individual is not perfectly self-possessed, his decisions must fail to command respect. The self-government of the teacher should be complete, in the following particulars:

1. *As to the passion of anger.* The exhibition of anger always detracts from the weight of authority. A man under its influence is not capable of doing strict justice to his pupils. Before entering upon teaching, therefore, a man should somehow obtain the mastery over his temper, so that under any provocation he can control it. He should consider that in school his patience will often be severely tried. He should not expect, indeed, that the current of affairs in school will for a single day run perfectly smooth. He should, therefore, prepare for the worst, and firmly resolve that whatever unpleasant thing shall occur, it shall not take him entirely by surprise. Such forethought will give him self-command. If, however, from his past experience, and from the nature of his temperament, he is satisfied he can not exercise this self-control, he may be assured he is the wrong man to engage in teaching. A man who has not acquired thorough ascendency over his own passions, is an unsafe man to be intrusted with the government of children.

2. *As to levity and moroseness of manner.* Either extreme is to be avoided. There are some teachers who exhibit such a *frivolity* in all their intercourse with their pupils, that they can never

command them with authority, or gain their cordial respect. This is a grievous fault; and the teacher should at once find an antidote for it, by serious reflection upon the responsibility of his position. If this will not cure it, nothing else can.

There are others who are characterized by a *perpetual peevishness*, so that a pleasant word from them is indeed a strange thing. They can never expect to gain the affection of their pupils; and without securing the *love* of children, the government of them will never be of the right kind. This habit of *snappishness* should be broken up at once.

There are some very young teachers, who sometimes *assume* one or the other of these peculiar modes of address, or perhaps both, to be used alternately,—fancying that they will gain popularity by the one, or give themselves greater authority by the other. This is a very mistaken notion; for children have more discernment than most men give them credit for, and they usually see directly through such a flimsy disguise,—and the teacher becomes ridiculous rather than great in their estimation, whenever he takes any such false position.

Mr. Abbott, in his "Teacher," states a fact which well illustrates this point. "Many years ago," says he, "when I was a child, the teacher of the school where my early studies were performed, closed his connection with the establishment; and, after a short vacation, another was expected. On the appointed day the boys began to collect, some from curiosity, at an early hour, and many speculations were started as to the character of the new instructor. We were standing near a table with our hats on,—and our position and the exact appearance of the group is indelibly fixed on my memory,—when a small and youthful-looking man entered the room and walked up toward us. Supposing him to be some stranger, or, rather, not making any supposition at all, we stood looking at him as he approached, and were thunderstruck at hearing him accost us with a stern voice and sterner brow:—'Take off your hats! Take off your hats, and go to your seats.' The conviction immediately rushed upon our minds that this must be the new teacher. The first emotion was that of surprise, and the second was that of the ludicrous; though I believe we contrived to smother the laugh until we got out into the open air."

The true rule is to act the part which is agreeable to nature. The teacher having gained the self-command just insisted upon, and having in him the spirit of kindness and a desire to be useful, should assume nothing unnatural for effect. His manner should be truly dignified, but courteous.

3. *As to his treatment of those pupils that are marked by some peculiarity.* There will usually be some pupils who are very backward, and per-

haps very dull,—or who may have some physical defect, or some mental eccentricity. The teacher should be able to govern himself in all his remarks concerning such pupils. He should avoid all allusion to such singularities before the school; and it is the height of injustice—I was about to say, of malevolence—for him ever to use those low and degrading epithets so often found upon the teacher's tongue,—such as dunce, thickskull, and the like. Is it not misfortune enough for a child to be backward or dull, without having the pain and mortification increased by the cruelty of an unfeeling teacher? The teacher should take a special interest in such children; he should endeavor to enter into the feelings of their parents, and to treat them in such a way as to encourage rather than crush them.

II. A CONFIDENCE IN HIS ABILITY TO GOVERN. We can generally do what we firmly believe we can do.* At any rate, a man is more likely to succeed in any enterprise, when he has the feeling of self-reliance. The teacher, by reflection upon the importance of good government to his success, and by a careful study of the means to be employed and the motives to be presented, should be able to bring himself to the determination to have good order in his school, and so fully to believe he *can* have it, that his pupils shall detect no misgivings in him on this point. Whenever they discover that he has doubts of

---

* *Possunt quia posse videntur.*—VIRGIL.

Views of government.—Not tyranny.

his success in governing, they will be far more ready to put his skill to the test. It would be better that a young teacher should decline to take a difficult school, rather than enter it without the full belief of his ability to succeed. I would not wish to be understood by these remarks to be encouraging an unreasonable and *blind presumption.* A confidence in one's ability should be founded upon a reasonable estimate of his powers, compared with the difficulties to be overcome. What I recommend is, that the teacher should carefully weigh the difficulties, and candidly judge of his own resources, and then undertake nothing which he thinks is beyond his ability. If, after this, he *believes* he can succeed, other things being equal, success is almost certain.

III. JUST VIEWS OF GOVERNMENT. 1. It is not *tyranny,* exercised to please the one who governs, or to promote his own convenience. The despot commands for the sake of being obeyed. But government in its proper sense, is an arrangement for the *general good,*—for the benefit of the *governed* as well as of the ruler. That is not good government which seeks any other object. The teacher should so view the matter; and in establishing any regulations in school, he should always inquire whether they are suggested by a selfish regard to his own ease, or whether they spring from a sincere and disinterested wish to promote the improvement of the school.

Uniformity.—Equality.—No aristocracy in school.

2. He should see the necessity of making the government *uniform;* that is, the same from day to day. If he punishes to-day what he tolerates to-morrow, he cannot expect the cordial respect of his pupils. Some teachers, not having learned the art of self-government, take counsel too much of their own *feelings.* To-day they are in good health and spirits, and their faces are clothed in *sunshine;* they can smile at any thing. To-morrow, suffering under bad digestion, or the want of exercise, or the want of sleep, the thunder-storm hovers about their brow, ready to burst upon the first offender. Woe to the luckless wight who does not seasonably discover this change in the condition of the weather. A teacher can not long *respect himself* who is thus capricious; he may also be sure that his school will not long respect him.

3. He should so view government as *to make it equal;* that is, equal in its application to the whole school,—the large as well as small scholars, the males as well as females. This is often a great fault with teachers. They raise up a sort of *aristocracy* in their schools, a privileged class, a miniature nobility. They will insist that the little boys and girls shall abstain from certain practices,—whispering, for instance,—and most promptly punish the offenders, while they tolerate the same thing among the larger pupils. This is cowardly in itself, and as impolitic as it is cowardly. The teacher makes a great mistake,

who begins his government with the small children, in the hope of frightening the larger ones into obedience. He should have the manliness and the justice to begin with the larger pupils; the smaller ones never resist, when authority is established with those above them. Besides this, the very class who are thus indulged, are the very ones who soonest despise, and justly too, the authority of the teacher.

He should make his government *impartial* in every respect. He should have no favorites—no *preferences*, based upon the outward circumstances of the child, his family, or his personal attractions and the like. The rich and the poor should be alike to the teacher. He should remember that each child has a soul; and it is with the soul, and not with the wealth of this world, that he has to do. He should remember that a gem, as bright as a sunbeam, is often concealed under a rough exterior. It should be his work, nay his delight—to bring out this gem from its hiding-place, and apply to it the polish of a "workman that needeth not to be ashamed."

IV. JUST VIEWS OF THE GOVERNED. Notwithstanding the imperfection of human nature, as developed in the young, they have some redeeming qualities. They are intelligent and reasonable beings. They have more or less love of approbation; they have affection, and, above all, they have a moral sense. All these qualities are considerably developed before they enter the school. The teacher should remember this, and prepare himself to address, as far as may be, all these. *Love of approbation*, as we have before seen, is not an unworthy motive to be addressed, and it is well known that many children are very easily controlled by it. It is not the highest motive, to be sure, nor is it the lowest. The *affection* for a teacher, which many children will exercise, is one of the most powerful instrumentalities in governing them with ease. The *conscience*, early trained, is all-powerful. I allude to these principles of action once more, in order to say that the peculiar character of each should be well studied by the teacher. He should understand the human mind so well, as to be able to find the avenues to these better parts of the child's nature, remembering that whenever several ways of doing the same thing, are presented, it is always wise to choose the best.

V. DECISION AND FIRMNESS. By *decision*, I mean a readiness to determine and to act in any event, just as duty seems to dictate; a willingness to take the responsibility just as soon as the way is plain. By *firmness* is meant that *fixedness of purpose* which resolutely carries out a righteous decision. Both of these qualities are essential to good government in the teacher. Much time is often lost by a teacher's vacillating when action is more important. Besides, if the pupils discover that the teacher hesitates, and dreads to take any responsibility, they very soon

The unjust judge.—A practical example.

lose their respect for him. I would not urge that a teacher should act *hastily*. He never should decide till he is confident he decides right: any delay is better than hasty error. But his delay, in all matters of government should have reference to a true knowledge of his *duty;* when that is clearly known, he should be decided.

Many teachers suffer in their government, for want of firmness. They act upon the principle of personal convenience, as did the unjust judge mentioned in the parable. "And he would not for a while: but afterward he said within himself, Though I fear not God nor regard man; *yet because this widow troubleth me,* I will avenge her, *lest by her continual coming she weary me.*" How often we hear something like this in the school-room. "May I go and drink"? —says James, in a peculiarly imploring tone. "No," says the teacher, promptly, and evidently without any reflection as to the decision he has made. James very composedly sits down, eyeing the countenance of the teacher expressively, as much as to say, "I'll try you again soon." Before long he observes the teacher quite busy with a class, and he again pops the question: "May I go and drink"? Stung at the moment with impatience at the interruption, the teacher answers instantly and emphatically, "No, no, James, sit down." James still watches his teacher's expression, and cannot discover there any signs of a mind seeking the path of duty, and he silently thinks to himself, "The third time never fails." So, after a minute or two, when the teacher is somewhat puzzled with a knotty question, and is on the *point* of nibbling a pen besides,—"*May I go and drink, sir?*" again rings upon the teacher's ear. "Yes, yes, yes! do go along; *I suppose you'll keep asking till you get it.*"

Now James goes to drink, and then returns to philosophize upon this matter, perhaps as follows:—"I don't believe he stopped to think whether I needed drink or not; therefore, hereafter I shall never believe he really means *no*, when he says it. He acts without thought. I have also found that if I will but ask several times, I shall get it. So I shall know how to proceed next time."—I do not know that any child would express this thought in so many words; but the impression upon his mind is none the less distinct.

Now the teacher should carefully consider the question addressed to him. How long since this child had water? Can it be necessary for him to drink so often? Then let the answer be given mildly, but decidedly—"No, James." The very manner, quite likely, will settle the question, so that James will not ask again. The answer once given should be *firmly* adhered to. It would even be better that James should suffer for the want of water, than for the want of confidence in his teacher's firmness. In this way the teacher

Moral and religious principle.—First impressions.

would establish his word with the school in a very few days; and his pupils would soon learn that with him "no means no," and "yes means yes"—a matter of no small importance to the teacher of a school.

VI. DEEP MORAL PRINCIPLE. The teacher should ever be a conscientious man; and in nothing is this more necessary than in the exercise of good government. In this matter the teacher can never respect himself when he acts from caprice or selfishness. His inquiry should be, What is right? What is justice—justice to my pupils—to myself? And if he could add to moral obligation the high sanctions of religious principle, and could habitually and sincerely turn his thoughts to his Maker, with the heartfelt inquiry—What wilt THOU have me to do?—then he would seldom err in the discharge of this trust. His pupils, seeing that he acted from fixed and deep principle, would respect his honesty, even if he should cross their desires.

Having now dwelt at some length upon the *requisites in the teacher for good government*, I shall next proceed to present some of the

SECTION II.—MEANS OF SECURING GOOD ORDER.

1. BE CAREFUL AS TO THE FIRST IMPRESSION YOU MAKE. It is an old proverb, that "what is well begun is half done." This holds true in schoolkeeping, and particularly in school government.

Respect precedes attachment.—The rough and the gentle way.

The young study character very speedily and very accurately. Perhaps no one pupil could express in words an exact estimate of a teacher's character after a week's acquaintance; but yet the whole school has received an impression which is not far from the truth. A teacher, then, is very unwise who attempts to *assume* to be any thing which he is not. He should ever be frank; and in commencing a school he should begin as he can hold out. Any assumption of an authoritative tone is especially ill-judged. The pupils at once put themselves in an attitude of resistance, when this is perceived by them.

A teacher should ever remember that among children—however it may be among adults—*respect* always precedes *attachment*. If he would gain the love of the children, he must first be worthy of their respect. He should therefore act deliberately, and always conscientiously. He should be firm, but never petulant. It is very important at the outset that he should be truly courteous and affable. It is much wiser to request than to command, at least until the request has been disregarded. There are usually two ways of doing a thing,—a gentle and a rough way. "John, go and shut that door," in a gruff tone, is one way to have a door closed. John will undoubtedly go and shut the door—perhaps with a *slam*,—but he will not thank the teacher for the rough tones used in commanding it. Now it costs no more time or breath to say, "John, I'll thank you if you will shut that door." Most cheerfully will John comply with the request, and he is grateful that he has heard these tones of kindness. If he could but know the teacher's wishes afterward, he would gladly perform them unasked. I would by no means recommend the adoption of the fawning tone of the sycophant, by the teacher. He should be manly and dignified; but the language of that courtesy which springs from real kindness, and which ever becomes the gentleman, is always the most suitable as well as most expedient for him.

II. AVOID EXHIBITING OR ENTERTAINING A SUSPICIOUS SPIRIT. It is a maxim of law, that one charged with crime is always to be presumed innocent, until *proved* guilty. This should be a maxim with the teacher who would govern well. There is no more direct way of making a school vicious, than by showing them that you suspect they are so. A good reputation is dear to all; and even a bad boy will be restrained from wicked acts as long as he thinks you give him credit for good intentions. But if he finds that he has lost your good opinion, he feels that he has nothing further to lose by being as bad as you suspect him to be. A teacher is wise, therefore, if he tries to see something good even in a vicious pupil. It may be, as it often has been, the means of saving such a pupil. I have known a very depraved boy entirely reformed in school, by his teacher's letting him know that he had noticed some good traits in his character. He afterward told his teacher that "he had been so often suspected to be a villain, that he had almost come to the conclusion that he would be one; but that, when he found one man who could do him the justice to give him credit for a few good feelings—(for he knew he had them)—he at once determined to show that man that his confidence had not been misplaced; and that he would sooner die than knowingly offend the only person who ever had understood him."

It is wise sometimes, not only to withhold the expression of suspicion, but to give some token of your confidence to the pupil who is troublesome. Intrust him with some errand involving responsibility, or assign to him some duty by way of assistance to yourself, and very likely you will gain his good-will ever after. This is founded upon the well-known principle in human nature acted upon by Dr. Franklin, who, when he would gain his enemy, asked him to do him a favor.

III. As soon as possible, give regular and full employment. It is an old proverb that "idleness is the mother of mischief." The nursery hymn also contains a living truth—

"And Satan finds some mischief still
For idle hands to do."

It is the law of a child's nature to be active; and as the teacher is placed in the school to give direction to such minds, he can hardly complain of their going upon forbidden objects, unless he seasonably provides something better for them to do.

Very early, then, the teacher should endeavor to classify his school, and furnish constant and full employment—whether of study, recitation, or relaxation—for every hour in the day. The teacher should have a plan when he opens the school, and the sooner it is carried into full operation the better.* Besides, when a teacher has given employment, he has a right to insist upon the pupil's being engaged in study. Nobody will question this *right;* and it is far more profitable to require a positive duty than to enjoin a negative,—such as abstinence from whispering or from mischief in general.

IV. MAKE BUT FEW RULES. It is a very common thing for teachers to embarrass themselves by a long code of requirements and prohibitions. Some go so far as to write out a system of laws; and, annexing to each the penalty for its infringement, post them up in a conspicuous place in the school-room. Others content themselves with a verbal announcement of them, and rely upon the memories of the pupils to retain the details of them and to govern themselves accordingly. This, it seems to me, is a great mistake. The multiplicity of specific rules for the government of a school, will naturally lead to a multiplicity of offenses. Children will be confused by the varying and sometimes conflicting demands of a for-

---

* See Chap. xi. of this work.

midable code of regulations, and in endeavoring to avoid Scylla will be likely to fall into Charybdis. It is believed by some honest statesmen that "the world has been governed too much"; and it is often alleged in support of this belief, that successful compliance with the laws requires far more wisdom than was displayed in making them; that is, the *science of obedience* is far more abstruse than the *science of legislation!* Whether this be true in the civil world or not, I shall not attempt to decide; I will only say that such has too often been the fact in the school-room.

It is, in my opinion, the part of wisdom, and I think also the teaching of experience, that it is best to make but few rules. The great rule of duty, quoted once before, "Do unto others as you would that they should do to you", comprises quite enough to begin with. The direction—Do RIGHT, is a very comprehensive one. There is in children an ability to distinguish between right and wrong, upon which the teacher may ever rely; and by insisting upon this as the standard, he daily brings into exercise the conscience of the child, who is called upon to decide, *is this right?* Besides, if a school is to be governed by a code of laws, the pupils will act upon the principle that *whatever is not proscribed is admissible.* Consequently, without inquiring whether an act is right, their only inquiry will be, *is it forbidden?* Now, no teacher was ever yet so wise as to make laws for every case; the consequence

Embarrassment in executing laws.—No discretion.

is, he is daily perplexed with unforeseen troubles, or with some ingenious evasions of his inflexible code. In all this matter the worst feature is the fact, that the child judges of his acts by the *law of the teacher*, rather than by the *law of his conscience*, and is thus in danger of perverting and blunting the moral sense.

To this it may be added, that the teacher will often find himself very much perplexed in attempting to judge the acts of his pupils by fixed laws, and in awarding to all violations of them a prescribed penalty. Cases will frequently occur in which two scholars will offend against a given prohibition, with altogether different intentions,— the one having a good motive and forgetting the law; the other with the law in his mind and having a wicked design to violate it. Now, the written code, with its prescribed penalty, allows the teacher no discretion. He must maintain his law and punish both offenders, and thus violate his own sense of justice; or he must pass both by, and thus violate his word. He can not excuse the one and punish the other, as justice would evidently demand, without setting at naught his own laws.

An example will illustrate this point. A teacher has made a rule that "any child who whispers without leave shall be *feruled.*" Now two little boys sit side by side. William is an amiable, obedient, and diligent little boy, who has never violated intentionally any wish of his teacher; while Charles is a sour-tempered, vicious, unprincipled fellow, who a dozen times within a week has sought to make his teacher trouble. Little John, who sits near to William, drops his pencil, and it falls under William's desk. John looks for his pencil on the right and left of his seat, grows anxious and perplexed. William has noticed him, and he carefully picks up the pencil, while John perhaps is looking for it in another direction,—and with the kind intention of relieving his neighbor's anxiety and restoring his property, he touches his elbow, and softly whispers, "Here is your pencil, John,"—then immediately resumes his own studies, and is probably entirely unconscious of having violated any law. At the same instant, the artful Charles, half concealing his face with his hand, with his wary eye turned to the teacher, willfully addresses another pupil on some point in no way connected with study or duty. The teacher sees both these cases and calls the offenders to his desk. The one trembles, and wonders what he has done amiss, while the other perhaps prepares himself to deny his offense, and thus to add falsehood to his other sins. The *rule* awards to both the *ferule*. It is applied to Charles with energy, and with the conviction that he deserves it; but I ask, can a man with any sense of justice raise his hand to punish William? If so, I see not how he can ever again hold converse with his own conscience. Yet the *rule* allows him no discretion. He must violate either the rule or his conscience; and too often in such cases, he chooses the latter alternative.

Now my advice is, *make but few rules*, and never multiply them till circumstances demand it. The rule of *right* will usually be sufficient without any *special* legislation; and it has this advantage, that it leaves the teacher the largest discretion.

I have been thus full on this point, because so many fail here, and especially young teachers. It has cost many a young teacher much bitter experience to make this discovery for himself, and I have desired to save others who may hereafter engage in teaching, the pain and perplexity which they may so easily and so safely avoid.

For similar reasons, I should also urge that the teacher should avoid the too common practice of *threatening* in his school. Threatening is usually resorted to as a means of frightening children into their duty,—and, too often, threats are made without any expectation of a speedy necessity either to execute or disregard them. The consequence is, they are usually more extravagant than the reality, and the teacher's word soon passes at a discount; his threats are viewed as very much like the barking of a dog who has no intention to bite. As threatening is, moreover, the language of impatience, it almost always leads to a loss of respect.

V. WAKE UP MIND IN THE SCHOOL, AND IN THE DISTRICT. There is usually but very little trouble in government where the scholars are deeply engaged in their studies or school exercises, and especially if, at the same time, the feelings of the parents are enlisted. To this end I would recommend that early attention should be given to some efforts to *wake up mind*, such as have been described in a former section of this work. It will be found, when skillfully conducted, one of the most successful instrumentalities in aid of good order and good feeling in the school.

An ingenious teacher, too, may introduce other varieties into the school exercises, and thus sometimes turn the attention of discontented pupils from some evil design to give him trouble. So long as the teacher keeps steadily the main object of his school in view, namely, progress in the studies, he is excusable if occasionally, to break up monotony and excite a deeper interest, he introduces a well-considered new plan of study or of recitation. Indeed, much of his success will depend upon his power to do this, and in nothing will its advantages appear more obviously than in the government of the school. A great portion of the disorder and insubordination in our schools, has its origin in a want of interest in the school exercises. He is the successful teacher and the successful disciplinarian who can excite and maintain the necessary interest.

As one of these varieties, I may mention the exercise of *vocal music* in school. I have already alluded to it. As a means of keeping alive the

German proverb.—Music in heaven.—Easily introduced in schools.

interest in a school, it is very important. Music is the language of the heart, and though capable of being grossly perverted—(and what gift of God is not?)—its natural tendency is to elevate the affections, to soothe the passions, and to refine the taste.

"The Germans have a proverb," says Bishop Potter, "which has come down from the days of Luther, that where music is not, the devil enters. As David took his harp, when he would cause the evil spirit to depart from Saul, so the Germans employ it to expel the obduracy from the hearts of the depraved. In their schools for the reformation of juvenile offenders (and the same remark might be applied to those of our own country), music has been found one of the most effectual means of inducing docility among the stubborn and vicious. It would seem that so long as any remains of humanity linger in the heart, it retains its susceptibility to music. And as proof that music is more powerful for good than for evil, is it not worthy of profound consideration that, in all the intimations which the Bible gives us of a future world, music is associated only with the employments and happiness of Heaven?"

Almost any teacher can introduce music into his school; because if he can not sing, he will always find that it will only require a little encouragement to induce the scholars to undertake to conduct it themselves. It will consume but very little time, and it is always that time which, if not employed in singing, would otherwise be unemployed or misemployed. It is the united testimony of all who have judiciously introduced singing into their schools, that it is among the best instrumentalities for the promotion of good feeling and good order.

VI. VISIT THE PARENTS OF YOUR SCHOLARS. I shall more particularly enjoin this, when I speak of the *teacher's relation to his patrons* [chap. xii.]; but I can not forbear in this place to urge it upon the teacher as one of the *means of securing good order* in school. A great deal of the insubordination in our schools, arises from some misunderstanding, or some dislike entertained by the parent toward the teacher, and spoken of in presence of the children. Whatever the pupils hear at home, they will be likely to exemplify in school. It should be the teacher's first object to become acquainted with the parent, and to let him understand, by a personal interview, all his plans and aims for the improvement of the school. This can be done best at the parent's own fireside. It has often happened, that by a friendly visit of an hour by the teacher, the parent's heart has been softened, his prejudices removed, his co-operation gained, and the cheerful and cordial obedience of his children in school secured.

These visits should of course be made in the true spirit of the teacher. They should be made in the honest desire of his heart to render his labors more successful. A visit made in such a spirit seldom fails to make the parents personal friends ever after; and, of course, in case of a collision afterward between him and their children, this is a very important point.

VII. REGISTERS OF CREDITS. Registers of the standing of pupils in their schools and their classes, are very highly recommended by some, whose experience is entitled to confidence. I am inclined to place this among the means of securing good order. I would recommend, however, that they should be registers of *credits* only. Some recommend the use of "*black marks*", that is, the record of prominent faults and perhaps of punishments. My own experience teaches me that this is unwise. The teacher should not show a willingness to record and publish the faults of a pupil. He should, on the contrary, show a tender regard for his reputation. Besides, the child is less likely to be mindful of his duty, when his reputation is already *blackened* by his teacher. If Registers are to be kept at all, they should record the successes and virtues of the child, rather than his failures and faults. And if, at the end of a week or a month, he is furnished with an abstract for the inspection of his parents, let it be so much of good character as he has earned for himself during the specified time.

I confess I am less sanguine than many others as to the utility of the register, either as an in-

Government not the business of the teacher.—Mr. Howard's remark.

centive to obedience or diligence; but, if used at all, I think the above restriction is highly important.

VIII. AVOID GOVERNING TOO MUCH. By this I would be understood to urge upon the teacher the fact that his main business in school is *instruction* and not *government*. Government is a *means* and not the *end* of school-keeping. A very judicious and practical teacher—Mr. R. S. Howard—has well remarked: "The real object to be accomplished, the real end to be obtained in school, is to assist the pupil in acquiring knowledge,—to educate the mind and heart. To effect this, good order is very necessary. But when order is made to take the place of industry, and discipline the place of instruction, where the time of both teacher and pupils is mostly spent in watching each other, very little good will be accomplished."

It is a mistake that many teachers fall into, that they seem to regard *government* as their chief occupation; and, as we should naturally expect in such cases, it is often very poorly exercised. That is not the best government which is maintained as a matter of formal business. The noiseless under-current is far more efficient. I have always noticed that men govern best *when they do not seem to govern;* and those who make most effort and bustle about it themselves, are pretty sure to have the most boisterous schools.

I once, in company with a friend, officially

visited a school, where the teacher, a man of strong frame—six feet high, and with *lungs in proportion*—was *laboring* to keep order. Every word he uttered was in a stentorian voice which would have been painful to the pupils in a quiet room; hence, they took care to keep up a constant clattering of books, slates, and rulers, mingled with the constant hum of their own voices, as if for self-defense. It seemed to be a mighty effort of each party to rise, if possible, above the noise of the other. "Silence! Order, I say!" was constantly ejaculated in a voice that was almost sufficient, as Shakspeare's Hamlet would say, to "split the ears of the groundlings."

One of the most ludicrous scenes I ever witnessed, occurred in this school during an exercise in English grammar. The class occupied the back seats, while the teacher stood by the desk in front of the school. The children between the teacher and his class were variously employed,—some manufacturing paper fly-boxes, some *whittling* the benches—(it was in New England); some were trying their skill at a spit-ball warfare; others were making voyages of exploration beneath the seats. The school, consisting of some seventy pupils, were as busy as the occupants of an ant-hill. The sentence to be parsed was, "A good boy loves study." No written description can present the scene as it was acted in real life.

It should be borne in mind that every word spoken by the teacher, whether to the class or to the school, was in a tone of voice which might have been heard at least an eighth of a mile, and that every exclamation was accompanied by several energetic *thumps* of a large oaken "*rule*" upon the lid of his desk. The language of the teacher is in italics. "*Mary, parse A.*" "A is an indefinite"—"*Silence! Order there!*"—"article, and is prefixed to"—"*John!*"—"No, sir, it is prefixed to"—"*Martha, Martha! sit up!*"—"it is prefixed to—boy."—"*Right.*"—"*Good, next.*"—"Good is an adjective,"—"*Order, order, order!*"—thump, thump, thump!—"*Go on, go on, I hear you!*"—thump, thump!—"and belongs to"—"*Speak louder! Sit up there! What are you doing? And belongs to?*"—"boy."—"*The Rule. The Rule! I say.*"—Here several children looked earnestly at the piece of timber he held in his hand.—"*The Rule, sir, the Rule!*"—thump, thump!—"You've got it in your hand," vociferated a little harmless-looking fellow on the front seat, while the scholar proceeded to recite the rule.—"Adjectives belong to"—"*Lazy, lazy fellow! sit up there.*"—Here the class smiled, and the scholar completed his rule, asserting, however, that "adjectives belong to nouns," and not to "*lazy fellows,*" as the class seemed to understand the master to teach. Word after word was parsed in this way (a way of teaching our language, which, if we could know it had been practiced at the erection of Babel, would sufficiently account for that memorable confusion of tongues without the

SCHOOL GOVERNMENT. 213

Who made it?—Another visit.—A new teacher.

intervention of a miracle), till the teacher, nearly exhausted by this strange combination of mental, oral, and *manual labor*, very much to the relief of all, vociferated, "*That'll do!*" and the scene was changed.

At the close of the afternoon, we were told that "it was a very hard school, that it was almost impossible to keep order, and that he *should* be discouraged were it not that he saw a manifest improvement within a few days past!"

Now this teacher *made* the school what it was, by his own manner. He would have done the same in any school. He taught in the most effectual way the science and art of confusion; and notwithstanding the hard name he gave his school, he was *emphatically* the most disorderly and noisy member of it.

There was a change. On another day, accompanied by the same friend, we presented ourselves at the door of this same room for admittance. We heard no sound as we approached the entrance, and almost began to suspect we should find there was no school within. We knocked; and presently, without our hearing the footstep of the person who approached, the door opened, and we passed in. The children looked up a moment as we entered, and then bent their eyes upon their lessons. The teacher softly handed us seats, and then proceeded with the recitation. His manner was quiet and deliberate, and the school was orderly and busy. He had no rule in

Good order.—The secret.—Excessive silence.

his hand, no heavy boots on his feet (he had exchanged them for slippers on entering the school), and no other means of giving emphasis to his words. He kindly requested,—never commanded,—and every thing seemed to present the strongest contrast with the former scene. The hour of dismission arrived, and the scholars quietly laid by their books, and as quietly walked out of the house, and all was still.

"How have you secured this good order?" said we to the teacher. "I really do not know," said he with a smile, "I have said nothing about order." "But have you had no difficulty from noisy scholars?" "A little at first; but in a day or two they seemed to become quiet, and we have not been troubled since."

Now the secret was, that this latter teacher had learned to govern himself. His own manner gave character to the school. So it will ever be. A man will govern more by his manner than in any other way.

There is, too, such a thing as keeping a school *too still* by over-government. A man of firm nerve can, by keeping up a constant constraint both upon himself and pupils, force a death-like silence upon his school. You may hear a pin drop at any time, and the figure of every child is as if molded in cast iron. But, be it remembered, this is the stillness of constraint, not the stillness of activity. It is an unhealthy state both of body and mind, and when attained by the most vigilant care of the teacher, is a condition scarcely to be desired. There should be silence in school, a serene and soothing quiet; but it should if possible be the quiet of cheerfulness and agreeable devotion to study, rather than the "palsy of fear."

Thus far I have confined myself to those qualifications in the teacher, and to those means which, under ordinary circumstances and in most districts, would in my opinion secure good order in our schools. With the qualifications I have described in the mental and moral condition of the teacher, and the means and suggestions above detailed—combined, I believe a very large majority of our schools could be most successfully governed without any appeal to *fear or force.*

But as some schools are yet in a very bad state, requiring more than ordinary talents and skill to control them; and as very many of those who must teach for a long time to come, have not, and can not be expected to have, all the qualifications described, and much less the moral power insisted on, it is unreasonable to expect, taking human nature as it is, and our teachers as they are, that all can govern their schools without some appeals to the lower motives of children and some resort to coercion as an instrumentality. I should leave this discussion very incomplete, therefore, were I not to present my views upon the subject of

SECTION III.—PUNISHMENTS.

As a great deal has been written and spoken upon the subject of school punishments, I deem it important that the term, as I intend to use it, should be defined at the outset. I submit the following *definition:*

PUNISHMENT IS PAIN INFLICTED UPON THE MIND OR BODY OF AN INDIVIDUAL BY THE AUTHORITY TO WHICH HE IS SUBJECT; WITH A VIEW EITHER TO REFORM HIM, OR TO DETER OTHERS FROM THE COMMISSION OF OFFENSES, OR BOTH.

It is deemed essential to the idea of punishment that the inflictor have legitimate authority over the subject of it,—otherwise, the act is an act of usurpation. It is also essential that the inflictor should have a legitimate object in view, such as the reformation of the individual or of the community in which his example has exerted an influence,—otherwise, the act becomes an abuse of power. Infliction for the purpose of retaliation for an insult or injury, is not punishment; it is revenge. Whenever, therefore, a teacher resorts to such infliction to gratify his temper, or to *pay off,* as it is expressed in common language, the bad conduct of a pupil, without any regard to his reformation or the prevention of similar offenses in the school, the pain he inflicts is not punishment; it is cruelty. Very great importance is to be attached to the motive in this matter; because the same infliction upon the same individual and for the same offense, may either be just and proper punishment, or it may be the most unjustifiable and revengeful abuse, according to the motive of the inflictor.

The *authority* to inflict punishment in general, is either by the constitution of God or of civil society. "The punishment of the faults and offenses of children by the parent," says Dr. Webster, "is by virtue of the right of government with which the parent is invested by God himself." The right to punish the offenses of children while at school, is by the common law vested in the teacher, as the representative of the parent for the time being. It is the declaration of this law as interpreted from time immemorial, that the teacher is *in loco parentis*—in place of the parent.

Some have alleged that *fear* and *shame*, the two principles addressed by punishment, are among the lowest in our nature; and have hence endeavored to show that punishment is always inexpedient, if not indeed always wrong. To this I answer, that both fear and shame are incorporated in our nature by God himself; and hence I infer they are there for a wise purpose. I find, moreover, that God himself, in his word and in his providence, does appeal to both of these principles; and hence I infer that punishment in the abstract is not wrong, and after the higher motives have been addressed, not altogether inexpedient.

The right assumed.—Plan of discussion.—Two classes.

Living in a community as we do, where the *right* of punishment in general, is assumed by our government, and the right of teachers to punish is conceded by our laws, I do not feel called upon to establish the *right* by argument; I shall assume that the *teacher has the right to punish*, in the sense in which I have defined punishment,—and shall therefore proceed to consider the various kinds of punishments used in our schools, and to distinguish those which are justifiable from those which are not; and also to consider some of the conditions and limitations of their use.

In preparing the way to do this, I may remark that punishments consist of two classes. 1. Those which address themselves directly to the mind; as privation from privileges, loss of liberty, degradation, some act of humiliation, reproof, and the like. 2. Those which address the mind through the body; as the imposition of a task—labor, for instance,—requiring the pupil to take some painful attitude, inflicting bodily chastisement, etc.

I have mentioned these two classes for the purpose of calling attention to the fact, that there are those who approve of the first class, and at the same time denounce the second, scouting the idea of reaching the mind through the senses of the body. This seems to me, however, to indicate a want of attention to the laws of our being; for in the economy of nature, we are made at every point sensitive to pain as a means of

SCHOOL GOVERNMENT. 219

Mind may be reached through the body.—Improper punishments.

guarding against injury. Why has the Creator studded the entire surface of our bodies with the extremities of nerves, whose function is to carry to the brain with lightning speed the intelligence of the approach of danger? And why should this intelligence be transmitted, if its object is not to influence the will, either to withdraw the suffering part from immediate danger, or to avoid those objects which cause the pain? The mind, then, by the economy of nature, or rather by the arrangement of God, is capable of being influenced through the bodily sensations; and those who deny this, either do not observe attentively, or, observing, do not reason fairly as to the laws of our being. With these preliminary observations, I now proceed to consider,

I. IMPROPER PUNISHMENTS. Some punishments are always wrong, or at least always inexpedient. The infliction of them either implies a wrong feeling on the part of the teacher, or it promises no wholesome result on the part of the pupil. I shall mention in detail, 1. *Those that from their nature excite the feeling in the pupil, that an indignity has been committed against his person.* No man is ready to forgive another for *wringing his nose.* There is almost a universal sentiment that this organ is specially exempted from such insult. Nearly the same feeling exists as to *pinching or pulling the ear,* or *twisting the hair,* or *snapping the forehead.* Each child feels that these parts of his person are not to be trifled

Head to be exempted from infliction.

with, and the feeling is natural and proper. Now, though it is not common for teachers to wring the noses of their pupils, it is very common for them to do each of the other things enumerated. I have often seen such punishments; but I think I never saw any good come of them. The pupil always looked as if the teacher had done despite toward his person. Whenever I have seen the teacher twist the locks of a child's hair about his finger till the tears would start in the eye, I have supposed the feelings called forth were any thing but desirable,—any thing but favorable to reformation. A pupil must love his teacher very strongly, to be able to keep his temper from rising under such circumstances; and there is great doubt whether either of these punishments does any thing to secure cheerful obedience in the child, one time in a hundred; probably in ninety-nine cases in the hundred, the evil passions are very much strengthened by them. Besides, these are undignified modes of punishment. They savor so much of a weak and childish impatience, that the pupils find it hard to respect a man, much more to love him, who will stoop to so *small* a way of giving vent to his angry feelings. Snapping the forehead is subject to strong physiological objections; and, as a general rule, *the head and its appurtenances* should be exempted from penal violence.

In this place I may very properly allude to another mode of assailing the ears of children, quite as undignified in itself, and quite as unprofitable in its results, as pulling them,—and until they are hardened to it by familiarity, probably more painful. I refer, I need not say, to *scolding.* This is a punishment altogether too common. There is a physiological law, that the exercise of any organ will give it greater strength and generally greater celerity. From this fact, and the additional one, that the more a child is scolded the harder his heart becomes, so that here, as in the Rule of Three, "more requires more,"—it follows that those who once begin to scold, are fortunate if they stop short of high attainments in the art.

There is no enterprise in which the investment yields so small a profit, as the business of scolding. It is really pitiable to witness the teacher given to this practice, making himself and *all* around him unhappy, without the hope of alleviation. The command of the tongue is a great virtue in a teacher; and it is to be feared that very many children still suffer in their moral feelings * as well as their ears; because so many teachers do not seasonably learn the right control of the "unruly member".

While upon this subject, I may allude to

---

* A blacksmith, it is said, who had been accustomed to scold his family, quite too freely, was one day attempting to harden a piece of steel; but failing after two or three attempts, his little son, who had been an observer of this as well as other operations of his father, is said to have exclaimed, "*Scold it, father, scold it—if that won't harden it, nothing else will.*"

another very objectionable mode of address practiced by some teachers toward their schools. I refer to a mixture of scolding with a species of low wit or cockney blackguardism, that should ever be banished from the school-room. Such expressions as, "Sit down, John, or I'll shiver your *top-timbers*,'—"Attend to your studies, or some of you will be a *head shorter*,"—"Keep quiet, or you'll hear thunder,"—and the like. To these I might add those empty and debasing threats which are too often and too thoughtlessly uttered; as, "I'll skin you alive," or "I'll shake you to pieces," or "I'll use you up,"—with others of the same character. I perhaps ought to beg pardon for placing these vulgarisms before the general reader; but they are so frequently employed in our schools, in some of our schools of good repute, too, that I thought it to be my duty to *quote* them (for they are all literal quotations), in order if possible to aid those who have fallen into such a low habit, *to see themselves as others see them.*

It is so very easy for a teacher to raise a laugh among his pupils, that he is in danger of being seduced into the use of coarse and quaint expressions by the supposition that they are *witty*. But the mirth of school-boys is not a more reliable criterion of wit in the modern teacher, than it was in the case of the school-master described by Goldsmith; and possibly the exercise of a little discernment on his part would convince him that children sometimes laugh, as they did of old, because they think it *prudent* to do so.

> "A man severe he was and stern to view,
> I knew him well, and every truant knew;
> Well had the boding tremblers learned to trace
> The day's disasters in his morning face;
> Full well they laughed, *with counterfeited glee*,
> *At all his jokes*, for many a joke had he!"

It is unquestionably true that there are schools and many such, now of high standing, the language of whose teachers, could it be noted down and printed for the parents, would perfectly astonish them; and such is the force of habit, it would very likely astonish the teachers themselves. Let all who mean to respect themselves, or who desire to be long respected by others, most carefully avoid the first approach to the use of such kind of language. Its influence in school is "only evil, and that continually."

2. *Those punishments that from their nature imply in the inflictor a love of prolonged torture.* These are quite numerous, and are resorted to, often for the purpose of avoiding what is usually deemed severer punishment. Some of them also have very serious physiological objections. As an instance, I may mention the holding of a weight at arm's length until the muscles of the arm become painful from over-exertion and fatigue. Sometimes the Bible, being the largest book at hand, is chosen as the weight; and thus that book, which should have no associations connected with it in the minds of the young, but those of rever-

ence and love, is made the instrument of torture—
the minister of cruelty!

Imagine that you see—what I have seen—an
offending boy called to the teacher's desk, and,
after words of reproach, sentenced to hold the
large Bible at arm's length for a specified time,
or until the teacher is willing to release him. At
first it is raised with a smile of triumph, almost
a smile of contempt. Soon the muscles thus exerted at disadvantage, begin to be weary and to
relax. "Hold it up!" exclaims the vigilant teacher,
and it is again brought to its position. Sooner
than before the muscles are fatigued, and they
almost refuse to obey the mandate of the *will*,
which itself is half *willing* to rebel against authority so unreasonable. "Up with it!"—again
brings it to its place, or perhaps a stroke of the
rattan repeats the command with more urgency.
At this moment every nerve sympathizes, and
the muscles are urged on to their greatest effort.
The limb is in agony,—and what agony can surpass that of an overstrained muscle?—and the
whole system reels and writhes with suffering.
Now look into that child's face, and tell me, what
is the moral effect of this sort of punishment?
Unless he is one of the most amiable of the sons
of Adam, he inwardly curses the cruelty that he
thinks is delighted with pangs like these, protracted yet intolerable. He almost curses the
blessed book which was given to warm his soul
into life and immortality. He cries with pain,

but not with penitence. He may submit, indeed, and he may abstain from similar offenses in time to come; but it is the submission of self-preservation, and the abstinence of an eye-servant.—while the stain that has thus been inwrought in his moral sensibilities, may long remain unexpunged. Such a punishment I unhesitatingly pronounce to be *improper*, whatever may be the circumstances.

Akin to this are those other contrivances to give prolonged pain, which in different parts of the country have taken a variety of forms, and as great a variety of names. One of these has been termed "*holding a nail into the floor.*" It consists in requiring the pupil to bend forward,—and, placing the end of a single finger upon the head of a nail, to remain in that position till the whole system is agonized. Another has, by some of its inflictors, been termed "sitting on nothing." The pupil is required to place his back against a wall of the room, and his feet perhaps a foot from its base, and then to slide his body down till the knees are bent at right angles, and his person is in a sitting posture without a seat! The muscles, acting over the knee at the greatest disadvantage, are now made to support the body in that position during the pleasure of the teacher. I have seen another mode of punishment practiced, and as I have heard no name for it, I shall give it the cognomen of "sitting on *worse* than nothing." The boy in this case was required to sit upon the floor, and then, placing the feet upon a bench or chair, to support the body in an erect position by reversed action of the muscles!

But I gladly turn away from a description of the punishments I have witnessed in the common schools of New England within a quarter of a century, exhibiting as they do so many characteristics of the *dark ages*. Some of these I have witnessed quite recently; and to what extent any or all of them are now in use, I am unable to say. I only desire to say, that they are all improper,—debasing to the morals of the pupils, and degrading to the profession of the teacher; and the sooner such punishments are entirely banished from our school-rooms, the sooner will the profession of the teacher rise to its proper level.

3. *Ridicule.* This is a weapon that should not be wielded as a school-punishment. It often cuts deeper than he who uses it imagines; and it usually gives most pain where it is least merited. Some physical defect, or some mental incapacity, or eccentricity, is most frequently made the subject of it; and yet nothing can be more unfeeling or more unjust than its use in such cases. If the designed failings of the indolent, or the premeditated mischief of the vicious, could be subjected to its influence, its use would be more allowable,— but even then it would be questionable. But the indolent and the vicious are usually unaffected by ridicule. They sin upon calculation, and not

without counting the cost; and they are therefore very willing to risk their reputation, where they have so little to lose. It is the modest, the conscientious, the well-meaning child, that is most affected by ridicule; yet it is such a one that, for various reasons, is oftenest made the subject of it, though of all children, his feelings should be most tenderly spared.

A strong objection to the use of ridicule, is the feeling which it induces between the teacher and pupil. The teacher, conscious that he has injured the feelings of the child, will find it hard to love him afterward; for we seldom love those whom we have injured. The child, on the other hand, loses confidence in his teacher; he feels that his sensibilities have been outraged before his companions, and that the teacher, who should be his best friend in the school, has invited the heartless laugh of his fellow-pupils against him. With a want of love on the one hand, and of confidence on the other, what further usefulness can reasonably be expected?

But the strongest objection of all to the use of ridicule, is the fact that it calls forth the worst of feelings in the school. Those who participate in the laugh thus excited, are under the influence of no very amiable motives. And when this is carried so far as to invite, by direct words, some expression from the school-mates, by pointing the finger of shame, and perhaps accompanying the act by a *hiss* of scorn, the most deplorable spirit of self-righteousness is cultivated.

Little Mary was detected one day in a wrong act by her teacher. "Mary, come here," said the teacher, sternly. Little thinking she had been seen, she obeyed promptly, and stood by the chair of her teacher, who, without giving Mary time to reflect, and thus allow the conscience opportunity to gain the mastery, immediately asked, "What naughty thing did I see you do just now?" "Nothing," said Mary, partly disposed to justify herself, and partly doubting whether indeed the teacher had *seen her* do any thing wrong. "Oh, Mary, Mary, who would think you would tell me a lie! Did you ever hear of Ananias and Sapphira?" Here a lecture followed on the sin and danger of lying, and particularly the danger of sudden death by the vengeance of God. Mary began to tremble, and then to weep, probably from terror. Now came the second part. "I should think you would be ashamed to be known to lie. All the children now know that you have lied. I should think they would feel ashamed of such a naughty little girl in the school. I should not wonder," she continued, "if all the little girls and boys *should point their fingers at you and hiss.*" In an instant, all the children who were not too old to be disgusted with the management and tone of the teacher, pointed their fingers, and uttered a long succession of hisses, while their faces beamed with all

Self-righteousness.—Defiance.—Freezing the affections.

the complacency of self-righteousness, triumphing over the fall of a companion, who perhaps was, after all, as good and as truthful a child as any of them. The poor child at first turned her back upon them; but soon, feeling that her reputation was gone, she turned, as woman ever will when her self-respect is blighted, with a look of indifference, almost a look of defiance. Fear was first swallowed up in shame, and shame gave place to reckless audacity. The whole scene was rendered still more ruinous to the child, from the fact that it took place in the presence of visitors!

When will our teachers learn the human heart well enough to be able to distinguish between a work of devastation and of true culture; between a process of blighting the sensibilities, searing the conscience, freezing up the fountains of sympathy, and of mutual love and confidence,—and a course of training which warms the conscience into activity, inculcates the reverence and love of God, instead of a slavish fear of his power, and instills into the soul a desire to *do right*, rather than to do that which will avoid the reproach of an unfeeling multitude, more wicked than those they censure? Goldsmith has shown that *woman* may "stoop to conquer"; but the above narrative shows how she may stoop, not to conquer, but to *lay waste* the youthful heart.

These punishments, and such as these, which I have classed under the list of *improper* punish-

Let teachers think.—Proper punishments.—Reproof in private.

ments, should all be carefully considered by the teacher. They should be considered before he enters his school. It would always be well for him to determine beforehand what punishments he will *not* use. It may save him many a serious mistake. I have written what I have under this head, in order to put teachers upon thought; believing that men seldom earnestly and honestly *inquire*, without arriving at the truth in the end.

II. PROPER PUNISHMENTS. Every teacher's mind should, if possible, be settled, as to what punishments are proper, so that when they are inflicted, it can be done in good faith and with an honest conviction of the performance of duty. Among the proper punishments, I may mention—

1. *Kind Reproof.* This will probably be conceded by all. I say *kind* reproof, because no other reproof can be useful. I would distinguish it from *reproach.* Reproof, judiciously administered, is one of the most effectual punishments that can be used. As a general rule, this is best administered privately. The child's spirit of obstinacy is very likely to exhibit itself in the presence of his fellows; but in private, the conscience is free to act, and the child very readily submits. It is always perfectly safe to reprove privately; that is, not in the presence of the school. The child has no motive to misrepresent the teacher; and if the teacher so far spares the reputation of the pupil, as to take him by him-

Loss of privileges, consequent upon abuse.—Confinement.

self, this very circumstance will often give the teacher access to his better feelings.

2. *Loss of Privileges.* By abuse of privileges we forfeit them. This is a law of Providence. It is unquestionably proper that this should be a law of our schools. All those offenses, therefore, against propriety in the exercise of any privilege, may be attended with a temporary or permanent deprivation of such privilege. A pupil who is boisterous at the recess, disturbing the quiet of the school or impeding the enjoyment of his playfellows, may be deprived of the recess. A child, who disfigures his seat with his knife, may be deprived of his knife; and so for any other similar offense. Some consider it proper to extend this punishment to other classes of offenses; as, for example, whispering or idleness. While I would not deny the right or the propriety of doing so, I should think it more expedient not thus to extend it. It is well, as far as it can be done, so to punish the child, that he shall see that his conduct naturally leads to its punishment as a consequence. And it is, moreover, very probable that in most schools there will be demand enough for this punishment, in its natural application, without extending it to other cases.

3. *Restraint, or confinement.* When liberty is abused, a scholar may be put under restraint. When duty is violated, and the rights of others are wantonly disregarded, confinement will afford time for reflection, and at the same time relieve

others from the annoyance and detriment of evil example. Such restraint is often a wholesome discipline; and confinement, if it be not too far protracted, is always safe. It should be remarked, however, that confinement in a *dark* apartment should never be resorted to by any teacher. There are insuperable objections to it, growing out of the fears which many children early entertain of being alone in the dark, as also the fact that light as well as air is necessary to the vigorous action of the nervous system during the waking hours, especially in the day-time. It is well known that a child shut up in a dark room even in the warmth of summer, speedily undergoes a depression of temperature; and if the confinement is unduly protracted, cold chills come over the system. For these reasons, and others, if confinement is ever used as a punishment, it should be in a room properly lighted and heated. Our prisoners enjoy, as far as may be, both of these favors.

4. *Humiliation.* This should be resorted to with great caution. When a fault has been openly committed, and attended with circumstances of peculiar obstinacy, it may sometimes very properly be required of the offender that he should confess the fault in a manner as public as its commission. This may be due to the school. Sometimes, when an offensive act is very strongly marked, a confession and a request for the forgiveness of the teacher or the individual injured

may be made a condition of restoration to favor. This is usually considered a very proper punishment. I would, however, suggest, that it be used with great care, and never unless the circumstances imperatively demand it. It may be the means of cultivating the grossest hypocrisy, or of inducing open rebellion; and it sometimes gives the other pupils an advantage over the culprit, which may do him personally much harm. The teacher should be convinced that this is the *best thing* he can do, before he resorts to it.

5. *The imposition of a task.* In every school there is more or less work to be done; such as sweeping the floors, washing the benches, preparing the fuel, and making the fires. Unless objection should be made by parents, this is one of the most effectual punishments, especially in cities and large villages, where work is a burden, and the attractions of play are most powerful. Some difficult schools have been governed for months with no other punishment than labor thus imposed. The plan is, that if two boys neglect their studies so as to attract the attention of the teacher, they shall be nominated as members of the committee on sweeping,—a duty to be performed after school hours. If one or two more are decidedly disorderly, they shall be required to make fires, bring up wood, or perhaps wash a certain portion of the room. This is always assigned pleasantly by the teacher, with

the understanding, however, that any failure to do the allotted work thoroughly and faithfully, will be attended with a *reappointment* till the object is secured.

If parents should object to this, it is not absolutely essential to the teacher's success; but where no objection is made, if judiciously managed, it may do very much in many of our schools toward producing that quiet order, which otherwise it might require more cogent and less agreeable means to secure.

It has sometimes been urged as an objection to this mode of punishment, that it would tend to attach the idea of *disgrace* to useful labor. It is conceived that this is by no means the necessary consequence. On the other hand, it would serve to teach the difference there always is between a duty imposed and one voluntarily undertaken. The same objection would apply to our prison discipline, where a man by a willful disregard of law and the rights of others, very justly forfeits his services for a time to the State.

I would not lay very much stress upon this mode of punishment, though I have known it resorted to, under favorable circumstances, with very good effect. It would, of course, be more effectual in a large town or city, than in the country, where boys are in the habit of laboring at home and would be quite as willing to labor after regular hours at school.

6. *Actual chastisement with the rod of correc-*

tion. I have no hesitation (though others have) in placing this among the class of *proper punishments*. As this involves a great question on the subject of school government, and one that is debated with great zeal and warmth in almost every educational meeting that is held, I shall feel justified in giving a little more space to the consideration of it.

SECTION IV.—CORPORAL PUNISHMENT.

I am aware that when I enter this field I am treading on ground every inch of which has been disputed. I come to the task of writing on this subject, however, I think, without prejudice or asperity. Having nothing to conceal, I shall express my own views honestly and frankly,—views which I entertain after diligently seeking the truth for some twenty years, during which time I have listened to a great deal of discussion, and have read carefully and candidly whatever has been written by others. Nor do I expect to give universal satisfaction. There are strong men, and I believe honest men, who run to the opposite extremes in their doctrine and practice, and who defend the one course or the other as if the existence of the world depended upon the issue. There are those who not only claim the right to chastise, but who insist that whipping should be the *first resort* of the teacher in establishing his authority; and to show that this is not a dormant article of their faith, they daily and almost hourly demonstrate their efficiency in the use of the rod, so that their pupils may be living witnesses that they act in accordance with their creed. Again, there are others who as earnestly deny the right of the teacher to resort to the rod at all, and who urge with all their power the efficacy of moral suasion to subdue and control the vicious and the stubborn in our schools; and who are ready to assert unequivocally that no man is fit to be employed to teach the young, who has not the ability to govern all the various dispositions he may meet in any school, without the use of corporal punishment.

I have no disposition to question the sincerity and honesty of each of these classes, knowing as I do, that different men see with different eyes, even when the circumstances are the same; much more when their circumstances are widely diverse. I have no bitterness of language to apply to those who go to the extreme of severity; nor any sneer to bestow upon the name of "moral-suasionist." But while I accord to other men the right of expressing their own opinions, I claim the same privilege for myself,—yet without wishing to obtrude my opinions upon other men any further than they will bear the test of reason and experience.

It is agreed on all hands *that the teacher must establish authority in some way, before he can pursue successfully the objects of his school.*

We must take the world as it is.—Mr. Mann quoted.

I have described the qualifications which the teacher should possess in order to govern well, and I have also given some of the means of securing good order without a resort to severity. Probably in a large majority of our schools, the teacher with these qualifications and the employment of these means, could succeed in establishing and maintaining good order without any such resort. This should, in my opinion, always be done, if possible,—and no one will rejoice more than myself to see the day, should that day ever come, when teachers shall be so much improved as to be able to do this universally. But in writing on this subject, it is the dictate of common sense to take human nature as it is, and human teachers as they are, and as many of them must be, for some time to come,—and adapt our directions to the circumstances. Human nature, as it is exhibited in our children, is far from being perfect; and I am sorry to say that the parents of our children often exhibit it in a still less flattering light. Perhaps no language of mine can so well represent the concurrence of circumstances making corporal punishment necessary in our schools, as it has been done by the Hon. Horace Mann in his lecture on "School Punishments." "The first point," says he, "which I shall consider, is, whether corporal punishment is ever necessary in our schools. As preliminary to a decision of this question, let us take a brief survey of facts. We have in this Commonwealth

[Massachusetts], above one hundred and ninety-two thousand children between the ages of four and sixteen years. All these children are not only legally entitled to attend our public schools but it is our great desire to increase that attendance, and he who increases it is regarded as a reformer. All that portion of these children who attend school, enter it from that vast variety of homes which exist in the State. From different households, where the widest diversity of parental and domestic influences prevails, the children enter the school-room, where there must be comparative uniformity. At home, some of these children have been indulged in every wish, flattered and smiled upon for the energies of their low propensities, and even their freaks and whims enacted into household laws. Some have been so rigorously debarred from every innocent amusement and indulgence, that they have opened for themselves a way to gratification, through artifice and treachery and falsehood. Others, from vicious parental example, and the corrupting influences of vile associates, have been trained to bad habits and contaminated with vicious principles, ever since they were born;—some being taught that honor consists in whipping a boy larger than themselves; others, that the chief end of man is to own a box that can not be opened, and to get money enough to fill it; and others again have been taught, upon their father's knees, to shape their young lips to the utterance

A dilemma.

of oaths and blasphemy. Now all these dispositions, which do not conflict with right more than they do with each other, as soon as they cross the threshold of the school-room, from the different worlds, as it were, of homes, must be made to obey the same general regulations, to pursue the same studies, and to aim at the same results. In addition to these artificial varieties, there are natural differences of temperament and disposition.

"Again: there are about three thousand public schools in the State, in which are employed, in the course of the year, about five thousand different persons, as teachers, including both males and females. Excepting a very few cases, these five thousand persons have had no special preparation or training for their employment, and many of them are young and without experience. These five thousand teachers, then, so many of whom are unprepared, are to be placed in authority over the one hundred and ninety-two thousand children, so many of whom have been perverted. Without passing through any transition state for improvement, these parties meet each other in the school-room, where mutiny and insubordination and disobedience are to be repressed, order maintained, knowledge acquired. He, therefore, who denies the necessity of resorting to punishment, in our schools,—and to corporal punishment, too,—virtually affirms two things:—first, that this great number of children, scooped up from all places, taken at all ages and in all conditions, can be deterred from the wrong and attracted to the right without punishment; and secondly, he asserts that the five thousand persons whom the towns and districts employ to keep their respective schools, are now, and in the present condition of things, able to accomplish so glorious a work. Neither of these propositions am I at present prepared to admit. If there are extraordinary individuals—and we know there are such—so singularly gifted with talent and resources, and with the divine quality of love, that they can win the affection, and, by controlling the heart, can control the conduct of children, who, for years, have been addicted to lie, to cheat, to swear, to steal, to fight,—still I do not believe there are now five thousand such individuals in the State, whose heavenly services can be obtained for this transforming work. And it is useless, or worse than useless, to say, that such or such a thing can be done, and done immediately, without pointing out the agents by whom it can be done. One who affirms that a thing can be done, without any reference to the persons who can do it, must be thinking of miracles. If the position were, that children *may* be so educated from their birth, and teachers *may* be so trained for their calling, as to supersede the necessity of corporal punishment, except in cases decidedly monstrous, then I should have no doubt of its truth; but such a position must

Divisions in district.—East end.—West end.—"We will see."

have reference to some future period, which we should strive to hasten, but ought not to anticipate."

Aside from the causes demanding punishment, so ably portrayed in the passage just quoted, there is still another, growing out of divisions and quarrels in the district. It is by no means uncommon, in our districts, owing to some local matter, or to some disunion in politics or religion, for the people to be arrayed, the one part against the other. The inhabitants of the *upper* road are jealous of the dwellers on the *lower* road; the *hill* portion of the district is aggrieved by the influence of the *valley* portion; the "east end" complains of the selfishness of the "west end," and so of the north and south. Whenever a school-house is to be built, these different interests are aroused, and a protracted and baleful quarrel is the result. One party "carries the day" by the force of numbers, but the prosperity of the school is impaired for years. At every district meeting, there will be the same strife for the mastery. If one division gains the power, the other bends its energies to cripple the school, and to annoy the teacher who may be employed by the dominant party, however excellent or deserving he may be. "We will see," say those who find themselves in the minority, "we will see whether this man can keep our school as well as it was done last year by *our* master." This is uttered in presence of their children—perhaps their half-grown sons,

Disobedience encouraged.—The teacher's course.

who will be very ready to meet their new teacher with prejudice, and to *act out* the misgivings of their parents as to his success. When the teacher first enters the school, he is met by opposition, even before he has time to make an impression for good; opposition, which he can scarcely hope to surmount as long as it is thus encouraged at home. Now, what shall he do? Shall he yield the point, abandon the idea of authority, and endeavor to live along from day to day, in the hope of a more comfortable state of things by and by? He may be sure that matters will daily grow worse. Shall he give up in despair and leave the school to some successor? This will only strengthen the opposition and make it more violent when the successor shall be appointed. It is but putting the difficulty one step farther off. Besides, if the teacher does thus give up, and leave the school, he loses his own reputation as a man of energy, and, in the eyes of the world, who perhaps may not know—or care to know—all the circumstances, he is held ever after as incompetent for the office.

Now, it would be very gratifying if the teacher, under any or all of these difficulties, *could* possess the moral power to quell them all by a look or by the exercise of his ingenuity in interesting his pupils in their studies. Undoubtedly there are some men who could do it, and do it most triumphantly, so as to make their most zealous enemies, in a few days their warmest friends.

Shall he yield? No, no.—Establish authority.

But there are not many who can work thus at disadvantage. What, then, shall be done? Shall the school be injured by being disbanded, and the teacher be stigmatized for a failure, when he has been employed in good faith? I say NO. *He has the right to establish authority by corporal infliction;* and thus to save the school and also save himself. And more than this;—if there is reasonable ground to believe that by such infliction he can establish order, and thus make himself useful, and save the time and the character of the school, he not only has the right, but *he is bound by duty to use it*. The lovers of order in the district have a right to expect him to use it, unless by express stipulation beforehand, they have exempted him from it. I repeat, then, that it is the teacher's duty to *establish authority;* "peaceably, indeed, if he may,—forcibly, if he must."

I ought in fairness here to add, as I have before hinted, that not unfrequently the necessity for corporal infliction exists in the teacher himself. This is often proved by a transfer of teachers. One man takes a school, and can only survive his term by the *exercise* of whipping. He is followed by another who secures good order and the love of the school without any resort to the rod. The first declared that whipping was necessary in his case to secure good order, and truly; but the necessity resided in him, and not in the school. So it often does,—and while teachers are zealously defending the rod, they should also feel the necessity of improving themselves as the most effectual way to obviate its frequent use.

When authority is once established in a school, it is comparatively easy to maintain it. There will, of course, be less necessity for resorting to the rod after the teacher has obtained the ascendancy, unless it be in the event of taking some new pupil into the school, who is disposed to be refractory. I have but little respect for the teacher who is *daily* obliged to fortify his authority by corporal infliction. Something must be fundamentally wrong in the teacher whose machinery of government, when once well in motion, needs to be so often forcibly wound up.

From what has already been said, it will be seen that I do not belong to the number who affirm that the *rod of correction should never be used in schools*. Nor am I prepared to advise any teacher *to publish beforehand* that he will not punish with the rod. It would always be wiser for the teacher to say nothing about it. Very little good ever comes of threatening the use of it. Threatening of any sort avails but little. A teacher may enter a school with the determination to govern it, if possible, without force. Indeed, I should advise one always to make this determination in his own mind. But whenever such a determination is published, the probability of success is very much diminished.

There is an arm of power.—Proposed substitutes.—Solitary confinement.

The true way and the safe way, in my opinion, is to rely mainly on moral means for the government of the school,—to use the rod without much threatening, if driven to it by the force of circumstances, and as soon as authority is established, to allow it again to slumber with the tacit understanding that it can be again awakened from its repose if found necessary. The knowledge in the school that there *is* an arm of power, may prevent any necessity of an appeal to it; and such a knowledge can do no possible harm in itself. But if the teacher has once pledged himself to the school that he will never use the rod, the necessity may soon come for him to abandon his position or lose his influence over the pupils.

As much has been said against the use of the rod in any case in school government, it may be proper to consider briefly some of the substitutes for it, which have been suggested by its opposers.

Some have urged solitary confinement. This might do in some cases. Undoubtedly an opportunity for reflection is of great use to a vicious boy. But then how inadequate are the means for this kind of discipline in our schools. Most of our school-houses have but one room. In such cases, solitary confinement is out of the question. In other instances, there may be (as there always should be) a room not constantly devoted to the purposes of the school. Here a pupil could be confined; and I have no objection whatever to this

Its futility.—Parental folly.

course, provided the room is not a dark one, and its temperature can be comfortable. But even with this facility, confinement can not be relied on as the only punishment, because if offenses should multiply, and the offenders should all be sent to the same place, then confinement would soon cease to be solitary! And suppose some philanthropist should devise a plan of a school-house with several cells for the accommodation of offenders; still this punishment would fail of its purpose. The teacher has no power to confine a pupil much beyond the limit of school-hours. This the obstinate child would understand, and he would therefore resolve to hold out till he must be dismissed, and then he would be the triumphant party. He could boast to his fellows that he had borne the punishment, and that, without submission or promise for the future, he had been excused because his time had expired.

This substitute is often urged by *parents*, who have tried it successfully in the case of their own children, in their own houses, where it was known that it could of course be protracted to any necessary length. Besides, if the confinement alone was not sufficient, the daily allowance of food could be withheld. Under such circumstances, it may be very effectual, as undoubtedly it often has been; but he is a very shallow parent who, having tried this experiment upon a single child, with all the facilities of a parent, prescribes it with the expectation of equal success in the government of a large school.

Others *have urged the expulsion of such scholars as are disobedient.* To this it may be replied, that it is not quite certain, under existing laws, whether the teacher has the *right* to expel a scholar from the common schools; and some deny even the right of the school officers to do it. Whether the *right* exists or not, it is very questionable whether it is ever *expedient* to expel a scholar for vicious conduct; and especially in cases where there is physical power to control him. The vicious and ignorant scholar is the very one who most needs the reforming influence of a good education. Sent away from the fountain of knowledge and virtue at this—the very time of need—and what may we expect for him but utter ruin? Such a pupil, most of all, needs the restraint and the instruction of a teacher who is capable of exercising the one and affording the other.

But suppose he is dismissed, is there any reason to hope that this step will improve the culprit himself, or better the condition of the school? Will he not go on to establish himself in vice, unrestrained by any good influence, and at last become a suitable subject for the severity of the laws, an inmate of our prisons, and, perhaps, a miserable expiator of his own crimes upon the gallows? How many youth—and youth worth saving, too—have been thus cast out perversely to procure their own ruin, at the very time when they *might have been saved* by sufficient energy and benevolence, no mortal tongue can tell! Nor is the school itself usually benefited by this measure. "For all purposes of evil," Mr. Mann justly remarks, "he continues in the midst of the very children from among whom he was cast out; and when he associates with them out of school, there is no one present to abate or neutralize his vicious influences. If the expelled pupil be driven from the district where he belongs into another, in order to prevent his contamination at home, what better can be expected of the place to which he is sent, than a reciprocation of the deed, by their sending one of their outcasts to supply his place; and thus opening a commerce of evil upon free-trade principles. Nothing is gained while the evil purpose remains in the heart. Reformation is the great desideratum; and can any lover of his country hesitate between the alternative of forcible subjugation and victorious contumacy?"

From all that has been said, it will be seen that I do not hesitate to teach *that corporal infliction is one of the justifiable means of establishing authority in the school-room.* To this conclusion I have come, after a careful consideration of the subject, modified by the varied experience of nearly twenty years, and by a somewhat attentive observation of the workings of all the plans which have been devised to avoid its use or to supply its place. And although I do not understand the Scriptures, and particularly the writings of Solomon, to recommend a too frequent and ill-considered use of it, I do not find any thing in the letter or spirit of Christianity inconsistent with its proper application. It is the *abuse*, and not the use of the rod, against which our better feeling, as well as the spirit of Christianity, revolts. It is the *abuse* of the rod, or rather the abuse of children under the infliction of the rod, that first called forth the discussion referred to, and awakened the general opposition to its use. I am free to admit there has been an egregious abuse in this matter, and that to this day it is unabated in many of our schools. I admit, too, that abuse very naturally accompanies the use of the rod, and that very great caution is necessary in those who resort to it, lest they pervert it. I feel called upon, therefore, before leaving this subject, to throw out, for the consideration of the young Teacher particularly, a few hints to regulate the infliction of chastisement, under the head of

SECTION V.—LIMITATIONS AND SUGGESTIONS.

1. The teacher should be thoroughly convinced that the rod is *the best thing for the specific case*, before he determines to use it. Nor should he hastily or capriciously come to this conviction. He should carefully and patiently

try other means first. He should study the disposition of the offender and learn the tendencies of his mind; and only after careful deliberation, should he suffer himself to decide to use this mode of punishment. In order that the punishment should be salutary, the scholar should plainly see that the teacher resorts to it from *deep principle*, from the full belief that under all the circumstances it is the *best thing that can be done*.

2. The teacher *should never be under the excitement of angry passion* when inflicting punishment. This is of the utmost importance. Most of the abuses before spoken of, grow out of a violation of this fundamental rule. A teacher should never strike for punishment till he is perfectly self-possessed, and entirely free from the bitterness which, perhaps, tinctured his mind when he discovered the offense. It was a wise remark of a young Shaker teacher, that "no teacher should strike a child *till he could hold his arm*." So long as the child discovers that the teacher is under the influence of passion, and that his lip trembles with pent-up rage, and his blood flows into his face as if driven by inward fires of wrath, he looks upon him, not as his friend seeking his welfare, but as his enemy indulging in persecution. This will call forth the evil passions of the child, and while he bears the pain, he feels no real penitence; and very likely, in the midst of his suffering, he resolves to go and do the same again, out of mere spite.

Public opinion.—In presence of the school.—Reasons for it.

It is, moreover, of great consequence in the infliction of a punishment, that the teacher should be fully sustained by the public opinion of the school. He can never expect this when he loses his self-control. If the pupils see that he is angry, they almost instinctively sympathize with the weaker party, and they associate the idea of injustice with the action of the stronger. A punishment can scarcely be of any good tendency, inflicted under such circumstances.

3. Corporal punishment, as a general rule, *should be inflicted in presence of the school.* I have before advised that *reproof* should be given in private, and assigned reasons for it, which were, perhaps, satisfactory to the reader. But in case of corporal punishment, the offense is of a more public and probably of a more serious nature. If inflicted in private, it will still be known to the school, and therefore the reputation of the scholar is not saved. If inflicted in the proper spirit by the teacher, and for proper cause, it always produces a salutary effect upon the school. But a still stronger reason for making the infliction public is, that it puts it beyond the power of the pupil to *misrepresent the teacher*, as he is strongly tempted to do if he is alone. He may misstate the degree of severity, and misrepresent the manner of the teacher; and, without witnesses, the teacher is at the mercy of his reports. Sometimes, he may ridicule the punishment to his comrades, and lead

Punishment delayed.—Reason for delay.

them to believe that a private infliction is but a small matter; again, he may exaggerate it to his parents, and charge the teacher most unjustly with unprincipled cruelty. Under these circumstances, I am of the opinion that the safest and most effectual way, is to do this work in presence of the school. An honest teacher needs not fear the light of day; and if he has the right spirit, he needs not fear the effect upon his other pupils. It is only the violent, angry punishment that needs to be concealed from the general eye, and that we have condemned as improper at any rate.

4. Punishment *may sometimes be delayed; and always delayed till all anger has subsided in the teacher.* It is often best for all concerned to defer an infliction for a day or more. This gives the teacher an opportunity in his cooler moments to determine more justly the degree of severity to be used. It will also give the culprit time to reflect upon the nature of his offense and the degree of punishment he deserves. I may say that it is generally wise for the teacher, after promising a punishment, to take some time to consider *what it shall be*, whether a corporal infliction or some milder treatment. If, after due and careful reflection, he comes conscientiously to the conclusion, that *bodily pain* is the *best thing*,—while he will be better prepared to inflict, the pupil, by similar reflection, will be better prepared to receive it and profit by it.

The instrument. —Punishment effectual.—Deliberation.

5. A *proper instrument* should be used and a *proper mode of infliction* adopted. No heavy and hurtful weapon should be employed. A light rule for the hand, or a rod for the back or lower extremities, may be preferred. Great care should be exercised to avoid injuring any of the joints in the infliction; and on *no account should a blow be given upon the head*.

6. *If possible, the punishment should be made effectual.* A punishment that does not produce thorough submission and penitence in the subject of it, can hardly be said to answer its main design. To be sure, in cases of general insubordination in the school, I have said that punishment may be applied to one, having in view the deterring of others from similar offenses. But such *exemplary* punishment belongs to extreme cases, while *disciplinary* punishment, which has mainly for its object the reformation of the individual upon whom it is inflicted, should be most relied on. Taking either view of the case, it should, if possible, answer its design, or it would be better not to attempt it. The teacher's judgment, therefore, should be very carefully exercised in the matter, and all his knowledge of human nature should be called into requisition. If, after careful and conscientious deliberation, he comes to the conclusion that the infliction of pain is the best thing, and to the belief that he can so inflict it as to show himself to the school and to the child, in this act as in all others, a true and

kind friend to the child,—then he is justified in making the attempt; and having considerately undertaken the case, it should be *so thorough as not soon to need repetition.*

I would here take the opportunity to censure the practice of those teachers who punish every little departure from duty with some trifling appliance of the rod, which the scholar forgets almost as soon as the smarting ceases. Some instructors carry about with them a rattan or stick, in order to have it ready for appliance as soon as they see any departure from their commands. The consequence is, they soon come to a frequent and inconsiderate use of it, and the pupils by habit become familiar with it, and of course cease to respect their teacher or to dread his punishments. I have seen so much of this, that whenever I see a teacher thus "*armed and equipped*," I infer at once that his school is a disorderly one, an inference almost invariably confirmed by a few minutes' observation. My earnest advice to all young teachers would be, next to the habit of *scolding* incessantly, *avoid the habit of resorting to the rod on every slight occasion.* When that instrument is not demanded for some special exigency, some great occasion or some high purpose, allow it to slumber in a private corner of your desk, not again to be called into activity till some moral convulsion shall disturb its quiet repose.

How to discuss this subject.—Experience of very young men.

I have a single caution to give in regard to the discussion of this subject, which in all our educational gatherings occupies so much time and talent. It is this:—*Do not adopt a general principle from too few inductions.* There is an old proverb that declares, "One swallow does not make a summer." Young teachers are very prone to rely on the experience of a single term. If they have kept one term without corporal punishment, they are very likely to instruct their seniors with their *experience;* and if they have happened to be so situated as to be compelled to save themselves by the rod, why then, too, their *experience* forever settles the question. It requires the experience of *more than one, or two, or three schools,* to enable a man to speak dogmatically on this subject; and I always smile when I hear men, and sometimes very young men, who have never kept school in their lives, perhaps, or at most but a single term, speaking as with the voice of authority. Experience is indeed one of our safest guides in this as in every other matter; but they who tell their experience should at least wait *till they have that which is worthy to be told.*

There is another point. It is quite fashionable at the present day, whenever this subject is to be discussed, to propose the matter in the form of a *resolution;* as, "Resolved, that no person is fit to be employed as a teacher, who can not govern his scholars by holier means than bodily chastisement"; or, "Resolved, that no limit should be set to the teacher's right to use the 'rod of correction,' and that they who denounce the teachers for resorting to it are unworthy of our confidence in matters of education." Now whoever presents the question in this form, assumes that he has drawn a line through the very core of the truth; and he undertakes to censure all those who are unwilling to square their opinions by the line thus drawn. In the discussion, a man must take one side or the other of the question as it is proposed, and consequently he may take a false position. The better way would be to present the whole subject as matter of free remark, and thus leave every one to present his own views honestly as *they lie in his own mind.* In this way no one is pledged to this or that party, but is left unprejudiced to discover and embrace the truth wherever it is found.

It should moreover be remembered, that *resolving* by the vote of a meeting in order to *force public opinion*, can never affect the truth. A few impious, heaven-daring men in France, at one of their revels, once *resolved,* "There is no God!"—but did this blasphemous breath efface the impress of Deity on all this fair creation of his power? And when they rose from their vile debauch, and sought with tottering step to leave the scene of madness and to court the dim forgetfulness of sleep,—rolled not the shining orbs in heaven's high arch above them as much in duty to His will, as when they sang together to usher in creation's morning? So it will ever be. Men may declare, and *resolve* as they please; but truth is eternal and unchangeable: and they are the wisest men who modestly seek to find her *as she is*, and not as their perverted imaginations would presume to paint her.

Yet, after all, in the government of schools, there is a more excellent way. There are usually easier avenues to the heart, than that which is found through the integuments of the body. Happy is that teacher who is so skillful as to find them; and gladly would I welcome the day when the number of such skillful and devoted teachers should render any further defense of the rod superfluous. Although I believe that day has not yet arrived, still, in the meantime, I most earnestly urge all teachers to strive to reach the higher motives and the finer feelings of the young, and to rely mainly for success, not upon appeals to fear and force, but upon the power of conscience and the law of reciprocal affection.

As I have placed the higher motives and the more desirable means first in order in these remarks on government, so I would always have them first, and perseveringly employed by the teacher; and if, by earnestness in his work, by unfeigned love for the young, by diligence in the study of their natures and the adaptation of means to ends, which true benevolence is sure to suggest, he can govern successfully without corporal punishment—as in a large proportion of cases I believe it can be done—none will rejoice more than I at such a desirable result;—and I most cordially subscribe to the principle so happily stated by another, that in the government of schools, if thorough obedience be but secured and order maintained, other things being equal, "THE MINIMUM OF PUNISHMENT IS THE MAXIMUM OF EXCELLENCE."

The three essential points of school management are organization, government, and instruction. The final purpose of a school is the instruction of its pupils; but to this end the school must first be organized; but that the organization may be preserved, there must be some system of government, or discipline. The condition under which the integrity of an organization can be preserved, is obedience to authority. In some way the wills of the governed must follow the lead of the one will that governs. In the last analysis, the direction of human wills depends on the deft manipulation of motive. Motives are of two sorts; they are either attractive or propulsive. There is either something ahead of us, inviting us forward; or there is a stimulus behind us, urging us forward. The attractive motives are the more economical, and the ingenuity of the teacher should be taxed to discover them and to employ them. But when these fail, as they sometimes will, then the propulsion, or painful motives, must be employed; the least painful first, but, in the last resort, as painful as may be necessary to secure obedience while the pupil is allowed to retain his membership in the school. When the limit of painful stimulation has been reached, membership must cease, through suspension or expulsion. This limit is determined by public opinion or by law.

The classification or gradation of motives may be exhibited as follows:

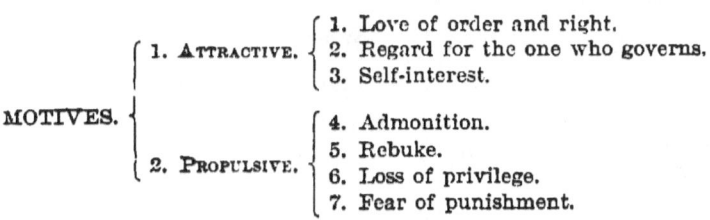

MOTIVES.
1. ATTRACTIVE.
 1. Love of order and right.
 2. Regard for the one who governs.
 3. Self-interest.
2. PROPULSIVE.
 4. Admonition.
 5. Rebuke.
 6. Loss of privilege.
 7. Fear of punishment.

A characteristic and very commendable feature of modern school discipline, is the large use that is made of the attractive motives; but with this better practice, there is sometimes joined the false assumption that this mode of government is adequate for all cases. In actual practice it often fails, and then there are but two courses to pursue; either the disobedient pupil must lose his membership in the school, or some form of painful stimulation must be employed. For the teacher, expulsion would doubtless be the preferable alternative; but, in most cases, public opinion will not justify expulsion save as a last resort.

It is a disputed question in the theory of the school, whether the exemplary or the remedial element in punishment should be kept uppermost in the thought of the disciplinarian. If we conceive that the organization is superior to the units that may chance to compose it, and that the units are to be affected mainly through the working of the organization, then the exemplary element in punishment becomes prominent, and a pupil may suffer chastisement, even when it is probable that his amendment may not be directly promoted by it. On the other hand, the remedial element in punishment assumes the first place when the individual, rather than the organization, holds the first place in thought. In the State, the exemplary character of punishment is primary and almost supreme, while in the family, the remedial character is chief; and as the school mediates between the State and the family, the two elements stand nearly in equipoise.

In the employment of censure, it should be noted that there is a vast difference between such charges as "You have told a falsehood," and "You are a liar." The first is an impeachment of conduct; the second, of character. In extreme cases, it may sometimes be justifiable to make censure general; but in all ordinary cases it ought to be specific. Thus Richter says: "What is to be followed as a rule of prudence, yea, of justice, toward grown-up people, should be much more observed toward children; namely, that one should never judgingly declare, for instance, 'You are a liar,' or even, 'You are a bad boy,' instead of saying, 'You have told an untruth,' or 'You have done wrong.'" (Levana, p. 114.)

CHAPTER XI.

SCHOOL ARRANGEMENTS.

EVERY teacher, before opening a school, should have some general plan in his mind, of what he intends to accomplish. In every enterprise there is great advantage to be derived from forethought,—and perhaps nowhere is the advantage greater than in the business of teaching. The day of opening a school is an eventful day to the young teacher. A thousand things crowd upon him at the same time, and each demands a prompt and judicious action on his part. The children to the number of half a hundred, all turn their inquiring eyes to him for occupation and direction. They have come full of interest in the prospects of the new school, ready to engage cheerfully in whatever plans the teacher may have to propose; and, I was about to say, just as ready to arrange and carry into effect their own plans of disorder and misrule, if they, unhappily for him and for themselves, find he has no system to introduce.

What a critical—what an eventful moment is this first day of the term to all concerned! The teacher's success and usefulness,—nay, his reputation as an efficient instructor,—now "hang upon

Angelic solicitude.—Low qualifications.

the decision of an hour." An hour, too, may almost foretell whether the precious season of childhood and youth now before these immortals, is to be a season of profit and healthful culture under a judicious hand, or a season of wasted— perhaps worse than wasted—existence, under the imbecility or misguidance of one who "knows not what he does or what he deals with."

If angels ever visit our earth and hover unseen around the gatherings of mortals, to survey their actions and contemplate their destiny as affected by human instrumentality, it seems to me there can be no spectacle so calculated to awaken their interest and enkindle their sympathy as when they see the young gathering together from their scattered homes in some rural district, to receive an impress, for weal or woe, from the hand of him who has undertaken to guide them. And, supposing them to have the power to appreciate to the full extent the consequences of human agency, how must they be touched with emotions of joy and gratitude, or shudder with those of horror and dread, as they witness the alternations of wisdom and folly, seriousness and indifference, sincerity and duplicity, purity and defilement, exhibited by him who has assumed to be at once the director and exemplar in the formation of human character, at such an important period. How deplorable is the thought that all the fond hopes of the parents, all the worthy aspirings of the children, and all

The first day.—A suggestion.—Its advantages.

the thrilling interests of higher beings, are so often to be answered by qualifications so scanty, and by a spirit so indifferent in the teacher of the young. How sad the thought that up to this very moment, so pregnant with consequences to all concerned, there has been too often so little of preparation for the responsibility.

I fain would impress the young teacher with the importance of having a plan for even the first day of the school. It will raise him surprisingly in the estimation of the pupils and also of the parents, if he can make an expeditious and efficient beginning of the school. While the dull teacher is slowly devising the plans he will *by and by* present for the employment and improvement of his school, the children taking advantage of their own exemption from labor, very promptly introduce their own plans for amusing themselves or for annoying him;—whereas, if he could but have his own plans already made, and could promptly and efficiently carry them into execution, he would forestall their mischievous designs and make co-operators out of his opposers.

In order to be sure of a successful commencement, I would recommend that the teacher should go into the district a few days before the school is to begin. By careful inquiry of the trustees or the school committee, he can ascertain what is the character of the district and the wants of the school. This will afford him considerable aid. But he should do more than this. He would do well to call on several of the families of the district, whose children are to become members of his school. This he can do without any ceremony, simply saying to them that, as he has been appointed their teacher, he is desirous as far as he may to ascertain their wants, in order to be as prompt as possible in the organization of his school. He will of course see the children themselves. From them he can learn what was the organization of his school under his predecessor; how many studied geography, how many arithmetic, grammar, etc.; and he can also learn whether the former organization was satisfactory to the district or not. The modes of government and the methods of interesting the pupils practiced by the former teacher, would be likely to be detailed to him; and from the manner of both parents and children, he could judge whether similar methods would still be desirable in the district. By calling on several of the largest families in this way, he would learn beforehand very accurately the state of the school and the state of the district.

I will take this occasion to insist that the teacher in these visits, should heartily discourage any forwardness, so common among children, to disparage a former teacher. It should be his sole object to gain useful information. He should give no signs of pleasure in listening to any unfavorable statements as to his predecessor;

Making personal friends.—A common error.

and I may add that during the progress of the school, he should ever frown upon any attempt on the part of the pupils to make comparisons derogatory to a former teacher. This is a practice altogether too prevalent in our schools; and I am sorry to say there are still too many teachers who are mean enough to countenance it. Such a course is unfair, because the absent party may be grossly misrepresented; it is dangerous, because it tends to cultivate a spirit of detraction in the young; and it is *mean*, because the party is absent and has no opportunity of defending himself.

Another important advantage of the visits proposed would be, that he would make the acquaintance of many of the children beforehand, and very likely, too, if he should go in the right spirit and with agreeable manners, he would make a favorable impression upon them, and thus he would have personal friends on his side to begin with. The parents, too, would see that he took an interest in his employment; that he had come among them in the spirit of his vocation—in the spirit of earnestness, and they would become interested in his success,—a point of no small importance.

I might here caution the teacher against a very common error. He should not confine his visits to the more wealthy and influential families. The poor and the humble should receive his attentions as soon as the rich. From the latter

Mr. Abbot.—Early at the school.—Why?

class very likely a large portion of his school will come; and it is wrong in principle as well as policy to neglect those who have not been as successful as others in the one item of accumulating property.

On the day of opening the school, he should be early at the school-house. Mr. Abbott, in his Teacher, has some valuable suggestions on this point. "It is desirable," he says, "that the young teacher should meet his scholars at first in an *unofficial* capacity. For this purpose, he should repair to the school-room, on the first day, at an early hour, so as to see and become acquainted with the scholars as they come in, one by one. He may take an interest with them in all the little arrangements connected with the opening of the school. The building of the fire, the paths through the snow, the arrangement of seats, calling upon them for information or aid, asking their names, and, in a word, entering fully and freely into conversation with them, just as a parent, under similar circumstances, would do with his children. All the children thus addressed will be pleased with the gentleness and affability of the teacher. Even a rough and ill-natured boy, who has perhaps come to the school with the express determination of attempting to make mischief, will be completely disarmed by being asked pleasantly to help the teacher fix the fire, or alter the position of a desk. Thus by means of the half hour during which the scholars are

It should be habitual.—Roguery promoted.

coming together, the teacher will find, when he calls upon the children to take their seats, that he has made a large number of them his personal friends. Many of these will have communicated their first impressions to others, so that he will find himself possessed, at the outset, of that which is of vital consequence in opening any administration—a strong party in his favor."

It will be well for the teacher, for several days, both in the morning and afternoon, to be early at the school-room. He can thus continue his friendly intercourse with the pupils, and effectually prevent any concerted action among them, at that hour, to embarrass his government. Many a school has been seriously injured, if not broken up, by the scholars being allowed to assemble early at the school, with nothing to occupy them and no one to restrain them. Having so convenient an opportunity for mischief, their youthful activity will be very likely to find egress in an evil direction. Many a tale of roguery could be told, founded upon the incidents of the school-room before school-hours, if those who have good memories would but reveal their own experience;—roguery that never would have occurred had the teacher adopted the course here suggested.

SCHOOL ARRANGEMENTS. 269

A day's work.—"What shall I do?"—"Yes, m'm."—Veto.

SECTION I.—PLAN OF THE DAY'S WORK.

It will be remembered by many of the readers of this volume, that in former times numerous teachers were accustomed to work without a plan, attempting to do their work just as *it happened* to demand attention, but never taking the precaution to have this demand under their own control. If one scholar or class was not ready to recite, another would be called; and there being no particular time for the various exercises, the school would become a scene of mere listlessness, and the teacher would hardly know how to find employment for himself in the school.

I shall make this point clearer by an example. Having occasion, in an official capacity, to visit a school which had been kept by a young teacher some two weeks, she very naturally asked— "What shall I do first, this afternoon?"

"Do precisely as you would if I had not come in," was the reply.

She looked a little perplexed. At length she doubtingly asked,—"Is the geography lesson ready?"

"Yes, m'm"—"No, m'm"—"Yes, m'm,"—was the ambiguous reply from the class. There was so much of *veto* in the looks of the young geographers that it amounted to prohibition.

"Well, are the scholars in Colburn's arithmetic ready?"

This was said with more of hope; but the

same equivocal answer was vociferated from all parts of the room. The teacher, placing her finger upon her lip, looked despairingly; but, recollecting one more resort, she said,—"Is the grammar class ready?"

Again came the changes on "Yes, m'm" and "No, m'm."

The teacher gave up, and asked what she *should* do. She was again told to go on as *usual* for that afternoon. It was a tedious afternoon to her, as it was to her visitor. She at length called one of the classes, unprepared as many of them said they were, and the exercise showed that none but those who said "Yes, m'm," were mistaken. The whole afternoon seemed to be one of pain and mortification to all concerned; and I fancied I could almost read in the knitted brow of the teacher a declaration that *that* should be her last school.

At the close of the afternoon, a single hint was suggested to her,—viz., that she should make out a list of her scholars' duties, and the times when they would be expected to recite their several lessons. She was told that it would be well to explain this plan of her day's work to her school in the morning, and then *never again ask whether a class was ready*. The hint was taken; and on subsequent visitations the several classes were ever ready to respond to the call of their instructor.

Now this matter is no unimportant one to the

Improvement.—A case supposed.—Classification.

teacher. Indeed, I judge of a teacher's ability very much by the wisdom and tact with which he apportions his time for his own duties, and divides the time of his scholars between their studies and recitations.

In order to aid the young teacher in forming a plan for himself, I subjoin a scheme of a *day's duties* adapted to a school of the simplest grade. Suppose a school to consist of thirty scholars, and that the teacher finds, by inquiry and by examination, that there may be four grand divisions; the first, which he designates [A,] may unite in pursuing Reading, Grammar, Mental Arithmetic, Written Arithmetic, and Writing. The second, [B,] can pursue Reading, Spelling, Writing, Geography, Mental and Written Arithmetic. The third, [C,] attend to Reading, Spelling, Mental Arithmetic, Writing, and Geography. The fourth, [D,] consisting of the small pupils, attend to Reading, Spelling, Tables, and sundry *slate exercises*.

Now, it is very desirable that as much time should be devoted to recitation as can be afforded to each class. It may be seen at once, that in certain studies, as geography, mental arithmetic, and spelling—the teacher can as well attend to fifteen at once as to seven. In these studies, unless the disparity in age and attainment is very great, two divisions can very properly be united. *All* can be taught writing at once, thus receiving the teacher's undivided attention for the

Preliminary considerations.—A scheme.

time. Besides, it is necessary to reserve some little time for change of exercises, and also for the *interruptions* which must necessarily occur. The recesses are to be provided for, and some time may be needed for investigation of violations of duty, and for the punishment of offenders. All this variety of work will occur in every school, even the smallest. Now, if the teacher does not arrange this in accordance with some plan, he will be very much perplexed, even in a small school; and how much more in a large one! He will do well to consider very carefully the relative importance of each exercise to be attended to, and then to write out his *scheme* somewhat after the following model. It must not be forgotten that *studying* is also to be provided for, and that it is just as important that the pupils should be regular in this as in recitation. Indeed, without such regularity, he can not expect acceptable recitations.

SCHOOL ARRANGEMENTS. 273

PROGRAM.
For the above supposed circumstances.

Time.	M.	Recitations, etc.	Studies.
9 to 9.15	15	READING SCRIPT, & PRAYER.	
9.15 to 9.40	25	D. Reading, Spelling, or Tables.	A. Reading; B. Arith.; C. Geography.
9.40 to 9.42	2	REST, CHANGE OF CLASSES, ETC.	
9.42 to 10	18	A. Reading.	B. Arith.; C. Geog.; D. Slates.
10 to 10.5	5	REST, SINGING, OR ANSWERING QUESTIONS.	
10.5 to 10.25	20	B. Arithmetic.	A. Gram.; C. Geog.; D. Books or Cards.
10.25 to 10.28	3	REST, ETC.	
10.28 to 10.48	20	B. & C. Geography.	A. Gram.; D. Recess.
10.48 to 11	12	RECESS.	
11 to 11.15	15	D. Reading, etc.	A. Gram.; B. M. Arith.; C. Spelling.
11.15 to 11.35	20	A. Grammar.	B. Spelling; C. Spelling; D. Slates.
11.35 to 11.50	15	B. & C. Spelling.	A. M. Arith.; D. Books or Cards.
11.50 to 12	10	GENERAL EXERCISE.	
		Intermission.	
2 to 2.15	15	D. Reading, Spelling, Tables.	A. Arith.; B. Reading; C. Reading.
2.15 to 2.45	30	A. B. & C. Writing.	D. Slates.
2.45 to 3.10	25	A. & B. Mental Arithmetic.	C. M. Arith.; D. Recess.
3.10 to 3.30	20	C. Reading.	A. Arith.; B. Arith.; D. Books, etc.
3.30 to 3.40	10	RECESS.	
3.40 to 4	20	B. Reading.	A. Arith.; C. M. Arith; D. Drawing.
4 to 4.5	5	REST, OR SINGING.	
4.5 to 4.25	20	C. Mental Arithmetic.	A. Read.; B. Arith. or Draw.; D. Slates.
4.25 to 4.55	30	A. Arithmetic.	B. Arith. or Draw.; C. Draw.; D. Dismissed.
4.55 to 5	5	GEN. EXER. AND DISMISSION.	

REMARKS.

In the foregoing Program, the first column shows the *division of time*, and the portion allowed to each exercise. I need not say the teacher should be strictly punctual. To this end a clock is a very desirable article in the school. Both teacher and pupils would be benefited by it. The second column shows the *recitations*, admitting, perhaps, some variety, especially in case of the younger children; while the third shows the *occupation* of those classes which are not engaged in recitation.

It will be seen that the classes are studying those lessons which they are soon to recite; and, as in this case it is supposed that all the lessons will be learned in school, each one has been provided for. It would be well, however, in practice to require one of the studies to be learned out of school, in which case no time should be allowed to the *study* of that branch in the program.

It will be perceived that *drawing* is placed as the occupation of the younger classes near the close of the afternoon. This is based upon the supposition that the teacher, during recess, has placed an example on the blackboard, to be copied by the children upon their slates. This is perhaps the most effectual way to teach drawing to children. Those more advanced, however, may use paper and pencil, and draw from an engraved copy, or from a more finished specimen furnished

An assistant.—A large school.—Alternation.—Thorough work.

from the teacher's portfolio. It is essential that the teacher should, if possible, give some specimens of his own in this branch. I have seldom known a teacher to excite an interest in drawing, who relied altogether upon engravings as models for imitation.

It should be remarked further, concerning such a program, that in case of an assistant in school, two columns under the head of *Recitations* should be formed—one for the principal's classes, and one for the assistant's. If there are a few talented scholars, who are able to do more than their class, they can be allowed to join some of the classes out of their division, or they may be provided with an extra study, which will not need daily recitation.

In case the school is much larger than the one supposed above, and the classes necessarily so numerous as to make the time allowed to each study very short, then the principle of *alternation* may be introduced; that is, some studies may be recited Mondays, Wednesdays, and Fridays,—and some other studies, with other classes, take their places on the alternate days. It is decidedly better for the teacher to meet a class, in arithmetic, for instance, especially of older pupils, but twice or three times a week, having time enough at each meeting to make thorough work, than to meet them daily, but for a time so short as to accomplish but little. The same remark may be applied to reading, and, indeed, almost any other branch. The idea is a mischievous one, that every class in reading, or in any other branch, must be called out four times a day, or even twice a day,—except in the case of very young children. It may be compared to nibbling at a cracker as many times a day, without once taking a hearty meal,—a process which would emaciate any child in the course of three months. These scanty nibblings at the table of knowledge, so often and so tenaciously practiced, may perhaps account for the mental emaciation so often discoverable in many of our schools.

The difficulty of classifying and arranging the exercises of a school, becomes greater as the number of teachers to be employed increases; and there is much greater inconvenience in allowing any pupils to study out of their own division, when the number of teachers is more than one or two. Few are aware of the difficulty of arranging the exercises of a large school, but those who have experienced it. It *can be done*, however; and it should always be done as soon as possible after commencing the school.

If at any time the arrangement, when made, is not found to be perfect, it is not wise to change it at once. Let it go on a few days, and watch its defects with great care; and in the meantime study, out of school, to devise a better. When this has been accomplished, and committed to paper, and perfectly comprehended by the teacher, it may be posted up in the school-room, and the

Models not to be copied.—Teacher must think.

day announced when it will go into operation. It will soon be understood by the pupils, and the change can thus be made without the loss of time.

Times for reviews of the various lessons could be found by setting aside the regular lessons for some particular day, once a week, or once in two weeks; and for composition, declamation, etc., a half day should be occasionally or periodically assigned.

If I have devoted considerable space to this subject, it is because I deem it of very great importance to the teacher's success. With one other remark I dismiss it. These models are not given to be servilely copied. They are given to illustrate the great principle. The circumstances of schools will be found to vary so widely, that no model, however perfect in itself, would answer for all. The teacher must exercise his own ingenuity and judgment to meet his own wants; and in general it may be remarked that where a teacher has not the skill to adapt his own plans to his own circumstances, he can hardly be expected to succeed in carrying out the plans of another.

The following general rules may serve a good purpose in constructing a teacher's time-table:

1. *The recitations of the youngest pupils should be short and frequent.* As the power of continuous attention, in the case of such pupils, is weak, the maximum time of recitation should not ex-

ceed fifteen minutes; and as they can be instructed only during the class exercise, not yet having learned the use of books, they should be called up as frequently as the teacher's time will permit.

2. *The exercises that require the greatest stress of mental effort should come in the earlier part of the day.* The working power of the mind is at its best from nine till twelve; and so a subject like arithmetic should come by preference in the forenoon, while penmanship, drawing, reading, etc., might come later in the day.

3. *Provide alternations that afford rest or an agreeable change.* To pass from an exercise in reasoning to another where memory is chiefly involved, is an agreeable change, for a new mode of mental activity is called into play, while the one just employed has a period of rest.

4. *Have as few classes as possible.* The reason for this rule is obvious, but it is often disregarded. Cases are on record where the teacher of a country school has had upward of forty classes during the day. One such teacher, in explanation of the apparent impossibility of attending to so many classes, said that he sometimes heard three at a time! By securing a uniformity of books, by conducting some recitations by topic, by uniting two classes in the same study, and by reducing the number of recitations in some subjects to two or three per week, it is quite possible to relieve an over-charged time-table.

Pupils without system.—Disorder.

SECTION II.—INTERRUPTIONS.

In every school consisting of pupils of different ages and circumstances, there will be more or less of interruption to the general order and employment of the school. Some of the pupils have never been trained to system at home; perhaps most of them have been positively taught to disregard it at school. At any rate, "it must needs be," in this particular, "that offenses come." Nor should the teacher lose his patience though he should be often disturbed by the thoughtlessness of his pupils. He should expect it as a matter of course, and exercise his ingenuity as far as possible to prevent it. It may well be one of his sources of enjoyment to witness an improvement in the habits of his pupils in regard to system.

These interruptions proceed from various causes,—such as soliciting leave to speak, or to go out; asking for some assistance in learning lessons, or for leave to drink, or to stand by the fire; requesting the teacher to mend pens or to set copies; disorderly conduct in pupils, making it necessary, in his judgment, to administer reproof or punishment in the midst of other duties,—and sometimes the vociferous and impatient making of complaints by one scholar against another.

How many times I have seen a teacher involved in indescribable perplexity, while trying to perform the duty of instruction, and to "get

SCHOOL ARRANGEMENTS.

Scene from nature.—Business accumulates.—A crisis.—A pail of water.

through" in time. While hearing a grammar lesson, a scholar brings up his atlas to have some place pointed out which he had upon one trial failed to find. The teacher, turning to look for the place, is addressed with "Please mend my pen," from another quarter. Having the knife in hand, as if such things were to be expected, the obliging teacher takes the pen, and, holding it between his eyes and the atlas, endeavors to shape its nib and to discover the city at the same glance. " Jane keeps a pinching me,"—vociferates a little girl who is seated behind the class. " Jane, Jane," says the teacher, turning away from both the nib and the city, "Jane, come to me instantly." Jane, with the guilty fingers thrust far into her mouth, makes her way sideling toward the teacher. "May I go out?"— says John, who is thinking only of his own convenience. " No, no," answers the teacher, a little pettishly, as if conscious that in a crisis like this, a request simply to breathe more freely is scarcely justifiable. "*Please, sir*, let me and Charles go out and get a pail of water?" This is said by a little shrewd-looking, round-faced, light-haired boy, who has learned how to select his time, and to place the emphasis upon the "*please, sir.*" The teacher, by this time being considerably fretted by such an accumulation of business on his hands, very naturally thinks of the refreshment contained in a pail of cool water, and very good-naturedly answers the little urchin

A juncture and a conjunction!—A truce.—Sunshine again.

in the affirmative, who most likely is, by this time, more than half way out of the door, so confident is he of success. Just at this juncture, a considerate-looking miss in the class earnestly appeals to the teacher, to know if the word next but three to the last, was not a *common noun*, though called a *conjunction!* This reminds the teacher that several words have been parsed without his notice, and he asks the class to "stop there." Glancing at his watch, he discovers that he has gone three minutes beyond the time for recess, and he relieves himself by saying, "boys may go out." This grants a truce to all parties. The pen goes back unmended; the atlas with its sought city undiscovered; John "goes out" now by common law, taking to himself the credit of this happy release, as he asked only to remind the master that it was time for recess; Jane takes both thumb and finger from her precious little mouth, and smiling, seats herself by the side of her late challenger, who is by this time more than half repentant of her own impatience; the shrewd-looking urchin and his companion return with the refreshing pail of water,—the boys and girls gather round to obtain the first draught, while the little chubby-faced lad comes forward, clothed in smiles, with a cup filled with the cooling liquid on purpose for the master; the boon is accepted, the perplexed brow becomes placid, and all is sunshine again.—This is not a very extravagant picture of the interruptions in a district school. Those who have been brought up in such a school will recognize the *fidelity* of the *likeness*, as it has been drawn from nature.

Now, whoever has any knowledge of human nature, and of school teaching, will at once see that this is all wrong. It is a law of our being, that we can do well but one thing at a time. He who attempts more, must do what he attempts but very imperfectly. There was a great deal of wisdom embodied in that motto which used to be placed in the old Lancasterian schools: "A TIME FOR EVERY THING, AND EVERY THING IN ITS TIME." It should be one of the mottoes of every teacher. In the construction of the *plan* or program for the day's duties, great care should be taken to provide for all these little things. If whispering is to be allowed at all in school, let it come into one of the intervals between recitations. If assistance in getting lessons is to be asked and rendered, let it be done at a time assigned for the special purpose. As far as possible, except in extreme cases, let the discipline be attended to at the time of general exercise, or some other period assigned to it, so that there shall not be a ludicrous mixture of punishments and instruction during the progress of a class exercise.

It is pleasant to visit a school, where every thing is done, and well done, at its proper time. Teaching under such circumstances, becomes a delightful employment. But where all is confusion, and the teacher allows himself, by the accumulation of irregularities, to be oppressed and perplexed, it is one of the most wearing and undesirable vocations on earth. The teacher goes to his lodgings harassed with care, oppressed with a consciousness of the imperfection of his labors, and exhausted by the unnatural and unwarrantable tax imposed upon his mental faculties. He groans under the burden incident to his calling, and longs to escape from it, never once dreaming, perhaps, that he has the power of relieving himself by the introduction of system, and thus changing his former *babel* into a scene of quietness and order.

SECTION III.—RECESSES.

In speaking of the arrangements of a school, the subject of recesses demands attention. It is the belief of many enlightened instructors, that the confinement in most of our schools is still too protracted, and that more time devoted to relaxation would be profitable, both to the physical and the mental constitution of our youth. Some have urged a recess of a few minutes every hour, in order to afford opportunity for a change of position and a change of air. This could better be done in schools composed only of one sex, or where the accommodation of separate yards and playgrounds permits both sexes to take a recess

One each session.—Ten minutes to each sex.—Separate playgrounds.

at the same time. Where these accommodations are wanting, and one sex must wait while the other is out, the time required for two recesses, in half a day, for the whole school, could scarcely be afforded. I am of the opinion, as our schools are at present composed, that one recess in the half day for each sex is all that can be allowed. The question then is, how can that one recess be made most conducive to the purposes for which it is designed?

1. *As to its duration.* Ten minutes is the least time that should be thought of, if the children are to be kept closely confined to study during the remainder of the three hours' session; that is, ten minutes for each sex. It would be a very desirable thing if our school-houses could be so furnished with separate playgrounds and separate out-door accommodations, that both sexes could take recess at the same time. This would save much time to the district in the course of a term, and it would also give opportunity for thoroughly ventilating the room during recess, while it would afford the teacher opportunity to take the air, and overlook the sports of the children to some extent,—a matter of no small importance.

Where these facilities are wanting, and the teacher must remain within to preside over the one half of the school while the others are out, he may still give at least ten minutes to each sex, contriving to employ the time profitably within doors. He may reserve this time for settling such difficulties as may have arisen in the school; he may administer reproofs, inflict his punishments if any are necessary, or he may spend the time in giving assistance to the pupils or in drawing upon the blackboard for the advantage of the younger pupils as they come in. In a large school, where a longer recess is the more necessary on account of the bad air of the school-room, he will find the more duty to be done at this time; so that in any event the time need not be lost, even if *fifteen* minutes be allowed to each sex.

2. *As to the proper hour for recess.* It was an old rule to have recess when " *school was half done.*" Indeed, this expression was often used as synonymous with recess in many districts twenty-five years ago. It is now generally thought better to have the recess occur later, perhaps when the school session is two thirds past. It is found that children, accustomed to exercise all the morning, can better bear the confinement of the first two hours than they can that of the third, even though the recess immediately precedes the third. In a school the half-daily sessions of which are three hours, I should recommend that the recess be introduced so as to terminate at the close of the second hour. As far as possible, it would be well to have all the pupils leave the room at the time recess is given them; and, as a general thing, they should not ask leave to go out at any

other time. A little system in this matter is as desirable as in any other, and it is quite as feasible.

In a school composed partly of very young children, there is no difficulty in giving such children two recesses each half day. Nor is there any objection to such a course. It is more irksome to young children to bear confinement than to the adult; especially as they can not be expected to be constantly occupied. It will relieve the teacher very much to have the children go out of the room as soon as they become fatigued; and, as it will promote their own health and happiness to go, it is very justifiable to grant them the privilege. This may properly and easily be provided for upon the Program.

SECTION IV.—ASSIGNING LESSONS.

Many teachers fail in this department. Judging of the difficulty of the lesson by the ease with which *they* can acquire it, even in a text-book new to themselves, they not unfrequently assign more than can possibly be learned by the children. They forget that by long discipline of mind, and by the aid of much previously acquired knowledge, the lesson becomes comparatively easy to them; they forget, too, the toil a similar lesson cost them when they were children. Now the effect of learning a lesson poorly is most ruinous to the mind of a child. He, by

Why?—Not how much, but how well.—Good habits of study.

the habit of missing comes to think it a small thing to fail at recitation. He loses his self-respect. He loses all regard for his reputation as a scholar. It is truly deplorable to see a child fail in a lesson with indifference. Besides, the attempt to acquire an unreasonable lesson induces a superficial habit of study,—a skimming over the surface of things. The child studies that he may live through the recitation; not that he may learn and remember. He passes thus through a book, and thinks himself wise while he is yet a fool,—a mistake that is no less common than fatal.

The motto of the wise teacher should be, "NOT HOW MUCH, BUT HOW WELL." He should always ask, is it *possible* that a child *can* master this lesson, and *probable* that he *will?* It is better that a class should make but very slow progress for several weeks, if they but acquire the habit of careful study, and a pride of good scholarship, —a dread of failure,—than that they should ramble over a whole field, firing at random, missing oftener than they hit the mark, and acquiring a stupid indifference to their reputation as marksmen, and a prodigal disregard to their waste of ammunition and their loss of the game.

In assigning lessons, the importance of good habits of study should be considered, and the lessons given accordingly. At the commencement of a term the lessons should always be short, till the ability of the pupils is well understood, and their habits as good students established. As the term progresses, they can be gradually lengthened as the capacity of the class will warrant, or their own desire will demand. It is frequently judicious to consult the class about the length of the lessons, though, to be sure, their judgment can not always be relied on, for they are almost always ready to undertake more than they can perform well. Assigning, however, somewhat less than they propose, will take from them all excuse for failure. When the lesson is given, a failure should be looked upon as a culpable dereliction of duty, as incompatible with a good conscience as it is with good scholarship. This high ground can not be taken, however, unless the teacher has been very judicious in the assignment of the lesson.

SECTION V.—REVIEWS.

In the prosecution of study by any class of students, frequent reviews are necessary. This is so because the memory is very much aided by repetition and by association. But, further, the understanding is often very much improved by a review. Many of the sciences can not be presented in independent parts, nor can all the terms employed be fully appreciated till these parts are again viewed as a whole. Many things which were but dimly seen the first time they were passed over, become perfectly clear to the mind

Application of principles to practical life.—A general review.

when viewed afterward in connection with what follows them.

In conducting reviews, regard must be had to the age and character of the pupils, and to the branch pursued. In arithmetic, and, indeed, in mathematics generally, where so much depends upon every link in the great chain, very frequent reviews are necessary. Indeed, almost daily it is profitable to call up some principle before gone over. In several branches, where the parts have a less intimate connection, as in geography, natural philosophy, and some others, the reviews may be at greater intervals. It would be well, I think, in every common school, to have a review-day once a week. This, besides the advantages already indicated, will lead the children to study for something *beyond* recitation. Nor is it enough at the review, that the questions of the text-book be again proposed to the children. If this be all, they will only exercise their *memories*. As far as possible, the *subject* should be called up, and the *application of principles to practical life* should be dwelt upon. If this course is expected by the learners, they will *think* during the week, in order to anticipate the examination of the teacher; and this *thinking* is more profitable to them than the knowledge itself.

It is always well, besides the periodical reviews, to have a general review at the close of any particular study. This enables the teacher to detect any false conceptions which the pupil has

An exception.

entertained during the first course. He can now present the subject as a whole, and view one part by the light of another. In natural philosophy, how much better the law of reflected motion can be appreciated after the subject of optics has been studied, in which the doctrine of reflection in general has been fully discussed and illustrated. In physiology, what light is thrown upon the process of growth in the system, by the subsequent chapters on absorption and secretion. How much clearer is the economy of respiration understood when viewed in connection with the circulation of the blood. A general review then is an enlightening process, and it is always profitable, with, perhaps, one exception. When it is instituted with reference to a public examination, it is very doubtful whether the evil is not greater than the good. It then degenerates into an effort to appear well at a particular time: again, it is studying in order to recite; and I look upon it as no small evil, that the mind should have any object in view which comes in between it and the grand *desire to know*,—to master the subject for its own sake, and not simply for the purpose of being able to talk about it on one great occasion.

SECTION VI.—PUBLIC EXAMINATIONS.

It is now the usage in all our schools to have public examinations,—generally at the close of a

Examinations not without objections.

term, or a portion of a term,—in order to test, in some measure, the industry and skill of the teacher, and the proficiency of the pupils. I am hardly prepared to oppose this usage, because I am inclined to believe examinations are of some utility as a means of awakening an interest in the parents of the children: perhaps they do something to stimulate school-officers, and also to excite both teacher and pupils to greater effort during the term. Still, public examinations, as frequently conducted, are not without *serious objections*.

1. They certainly can not be looked upon as criterions of the faithfulness or success of teachers. A man *with* tact, and *without* honesty, may make his school appear to far greater advantage than a better man can make a better school appear. This has often happened. It is not the most faithful and thorough teaching that makes the show and attracts the applause at a public exhibition. It is the superficial, mechanical, *memoriter* exercise that is most imposing. Who has not seen a class, that recited by rote and *in concert* at a celebration, win the largest approbation, when many of the individuals knew not the import of the *words* they uttered. *Names* in geography have been thus "said or sung," when the things signified were to the children as really *terræ incognitæ* as the fairy lands of Sindbad the Sailor.

2. Nor can such exhibitions be claimed justly to indicate the proficiency of the pupils. Every

Not to be taken as indices of proficiency.—Encourage deception.

experienced teacher knows that the best scholars often fail at a public examination, and the most indolent and superficial often distinguish themselves. The spectators, not unfrequently, in pointing out the *talent* of the school, make the teacher smile at their blunders.

3. They present a strong temptation to dishonesty on the part of the teacher. Since so much stress is laid upon the examination, and particularly, in some regions, upon the *Celebration*, where several schools are brought together to make a show for few hours, it must be rather an uncommon man who will have sufficient principle to exhibit his school *as it is*, and refuse to make those efforts so very common to have it appear *what it is not*. The wish, expressed or implied, of the parents, and the ambition of the children, all conspire to make the teacher yield to a usage so common. Consequently, several weeks will be spent to *prepare* the children to appear in public. During this time, they study not for improvement, not for future usefulness, but simply to *make a show* at the public celebration. An unworthy and unwarrantable motive actuates them during all this process; and, at last, unless strangely benighted, they are conscious of holding up a false appearance to the world. Now, under such circumstances, whatever of good is effected, by way of enkindling a zeal in the parents, is dearly purchased. The sacrifice of principle in a teacher—much more in

the children—is a large price to pay for the applause of a few visitors, or even for an increase of interest among them in the cause of popular education.

Examinations, however, which are less showy, and which are of such a character as thoroughly to sift the teachings that have been given, and to thwart any ingenious efforts specially to prepare for them—examinations that look back to the general teaching of the term or the year, and test the accuracy and thoroughness of the instructions—are unquestionably very desirable and useful. To make them so in the highest sense, and to exempt them from an evil tendency upon the minds of the young themselves, the *teacher should be strictly honest*. Not a lesson should be given with sole reference to the exhibition at the close; not an exercise should be omitted because the examination approaches. The good teacher should keep those great motives before the mind, which look to future usefulness, and to the discharge of duty. The child should be taught that he is accountable for what he acquires, and what he *may* acquire, and not for what he may *appear* to have acquired; and that this accountability is not confined to a single day, soon to pass and be forgotten; but it runs through all time and all eternity.

I know not but the expectation of an examination may stimulate some to greater exertion, and make them better scholars. If this be so, it

Restrictions and limitations.

may be well enough; and yet I should be slow to present such a motive to the mind of a child, because a special or secondary accountability always detracts from the general and chief.

A strong reason, in addition to those already assigned, why special preparation should not be made for the examination, is, that where such preparation is expected, the pupils become careless in their ordinary exercises.

While, then, I think too much stress is at present placed upon showy exhibitions and celebrations, and that objections and dangers attend *examinations*, as frequently conducted, I would not recommend altogether their discontinuance. I would rather urge that the teacher, by his inflexible honesty, should make them fair representations of the actual condition of his school, without relying very much upon them as a means of stimulating the pupils to exertion; that the pupils should be made to feel that the results of their exertion through the term, rather than a few special efforts near its close, would be brought into review; that no hypocrisy or management should ever be tolerated, in order to win the applause of the multitude; that no particular lessons should ever be assigned for the occasion; that it should be remembered, that the moral effect of an occasional failure at examination, will be more salutary upon the school than unbroken success; and that the children are irreparably injured, when they are made in

Profitable examinations.

any way the willing instruments of false pretension.

Under such circumstances, examinations may be profitable to all concerned. If teacher and pupils have done well, they have the opportunity of showing it without violence to their own consciences. The employers, and patrons too, have some means of forming a correct estimate of the value of their school; and all parties may be encouraged and stimulated. But above all things, LET THE TEACHER BE HONEST.

CHAPTER XII.

THE TEACHER'S RELATION TO THE PARENTS OF HIS PUPILS.

IN the choice of a clergyman, after estimating his moral and religious character, and ascertaining the order of his *pulpit* talents, a third question remains to be answered, viz.:—What are his qualifications as a *pastor?* How is he adapted to fulfill the various relations of private friend and counselor; and in the family circle, in his intercourse with the aged and the young, how is he fitted to

"Allure to brighter worlds and lead the way"?

In that sacred profession, every one knows that nearly as much good is to be done by private intercourse as in the public ministration. Many a heart can be reached by a friendly and informal conversation, that would remain unmoved by the most powerful eloquence from the pulpit. Besides, many are *prepared* to be profited in the public exercises by that intercourse in private which has opened their hearts, removed prejudice, and engendered a feeling of friendly interest in the preacher. The admonitions of the gospel thus have the double power of being truth,

Social qualities in a teacher.—He should call on the parents.

and truth uttered by the lips of a valued friend.

It is, to some extent, thus with the school teacher. He may be very learned and very apt to teach, and yet fail of success in his district. Hence, it is highly important that he should possess and carefully cultivate those social qualities, which will greatly increase his usefulness. The teacher should consider it a part of his duty, whenever he enters a district, to excite a deeper interest there, among the patrons of the school, than they have ever before felt. He should not be satisfied till he has reached every mind connected with his charge in such a way that they will cheerfully co-operate with him and sustain his judicious efforts for good. Being imbued with a deep feeling of the importance of his work, he should let them see that he is alive to the interests of their children. To this end,—

1. *He should seek frequent opportunities of intercourse with the parents.* Though the advances toward this point, by the strict rules of etiquette, should be made by the parents themselves (as by some it is actually and seasonably done)—yet, as a general thing, taking the world as we find it, the teacher must lead the way. He must often introduce himself uninvited to the people among whom he dwells, calling at their homes in the spirit of his vocation, and conversing with them freely about his duty to their children and to themselves. Every parent,

Object of his calls.—He should explain his plans.

of course, will feel bound to be courteous and civil in his own house; and, by such an interview, perhaps a difference of opinion, a prejudice, or a suspicion may be removed, and the foundation of a mutual good understanding be laid, which many little troubles can never shake. It may be very useful to have an interview with such parents as have been disturbed by some administration of discipline upon members of their families. Let me not be understood, however, to recommend that the teacher should ever go to the parent in a cringing, unmanly spirit. It would probably be far better that the parties should ever remain entire strangers, than that their meeting should necessarily be an occasion of humiliating retraction on the part of the teacher. Neither should the parents ever be allowed to expect that the teacher always will, as a matter of duty, come to their *confessional*. But it is believed, if there could be a meeting of the parties as men, as gentlemen, as Christians, as coadjutors for the child's welfare, it would always be attended with good results.

2. *He should be willing to explain all his plans to the parents of his pupils.* If they had implicit confidence in him, and would readily and fully give him every facility for carrying forward all his designs without explanation, then, perhaps, this direction might not be necessary. But, as the world is, he can not expect spontaneous confidence. They wish to know his designs, and it

Encourage inquiry.—No mystery.

is best they should be informed of them by himself. The best way for the teacher to interest them in the business of education, will be freely to converse with them concerning the measures he intends to adopt. If his plans are judicious, he of course can show good reasons why they should be carried into effect; and parents are generally willing to listen to reason, especially when it is directed to the benefit of their own children. Many a parent, upon the first announcement of a measure in school, has stoutly opposed it, who, upon a little explanatory conversation with the teacher, would entertain a very different opinion, and ever after would be most ready to countenance and support it.

It seems to me a teacher may safely *encourage inquiry* into all his movements in school. There is an old saying—in my opinion a mischievous one,—which enjoins it as a duty upon all, to "tell no tales out of school." I see no objection to the largest liberty in this matter. Why may not every thing be told, if told correctly? Parents frequently entertain a suspicious spirit as to the movements of the teacher. Would not very much of this be done away, if it was understood there was no *mystery* about the school? The teacher who would thus invite inquiry, would be very careful never to do any thing which he would not be willing to have related to the parents, or even to be witnessed by them. I would have no objection, if it were possible, that the walls of our school-rooms, as you look inward, should be transparent, so that any individual unperceived might view with his own eyes the movements within. The consciousness of such an oversight would work a healthy influence upon those who have too long delighted in mystery.

3. *The teacher should encourage parents to visit his school frequently.* There is almost everywhere too great backwardness on the part of parents to do this duty. The teacher should early invite them to come in. It is not enough that he do this in *general* terms. He may fix the time, and arrange the party, so that those who would assimilate, should be brought together. It will frequently be wise to begin with the mothers, where visitation has been unusual. They will soon bring in the fathers. As often as they come they will be benefited. When such visits are made, the teacher should not depart from his usual course of instruction on their account. Let all the recitations and explanations be attended to, all praises and reproofs, all rewards and punishments be as faithfully and punctually dispensed as if no person were present. In other words, let the teacher faithfully exhibit the school *just as it is*, its lights and its shadows, so that they may see all its workings, and understand all its trials as well as its encouragements.

Such visitations under such circumstances, it is believed, would ever be highly beneficial. The teacher's difficulties and cares would be better

Be frank and true with parents.

understood, and his efforts to be useful appreciated. The hindrances, thus *seen* to impede his progress, would be promptly removed, and the teacher would receive more cordial sympathy and support.

But if the teacher makes such visits the occasion for putting a false appearance upon the school; if he takes to himself unusual airs, such as make him ridiculous in the eyes of his pupils, and even in his own estimation; if he attempts to bring before the visitors his best classes, and to impress them with his own skill by showing off his best scholars, they will, sooner or later, discover his hypocrisy, and very likely despise him for an attempt to deceive them.

4. *The teacher should be frank in all his representations to parents concerning their children.* This is a point upon which many teachers most lamentably err. In this, as in every other case, "honesty is the best policy." If an instructor informs a parent during the term that his son is making rapid progress, or, as the phrase is—"doing very well," he excites in him high expectations; and if at the end of the term, it turns out otherwise, the parent, with much justice, may feel that he has been injured, and may be expected to load him with censure instead of praise. Let a particular answer, *and a true one*, always be given to the inquiry—"How does my child get along?" The parent has a right to know, and the teacher has no right to conceal the truth.

No evasion.—Study the art of conversation.—Be modest.

Sometimes teachers, fearing the loss of a pupil, have used some *indefinite expression*, which, however, the doting parent is usually ready to interpret to his child's advantage. But sooner or later the truth will appear; and when the teacher is once convicted of any misrepresentation in this particular, there is rarely any forgiveness for him. For this reason and for his own love of truth, for his own reputation and for the child's welfare, he should keep nothing back. He should tell the whole story plainly and frankly,—and the parent, if he is a gentleman, will thank him for his faithfulness to him; and if he has any sense of justice, he will be ready to co-operate with him for his child's improvement. At any rate, such a course will insure the reward of a good conscience.

The teacher, as I have before urged, should have the habits and manners of a gentleman. He should strive also to acquire the ability to converse in an easy and agreeable way, so that his society shall never be irksome. He, in other words, should be a man who does not require *much entertaining.* Modesty, withal, is a great virtue in the teacher;. especially in his intercourse with the people of his district. Teachers, from their almost constant intercourse with their pupils, are apt to think their own opinions infallible; and they sometimes commit the ridiculous error, of treating others wiser than themselves, as children in knowledge. This infirmity, incident to

"Out-door work."—Its result.

the profession, should be carefully avoided; and while the teacher should ever endeavor to make his conversation instructive, he should assume no *airs* of superior learning or infallible authority He should remember the truth in human nature, that men are best pleased to learn without being reminded that they are learners.

I have known some teachers who have sneered at what they have termed the "out-door work" here recommended. They have thrown themselves upon their dignity, and have declared that when they had done their duty within the schoolroom, they had done all that could be expected, and that parents were *bound* to co-operate with them and sustain them. But, after all, we must take the world as we find it; and since parents *do not* always feel interested as they should, I hold it to be a part of the teacher's duty to *excite* their interest, and to *win* them to his aid by all the proper means in his power. In doing this he will, in the most effectual way, secure the progress of his school, and at the same time advance his own personal improvement.

CHAPTER XIII.

TEACHER'S CARE OF HIS HEALTH.

NO employment is more wearing to the constitution than the business of teaching. So many men falter in this employment from ill health, so many are deterred from entering it, because they have witnessed the early decay and premature old age of those who have before pursued it, and so many are still engaged in it, who almost literally "drag their slow length along," groaning under complicated forms of disease and loss of spirits, which they know not how to tolerate or cure,—that it has become a serious inquiry among the more intelligent of the profession, "Can not something be known and practiced on this subject, which shall remove the evils complained of?" Is it absolutely necessary that teachers shall be dyspeptics and invalids? Must devotion to a calling so useful be attended with a penalty so dreadful?

A careful survey of the facts, by more than one philanthropist, has led to the conclusion that the loss of health is not necessarily attendant upon the teacher of the young. It is believed, indeed, that the confinement from the air and sunlight, and the engrossing nature of his pur-

Laws of health should be studied.—Effect of a change of employment.

suits, have a *strong tendency* to bring on an irritability of the nervous system, a depression of spirits, and a prostration of the digestive functions; but it is also believed that, by following strictly and systematically, the known laws of health, this tendency may be successfully resisted, and the teacher's life and usefulness very much prolonged. The importance of the subject, and a desire to render this volume as useful as possible, has induced me to ask leave to transfer to its pages, with slight abbreviation, the very judicious and carefully written chapter on "Health—Exercise—Diet," contained in the "School and School-master," from the gifted pen of George B. Emerson, Esq., of Boston,—one of the most enlightened educators of the present age.

HEALTH—EXERCISE—DIET.

"The teacher should have perfect health. It may seem almost superfluous to dwell here upon what is admitted to be so essential to all persons; but it becomes necessary, from the fact that nearly all those who engage in teaching, leave other and more active employments to enter upon their new calling. By this change, and by the substitution of a more sedentary life within-doors, for a life of activity abroad, the whole habit of the body is changed, and the health will inevitably suffer, unless precautions be taken which have never before been necessary. To all such persons—to all, especially, who are entering upon the work of teaching, with a view of making it their occupation through life, a knowledge of the laws of health is of the utmost importance, and to such this chapter is addressed. I shall speak of these laws briefly, under the heads of Exercise, Air, Sleep, Food, and Dress.

"EXERCISE. So intimate is the connection between the various parts of our compound nature, that the faculties of the mind can not be naturally, fully, and effectually exercised, without the health of the body. And the first law of health is, that which imposes the necessity of *exercise.*

"The teacher can not be well without exercise, and usually a great deal of it. No other pursuit requires so much,—no other is so exhausting to the nerves; and exercise, air, cheerfulness, and sunshine, are necessary to keep them in health. Most other pursuits give exercise of body, sunshine, and air, in the very performance of the duties that belong to them. This shuts us up from all.

"One of the best, as one of the most natural modes of exercise, is *walking.* To give all the good effects of which it is susceptible, a walk must be taken either in pleasant company, or, if alone, with pleasant thoughts; or, still better, with some agreeable end in view, such as gathering plants, or minerals, or observing other natural objects. Many a broken constitution has been built up, and many a valuable life saved and prolonged, by such a love of some branch of natural history as has led to snatch every opportunity for a walk, with the interest of a delightful study,

> 'Where living things, and things inanimate
> Do speak, at Heaven's command, to eye and ear.'

The distinguished geologist of Massachusetts, President Hitchcock, was once, when teacher of a school, reduced to so low a state by disease of the nerves, which took the ugly shape of dyspepsia, that he seemed to be hurrying rapidly toward the grave. Fortunately, he became interested in mineralogy, and this gave him a strong motive to spend all his leisure time in the open air, and to take long circuits in every direction. He forgot that he was pursuing health, in the deeper interest of science; and thus, aided by some other changes in his habits, but not in his pursuits, he gradually recovered the perfect health which has enabled him to do so much for science, and for the honor of his native State.

"*Riding on horseback* is one of the best modes of exercise possible for a sedentary person. It leads to an erect posture, throws open the chest, gives a fuller breathing, and exercises the muscles of the arm and upper part of the frame. * * * In weakness of the digestive organs its efficacy is remarkable. * * *

"*A garden* furnishes many excellent forms of

Farm labor.—Rowing.—Sawing and splitting wood.

exercise, and the numerous labors of a *farm* would give every variety, if the teacher could be in a situation to avail himself of them. This is not often the case. When accessible, the rake, the pitchfork, moderately used, can not be too highly recommended. A garden is within the reach of most teachers in the country. It has the advantage of supplying exercise suited to every degree of strength, and of being filled with objects gratifying to the eye and taste. * * * The flower-garden and shrubbery commend themselves to the female teacher. To derive every advantage from them, she must be willing to follow the example often set by the ladies of England, and use the hoe, the rake, the pruning-hook, and the grafting-knife, with her own hands.

"*Rowing*, when practicable, is a most healthful exercise. It gives play to every muscle and bone in the frame. * * * When the river is frozen, *skating* may take the place of rowing; and it is an excellent substitute. * * * *Driving* a chaise or a sleigh, is a healthful exercise, if sufficient precaution be used to guard against the current which is always felt, as it is produced by the motion of the vehicle, even in still air.

"*Sawing* and *splitting* wood form a valuable exercise, particularly important for those who have left an active life for the occupation of teaching.

"Exercise should be taken in the early part of the day. Warren Colburn, the author of the

Warren Colburn.—In the morning.—In open air.—In the light.

Arithmetic, whose sagacity in common things was as remarkable as his genius for numbers, used to say, that half an hour's walk before breakfast did him as much good as an hour's after. Be an early riser. The air of morning is more bracing and invigorating; the sights, and sounds, and odors of morning are more refreshing. A life's experience in teaching declares the morning best. * * *

"Exercise must always be taken, if possible, in the open air. Air is as essential as exercise, and often, in warm weather particularly, more so. They belong together. The blood flows not as it should, it fails to give fresh life to the brain, if we breathe not fresh air enough. The spirits can not enjoy the serene cheerfulness which the teacher needs, if he breathe not fresh air enough. The brain can not perform its functions; thought can not be quick, vigorous, and healthy, without ample supplies of air. Much of the right moral tone, of habitual kindliness and thankful reverence, depends on the air of heaven.

"Exercise must be taken in the light; and if it may be, in the sunshine. Who has not felt the benignant influence of sunshine? The sun's light seems almost as essential to our well-being as his heat, or the air we breathe. It has a great effect on the nerves. A distinguished physician of great experience, Dr. J. C. Warren, of Boston, tells me that he almost uniformly finds diseases that affect the nerves, exasperated by the darkness of night and mitigated by the coming on of day. All plants growing in the air lose their strength and color when excluded from light. So in a great degree does man. They lose their fine and delicate qualities, and the preciousness of their juices. Man loses the glow of his spirits, and the warmth and natural play of his finer feelings. * * *

"Next to air and light, water is the most abundant element in nature. It can hardly be requisite to enjoin upon the teacher the freest use of it. The most scrupulous cleanliness is necessary, not only on his own account, but that he may be able always to insist upon it, with authority, in his pupils. The healthy state of the nerves, and of the functions of digestion, depends in so great a degree on the cleanliness of the skin, that its importance can hardly be overstated. * * *

"SLEEP. No more fatal mistake in regard to his constitution can be made by a young person given to study, than that of supposing that Nature can be cheated of the sleep necessary to restore its exhausted, or strengthen its weakened powers. From six to eight hours of sleep are indispensable; and with young persons, oftener eight or more, than six. It is essential to the health of the body, and still more to that of the mind. It acts directly on the nervous system; and irritability, or what is called *nervousness*, is the consequence of its loss. This, bad in any person, is

| Diet.—Simple food.—Extremes in kind and quantity. |

worse in the teacher than in any one else. It is an unfailing source of unhappiness to himself and to all his school. He would be unwise to subject himself to the consequences of the loss of sleep; he *has no right* to subject others. * * *

"DIET. To no person is an attention to diet more important than to the teacher. For his own guidance, and that he may be able to give proper instructions in regard to this subject to his pupils, the conclusions of experience, or what we may consider the laws of diet, should be familiar to him. Some of these are the following:

"1. Food should be simple; not of too little nor too great variety. The structure of the teeth, resembling at once those of animals that naturally subsist on flesh, and of animals that take only vegetable food, and the character and length of the digestive organs, holding a medium between the average of these two classes, indicate that a variety of food, animal and vegetable, is natural to man, and in most cases probably necessary. The tendency in most parts of this country, from the great abundance of the necessaries of life, is to go to excess in the consumption of food, particularly of animal food. The striking evils of this course have led many to the opposite extreme—to renounce meats entirely. Experience of the evils of this course also has in most cases brought men back to the safe medium. No person needs to be more careful in

True medium.—Taken at intervals.—Moderate quantity.

regard to the quality and nature of his food than the teacher, as his exclusion from air for a great part of the day leaves him in an unfit condition to digest unwholesome food, while the constant use of his lungs renders his appetite unnaturally great, or destroys it altogether. Animal food seems to be necessary, but not in great quantities, nor oftener, usually, than once a day. * * * In winter, the food should be nourishing, and may be more abundant; in summer, less nutritious, less of animal origin, and in more moderate quantity.

"2. Food should be taken at sufficiently distant intervals. * * * The operation of digestion is not completed, ordinarily, in less than four hours. Food should not be taken at shorter intervals than this; and intervals of five or six hours are better, as they leave the stomach some time to rest.

"3. It should be taken in moderate quantity. In the activity of common life excess is less to be dreaded than with the sedentary habits and wearying pursuits of the teacher. * * * The exhaustion of teaching is that of the nervous power, and would seem to call for hours of quiet, and freedom from care, with cheerful conversation, and the refreshment of air and gentle exercise. Probably all the kinds of food in general use are wholesome when partaken of moderately. Those who, from choice or compulsion, pass from an active to a sedentary life, should at the same time restrict themselves to one half their accustomed quantity of food.

"4. As a general rule, *fat* should be avoided. * * * None but a person who takes a great deal of most active exercise, or is much exposed to cold, can long bear its use with impunity. If taken, fat in a solid form is less injurious than liquid fat.

"5. Fruit may be eaten with the recollection of the proverb of fruit-producing countries: 'It is gold in the morning, silver at noon, and lead at night.' Ripe fruit in its season is wholesome, and preferable for a person of sedentary habits, to more nourishing and exciting food. But it should be a substitute for other food, not an addition. A bad practice, common in some places, of eating fruit, especially the indigestible dried fruits, raisins, and nuts, in the evening, should be avoided by the teacher. He must have quiet and uninterrupted sleep and early hours, to be patient, gentle, and cheerful in school.

"6. The drink of a sedentary person should be chiefly water, and that in small quantities, and only at meals. The intelligent Arab of the desert drinks not during the heat of the day. He sees that watering a plant in the sunshine makes it wither; and he feels in himself an analogous effect from the use of water. There are few lessons in regard to diet so important to be inculcated as this: 'Drink not between meals.'

"7. The last rule to be observed is, that no

Dress.—Cheerfulness.

unnecessary exertion of mind or body should be used immediately after a meal. If a walk must be taken, it should rather be a leisurely stroll than a hurried walk.

"DRESS. The teacher should be no sloven. He should dress well, not over nicely, not extravagantly; neatly, for neatness he must teach by example as well as by precept; and warmly, for so many hours of the day shut in a warm room will make him unusually sensitive to cold. The golden rule of health should never be forgotten: 'Keep the head cool, the feet warm, and the body free.' The dress of the feet is particularly important. Coldness or dampness of the feet causes headache, weakness and inflammation of the eyes, coughs, consumptions, and sometimes fevers. A headache is often cured by sitting with the feet long near a fire. Keeping the feet warm and dry alleviates the common affections of the eyes, repels a coming fever, prevents or quiets coughs, and serves as one of the surest safeguards against consumption. Many of our most sensible physicians trace the prevalence of consumption in Northern States, not to our climate, but to the almost universal custom of wearing insufficient clothing, especially on the feet.

"There is another subject intimately connected with health, which has been alluded to, but which ought, from its importance, to receive more than a passing remark. It is *cheerfulness*. This should be one of the ends and measures of health. It

Cause of low spirits.—A home.—Sociality.

ought to be considered the natural condition of a healthy mind; he who is not cheerful is not in health. If he has not some manifest moral cause of melancholy, there must be something wrong in the body, or in the action of the powers of the mind.

"A common cause of low spirits in a teacher is anxiety in regard to the well-doing of his pupils. This he must feel; but he must endeavor, as far as possible, to banish it from his hours of relaxation. He must leave it behind him when he turns from the school-house door. To prevent its haunting him, he must seek pleasant society. He must forget it among the endearments of home, the cheerful faces and kind voices of friends. This is the best of all resources, and happy is the man who has a pleasant home, in the bosom of which he may rest from labor and from care. If he be among strangers, he must endeavor to find or make friends to supply the place of home. He must seek the company of the parents and friends of his pupils, not only that he may not be oppressed by the loneliness of his situation, but that he may better understand the character of his pupils and the influences to which they are subjected. The exercise of the social affections is essential to the healthy condition of a well-constituted mind. Often he will find good friends and pleasant companions among his pupils. Difference of years disappears before kindliness of feeling, and sympathy may exist between those most remote in age, and pursuit, and cultivation.

* * * * * * *

"A delightful, but somewhat dangerous recreation is offered by music; delightful, as always soothing to the wearied mind; but dangerous, because liable to take to itself too much time. It would be desirable if every instructor could himself sing or play. If he can not, let him listen to songs or cheerful music from voice or instrument, or to the notes of birds.

"'I'm sick of noise and care, and now mine ear
Longs for some air of peace.'"

To the foregoing excellent remarks, I could scarcely wish to add any thing, save to call attention to that pernicious habit among both clergymen and teachers, of dressing the neck too warmly whenever they go into the open air. There seems to have obtained an impression that those who have occasion to *speak* often, should be peculiarly careful to guard their throats from the cold. Hence many are seen in a winter's day with a collar of fur, or a woolen "comforter," or at least a silk handkerchief of extraordinary dimensions, around their necks, and often extending above their mouths and nostrils. If they have occasion to step out but for a moment, they are still subject to the slavery of putting on this unnatural incumbrance.

Bronchitis.—"Lung complaint."—Experience.

Now, I believe that this extra covering for the neck, instead of preventing disease of the throat and lungs, is one of the most fruitful sources of such disease. These parts being thus thickly covered during exercise, become very warm, and an excessive local perspiration is excited; and the dampness of the throat is much increased if the covering extends above the mouth and nose, thus precluding the escape of the exhalations from the lungs. When, therefore, this covering is removed, even within-doors, a very rapid evaporation takes place, and a severe cold is the consequence. In this way a cold is renewed every day, and hoarseness of the throat and irritation of the lungs is the necessary result. Very soon the clergyman or teacher breaks down with the *bronchitis*, or the "lung complaint," and is obliged for a season, at least, to suspend his labors. This difficulty is very much enhanced, if the ordinary neck-dress is a stiff stock, which, standing off from the neck, allows the ingress of the cold air as soon as the outer covering is removed.

Having suffered myself very severely from this cause, and having seen hundreds of cases in others, I was desirous to bear the testimony of my experience against the practice,—and to suggest to all who have occasion to speak long and often that the simplest covering for the neck is the best. A very light cravat is all that is necessary. If the *ordinary* cravat be too thick and too warm, as the large-sized white cravats, so fashionable with the clergy, usually are, during the exercise of speaking, an unnatural flow of blood to the parts will be induced, which, after the exercise ceases, will be followed by debility and prostration. A cold is then very readily taken, and disease follows. I am confident, from my own experience and immediate observation, that this unnatural *swaddling* of the neck is one of the most fruitful causes of disease of the lungs and throat that can be mentioned.

CHAPTER XIV.

TEACHER'S RELATION TO HIS PROFESSION.

IT has long been the opinion of the best minds in our country, as well as in the most enlightened countries of Europe, that teaching should be a profession. It has been alleged, and with much justice, that this calling, which demands for its successful exercise the best of talents, the most persevering energy, and the largest share of self-denial, has never attained an appreciation in the public mind at all commensurate with its importance. It has by no means received the emolument, either of money or honor, which strict justice would award, in any other department, to the talents and exertions required for this. This having been so long the condition of things, much of the best talent has been attracted at once to the other professions; or, if exercised awhile in this, the temptation of more lucrative reward, or of more speedy, if not more lasting honor, has soon diverted it from teaching, where so little of either can be realized, to engage in some other department of higher promise. So true is this, that scarcely a man can be found, having attained to any considerable eminence as a teacher, who has not been several times solic-

Some noble souls.—Some small men.—Two evils.

ited—and perhaps strongly *tempted*—to engage in some more lucrative employment; and while there have always been some strong men, who have preferred teaching to any other calling,— men who would do honor to any profession, and who, while exercising this, have found that highest of all rewards, the consciousness of being useful to others,—still it must be confessed that teachers have too often been of just that class which a knowledge of the circumstances might lead us to predict would engage in teaching; men of capacity too limited for the other professions, of a temperament too sluggish to engage in the labors of active employment, of manners too rude to be tolerated except in the society of children (!), and sometimes of a morality so pernicious, as to make them the unfailing contaminators of the young whenever permitted—not to teach—but to "keep school." Thus, two great evils have been mutually strengthening each other. The indifference of the employers to the importance of good teachers, and their parsimony in meting out the rewards of teaching, have called into the field large numbers, in the strictest sense, unworthy of all reward; while this very unworthiness of the teachers has been made the excuse for further indifference, and, if possible, for greater meanness on the part of employers. Such has been the state of the case for many years past, and such is, to a great extent, the fact at present.

Educational millennium.—How ushered in?—Different views.

It has been the ardent wish of many philanthropists that this deplorable state of affairs should be exchanged for a better. Hence, they have urged that teaching should be constituted a profession; that none should enter this profession but those who are thoroughly qualified to discharge the high trust; and, as a consequence, that the people should more liberally reward and honor those who are thus qualified and employed. This would, indeed, be a very desirable change; it would be the educational millennium of the world. For such a period, we all may well devoutly pray.

But how shall this glorious age—not yet arrived —be ushered in? By whose agency, and by what happy instrumentality must its approach be hastened? Here, as in all great enterprises, there is some difference of opinion. Some have urged that the establishment of normal schools and other seminaries for the better education of teachers, and the institution of a more vigilant system of supervision, by which our schools should be effectually guarded against the intrusion of the ignorant and inefficient teacher, is all that is necessary to bring in this brighter day. Others have zealously urged that such preparation and such supervision are entirely superfluous and premature in the present state of the public mind. *They* say that the public must first become more liberal in its appropriations for schools; it must at once double the amount it has been

Truth between the extremes.—A mutual evil, and a mutual remedy.

accustomed to pay to teachers, and thus secure to this vocation the best talent without further trouble. To this the former class reply, that the public has seldom been known to raise its price, so long as its wants could be supplied at the present rates. *They* say that the last century has afforded ample opportunity for the exhibition of this voluntary generosity of the public, and yet we still wait to see this anomaly in human prudence, of offering in advance to pay double the price for the same thing; for until better teachers are raised up, it must be an advance upon the present stock. So there is a division among them, "for some cry one thing, and some another."

Now, I believe, in this case as in most others, the truth lies between the extremes. As the evil complained of is a *mutual* one, as has already been shown,—that is, an illiberal public has tolerated incompetent teachers, and the incompetence of teachers has enhanced in turn the parsimony of the public,—so the remedy must be a mutual one; the public must be enlightened and teachers must be improved; the pay of teachers must be raised, but there must be also something to warrant the higher rate. Nor is it easy to determine which shall begin first. We can hardly expect the people to pay more, till they find an article worth more; nor, on the other hand, can we expect the teachers to incur any considerable outlay to improve themselves, until better encour-

Teachers should elevate their calling.—Encouragements.

agement shall be held out to them by their employers. The two must generally proceed together. Just as in the descending scale, there was a mutual downward tendency, so here, better service will command better pay, and in turn, the liberality of employers will stimulate the employed to still higher attainments in knowledge and greater exertions in their labors.

In this condition of things, the question recurs, What is the duty of teachers in relation to their calling? I answer, they are bound to do what they can to elevate it. Lord Bacon said, "Every man owes a debt to his profession." Teachers being supposed to be more intelligent than the mass of the community, may justly take the lead in the work of progress. They should, as a matter of *duty*, take hold of this work,—a work of sacrifice and self-denial as it will be, at least for some time,—and heartily do what they can to magnify their office and make it honorable. In the meantime they may do what they can to arouse the people to a sense of their duty. The more enlightened are to some extent with them already. The press, the pulpit, the legislative assemblies, all proclaim that something must be done. All admit the faithful teacher has not been duly rewarded, and *some* are found who are willing to *do* something for the improvement both of the mind and condition of the teacher. This is encouraging; and while we rejoice at the few gleams of light that betoken our dawning,

Public safety restricts membership of professions.

let us inquire, for a little space, how we can hasten the "coming in of the perfect day."

Any one who will may become a tailor, a carpenter, or a mason; but the practice of surgery, dentistry, and law, is restricted to a privileged few. Why are there thus open occupations (trades), and closed occupations (professions)? The reason lies in the fact that it is easy to judge of the quality of the service rendered in one case, and very difficult in the other; or that the public needs no formal protection against the incompetence of masons, while there is need of such protection against the incompetence of surgeons. It is therefore a measure of public safety that restricts the membership of professions to those who have given a formal proof of their competence.

On the other hand, as it requires a high grade of ability, a high degree of skill and peculiar knowledge, that can be obtained only at a great expense of time, labor, and money, to become qualified for the difficult and highly responsible duties of a profession, some hope of reward must be held out to induce men to undertake this arduous preparation. The most direct way to insure this reward has been found to be to protect such men by cutting off unjust competition; and this is effected by forbidding the incompetent to practice. It thus happens that by protecting the professions, society protects itself; and that the lowering of professional standards

Teaching requires to be treated as a profession.

is equivalent to exposing the public to the dangers of incompetence and pretense.

So long as we regard general scholarship as constituting fitness for teaching, it is merely an occupation open to all the well educated. But, under the conception that to scholarship must be added skill and science, and that these elements of fitness are of difficult attainment, there emerges the notion that the public should be protected in their dearest interests against incompetence and pretense; and, as in the cases cited, the measure of public protection will be in exact ratio to the teacher's protection against unjust competition; so that the whole case may be summed up as follows:

1. Skill gained through the study of educational science, should be counted as the professional mark of competence for teaching.

2. The practice of teaching should be gradually restricted to those who furnish formal proof of this professional competence.

3. This protection against unjust competition will attract men and women of talent into the profession of teaching.

4. There will be a gradual rise in the degree of public protection against incompetence in teaching.

SECTION I.—SELF-CULTURE.

The teacher should labor diligently to improve himself. This is a duty incumbent on all persons,

Teachers should possess general information.

but particularly upon the teacher. The very nature of his employment demands that his mind should be frequently replenished from the storehouses of knowledge. To interest children in their studies, how necessary is it that the teacher's mind should be thoroughly furnished with the richest thoughts of the wise; to inspire them with a desire to learn, how important that he should be a living example of the advantage and enjoyment which learning alone can bestow; to strew the path of knowledge with flowers, and thus make it the path of pleasantness, how desirable that he should abound with the aptest illustrations, drawn from all that is wonderful and curious in nature and art; to awaken the young mind to a consciousness of its capacities, its wants, its responsibilities, how thoroughly should he know all the workings of the human soul,—how wisely and carefully should he touch the springs of action,—how judiciously should he call to his aid the conscience and the religious feelings!

Besides, let it be remembered that in this, as in other things, the teacher's *example* is of great importance. The young will be very likely to judge of the importance of their own improvement by the estimate the teacher practically places upon his; nor can he, with any good grace, press his pupils to exertion, while they see that he makes none whatever himself.

There is great danger, in the midst of the

Stagnation accounted for.—The teacher has time.

confinement and fatigue of the school-room, and the pressure of anxiety and care out of school, that the teacher will yield to the temptations of his position, and fall into habits of indolence as to his own improvement. Compelled, as he often is, to labor at great disadvantage, by reason of a small and poorly furnished school-room; confined through the day from the sunshine and the fresh breeze; subjected to a constant pressure of duty amid untold trials of his patience, arising from the law that impels children to be active as well as inconsiderate; required to concentrate his powers upon the double duty of governing and teaching at the same instant, and all through the session,—it is not strange, when the hour of release comes, that he should seek rest or recreation at the nearest point, even to the neglect of his own mental or moral culture. I am of the opinion that this accounts for the fact that so many persons enter the work of instruction, and continue in it for a longer or a shorter period, without making the slightest progress either in the art of teaching or in their own intellectual growth. Their first school, indeed, is often their best. This tendency or temptation, incident to the calling, it is the teacher's duty constantly and manfully to resist. *He can do it.*

1. *He has the time to do it.* He is usually required to spend but six hours in the day in the school-room. Suppose he add two hours

more for the purpose of looking over his lessons and devising plans for improving his school,—he will still have sixteen hours for sleep, exercise, recreation, and improvement. Eight hours are sufficient for sleep, especially for a sedentary man (some say less), and four will provide for meals, exercise, and recreation. *Four still remain for improvement.* Any teacher who is systematic and economical in the use of his time, can reserve, for the purpose of his own improvement, *four hours in every twenty-four*, and this without the slightest detriment to his school duties, or to his health. To be sure, he must lead a regular life. He must have a plan, and systematically follow it. He must be *punctual*, at his school, at his meals, at his exercise or recreation, at his hour of retiring and rising, and at his studies. Nor should he ordinarily devote more time than I have mentioned directly to his school. He should labor with his whole soul while he does work, and he will the more heartily do this, if he has had time to think of something else during the season of respite from labor. It is a great mistake that teachers make when they think they will be more successful by devoting all their thoughts to their schools. Very soon the school comes to occupy their sleeping as well as waking hours, and troublesome dreams disturb the repose of night. *Such men must soon wear out.*

But according to the laws of our nature, by

Immediate reward.—Proof.—*How to improve.*

a change of occupation the jaded faculties find rest. By taking up some new subject of inquiry, the intellect is relieved from the sense of fatigue which before oppressed it, the thoughts play freely again, the animation returns, the eye kindles, and *the mind expands.*

2. *Such labor finds immediate reward.* The *consciousness of growth* is no small thing toward encouraging the teacher. He feels that he is no longer violating his nature by allowing himself to *stagnate.* Then he will find every day that he can apply the newly-acquired truth to the illustration of some principle he is attempting to teach. He has encouraging and immediate *proof* that he is a better teacher, and that he has made himself so by timely exertion. He is thus again stimulated to rise above those temptations before described,—this immediate availability of his acquirements being vouchsafed to the teacher, as it is not to most men, in order to prompt him to stem the current which resists his progress.

And now, if I have shown that a teacher is bound to improve himself, both from a regard to his own well-being, and the influence of his example upon others,—and if I have also shown that he *can* improve himself, I may be indulged in making a few suggestions as to the *manner* of his doing it.

1. *He should have a course of professional reading.* It will do much for his improvement to read the works of those who have written on the

A course of professional reading.—The books.

subject of education, and the art of teaching. If possible, he should collect and possess a small educational library. It will be of great service to him to be able to read more than once such suggestions as are abundantly contained in the "School and School-master," by Potter and Emerson; the "Teacher," by Abbott; "Lectures," by Horace Mann; "Lectures of the American Institute of Instruction;" "Thoughts on Education," by John Locke; "Education," by Spencer; "Essays on Educational Reformers," by Quick; "Émile," by Rousseau; "Leonard and Gertrude," by Pestalozzi; "Education as a Science," by Bain; "John Amos Comenius," "Primary Instruction," and the "Training of Teachers," by Laurie; "Home Education," by Isaac Taylor; "Household Education," by Miss Martineau; "The Cyclopedia of Education," by Kiddle and Schem; "Theory and Practice of Teaching," and "Education and School," by Thring; "Day Dreams of a School-master," by Thompson; "School Management," by Landon; "Lectures on Teaching," by Fitch; "Histoire de la Pédagogie," by Compayré; "Levana," by Richter; "School and Industrial Hygiene," by Lincoln; "The Law of Public Schools," by Burke; the writings, if they can be obtained, of Wyse, of Cousin, of Lalor, of Lord Brougham on Education, together with such other works as are known to contain sound and practical views. It is not to be expected that every teacher will possess all these, or that he

A course of *general* study.—One thing at a time.

will read them all in a single term. But it is well to hold converse with other minds, and to have it in our power to review their best thoughts whenever our own need refreshing. I have given a somewhat extended list of books, because the inquiry is now so often made by teachers, what they shall read.

2. *By pursuing systematically a course of general study.* Many teachers who have a desire to improve themselves, still fritter away their time upon little miscellaneous matters, without making real progress. It is well in this to have a plan. Let some one study,—it may be geology, or astronomy, or chemistry, or botany, or the pure mathematics,—let some one study receive constant attention till no mean attainments have been made in it. By taking one thing at a time, and diligently pursuing it, at the end of a term the teacher feels that he has something to show for his labor,—and he is, by the advance already made, prepared to take the next and more difficult step. In a course of years, while a neighbor, who began teaching at the same time, has been stagnating or even retrograding, for the want of a plan and a purpose, a diligent man, by system and perseverance, may make himself at least equal to many who have enjoyed better advantages in early life, and at the same time have the superadded enjoyment of feeling that he has been his own teacher.

3. *Keep a journal or commonplace-book.* The

A journal or commonplace-book.—Why?—A demonstration.

habit of composing daily is very valuable to the teacher. In this book he may record whatever plans he has devised with their results in practice. He may enter remarkable cases of discipline,—in short, any thing which, in the course of his practice, he finds interesting. Those valuable suggestions which he receives from others, or hints that he may derive from books, may be epitomized here, and thus be treasured up for future reference. Sometimes one's best thoughts fade from his own mind, and he has no power to recall them. Such a book would preserve them, and would, moreover, show the character of one's thoughts at any particular period, and the *progress* of thought, from one period to another, better than any other means.*

To these means of self-culture I would add the practice of carefully reading and writing on chosen subjects, more fully described in the chapter on Habits of the Teacher.

By all these means and such others as may come within his reach, if a teacher succeeds in his attempts at progress, *he does much for his profession.* The very fact that he has given practical demonstration that a man may teach and still improve; that the temptations of his profession may be resisted and overcome; that the life of the pedagogue which has required him to keep the company of small minds, and to be occupied

---

* For further remarks on the Commonplace-book, see Chap. viii., p. 142. Note.

Encouragement to others.—Mutual aid.—Selfishness.

with minute objects, has never prevented his holding communion with the greatest men our earth has known, nor circumscribed in the least the sphere of his grasping research,—I say the very fact that he has thus shown what a man may do under such circumstances, may do much to encourage others to like effort.

But there are other and direct duties which he owes to his profession, which I proceed to consider under the head of

SECTION II.—MUTUAL AID.

Every teacher should be willing to impart as well as to receive good. No one, whatever may be his personal exertions, can monopolize all the wisdom of the world. The French have a proverb that "Everybody is wiser than anybody." Acting on this principle, the teacher should be willing to bring his attainments into the common stock, and to diffuse around him, as far as he is able, the light he possesses. I have no language with which to express my abhorrence of that selfishness, which prompts a man, after attaining to some eminence as a teacher by the free use of all the means within his reach, self-complacently to stand aloof from his fellow-teachers, as if he would say, "Brethren, help yourselves—I have no need of you, and you have no *claim* upon me. I have toiled hard for my eminence, and the secret is with me. I will enjoy it alone. When you have toiled as long, you *may* be as wise. Brethren, help yourselves." Such a spirit would perhaps be tolerated by the world in an avaricious man, who had labored to treasure up the shining dust of earth. But no man may innocently monopolize knowledge. The light of the sun is shed in golden refulgence upon every man, and no one if he would, may separate a portion for his own exclusive use, by closing his shutters about him,— for that moment, his light becomes darkness. It is thus with the light of knowledge. Like the air we breathe, or like the rain from heaven, it should be free to all. The man who would lock up the treasures of learning from the gaze of the whole world, whether in the tomes of some dusty library, as of old it was done, or in the recesses of his narrower soul, is unworthy of the name of man; he certainly has not the spirit of the teacher.

An exclusive spirit may be borne where meaner things, as houses, and lands, and gold, are at stake; but in education and religion—light and love,—where giving doth not impoverish nor withholding make rich, there is not even the shadow of an excuse for it. The man who is exclusive in these things, would be so, I fear, in heaven.

How can teachers encourage each other?

1. *By mutual visitation.* Very much may be done by social intercourse. Two teachers can scarcely converse together an hour without benefiting each other. The advantages of intercourse

with friends, as delineated by Dr. Young, may not be denied to teachers:

> "Hast thou no friend to set thy mind abroach?
> Good sense will stagnate. Thoughts shut up want air,
> And spoil like bales unopened to the sun.
> Had thought been all, sweet speech had been denied.
> * * * * * * * * *
> Thought, too, delivered, is the more possessed:
> Teaching, we learn; and giving, we retain
> The births of intellect; when dumb, forgot
> Speech ventilates our intellectual fire;
> Speech burnishes our mental magazine,
> Brightens for ornament, and whets for use."

But not only should teachers visit one another,—it is profitable also for them to visit each other's schools. I have never spent an hour in the school of another without gaining some instruction. Sometimes a new way of illustrating a difficult point, sometimes an exhibition of tact in managing a difficult case in discipline, sometimes an improved method of keeping up the interest in a class, would suggest the means of making my own labors the more successful. And even should one's neighbor be a bad teacher, one may sometimes learn as much from witnessing glaring defects as great excellences. Some of the most profitable lessons I have ever received, have been drawn from the deficiences of a fellow teacher. We seldom "see ourselves as others see us"; and we are often insensible of our own faults till we have seen them strikingly exhibited by another; and then by a comparison we correct our own.

Besides, by a visitation of a friend's school we may not only receive good, but we may impart it. If there is mutual confidence, a few words may aid him to correct his faults, if he has any,—faults which, but for such suggestion, might grow into confirmed habits, to his permanent injury.

So important is this mutual visitation among teachers, as a means of improvement, that I doubt not employers would find it for their interest to encourage it, by allowing the teachers to set apart an occasional half day for this purpose.

It would, moreover, be very useful for the teachers of a town to hold stated meetings, as often as once a month, for the purpose of mutual improvement. It would cultivate a fellow-feeling among them, and it would afford them an opportunity to exchange thoughts on most of the difficulties which they meet in their schools, and the best methods of surmounting them. At these meetings, a mutual exchange of books on the subject of teaching, would extend the facilities of each for improving his own mind, and his methods of instruction and government.

2. *By the use of the pen.* Every teacher should be a ready writer. Nearly every teacher could gain access to the columns of some paper, through which he could impart the results of his experience, or of his reflection. Such a course would benefit him specially, and, at the same time, it would awaken other minds to thought and action. In this way the attention, not only

of teachers, but also of parents, would be called to the great work of education. One mind in this way might move a thousand. If a teacher does not feel qualified to *instruct*, let him *inquire*, and thus call out the wisdom of others. This could be done in nearly every village. The press is almost always ready to promote the cause of education. By the use of it, teachers may profitably discuss all the great questions pertaining to their duty, and at the same time enlighten the community in which they live. This is an instrumentality as yet too little employed.

3. *By Teachers' Associations or Institutes.* These are peculiarly adapted to the diffusion of the best plans of instruction. Rightly conducted, they can never fail of being useful. Every man who lectures or teaches, is profited by the preparation. If he is a man of wisdom and experience, he will benefit his hearers. If otherwise, the discussion, which should ever follow a lecture, will expose its fallacies. It has often happened, in such associations, that an honest and experienced man has, in a half-hour, given to the younger portion of the members, lessons of wisdom which it would take them years to learn by their own observation. Errors in principle and practice have been exposed, into which many a young teacher was unconsciously falling, and hints have been given to the quicker minds, by which their own modes of teaching and governing have been speedily improved.

Should be practical.—A perversion.—Talk.

As far as possible, such meetings should be made strictly practical. The older teachers, who usually have the most to do with the management of them, should bear in mind that they are mainly designed to diffuse practical ideas of teaching, particularly among the younger members. Too often these meetings are made the arena of debate upon questions of very little practical importance to the teacher. I have seen a body of men spend an entire session of a half-day, in discussing a series of over-wrought *resolutions*, upon some topic scarcely at all connected with any duty of the teacher, frequently leaving the main question to wrangle about some point of order, or of "parliamentary usage"; and after the resolutions were passed or rejected, as the case might be,—(and it was of very little consequence whether "carried" or "lost,")—the ladies and younger teachers, who had borne no part in the *talk*, would find it difficult to tell "wherefore they had come together." Nothing had been said or done, by which they could be aided in their schools. *Lecturers*, too, have frequently mistaken their aim. Ambitious to shine out as literary men, they have given orations instead of practical lessons. In these meetings, it seems to me, nothing ostentatious, nothing far-fetched is what we need; but rather the modes and experience of practical men. We need to come down to the school-room, to the every-day business of the teacher, and thus prepare him to do his

Encouragement by meeting friends.—Illustration.—*Professional* feeling.

work more successfully on his return to his duties.

Another, and no inconsiderable advantage of such associations, is, that the teacher gains encouragement and strength, by being thus brought in contact with others engaged in the same pursuit. Toiling on alone, in his isolated district, surrounded by obstacles and discouragements, weighed down by care, and finding none to sympathize with him, he is almost ready to faint in his course, and perhaps to abandon his calling. At this crisis, he reads the notice for the teachers' meeting, and he resolves to go up once more to the gathering of his friends. From the various parts of the county, from the populous and crowded city, and from the by-ways of the country towns, a goodly number collect together and greet each other. Smile answers to smile, the blood courses more freely through the veins, the spirits, long depressed perhaps, partake of the general glow, and each feels that *he is not toiling alone.* He feels that a noble brotherhood of kindred spirits are laboring in the same field, under trials and discouragements similar to those which have oppressed him. He derives new strength from the sympathy of friends.

A *professional* feeling is engendered, which will accompany him to his school-room; and when he goes home, it is with renewed vigor and fresh aspirings to be a better man, and a better teacher. He labors with more confidence in himself; and, enlightened by what he has seen and heard, he is far more successful than before. His pupils, too, respond to the new life they see enkindling in him, and go to their work more cheerfully. One difficulty after another vanishes, and he begins to think teaching, after all, is not the *worst* employment in the world, but that it has some flowers as well as thorns; and he concludes to remain in the profession. This has been the history of at least *one* man. Long may many others have occasion to exercise gratitude like his, for the enjoyment of similar privileges.

The Teachers' Institute may be defined as a normal school having a very short course of study. Owing to this limitation of time, instruction must be given mainly by lecture, and must bear on methods and principles rather than on subjects. It should not be presumed that an Institute can make any considerable addition to a teacher's general scholarship; but it may and should do the following things:

1. It should make clear the nature of education and of instruction, and the purposes of the school.

2. It should present the best current methods of instructing and governing.

3. It should awaken a zeal in teaching, and provoke to higher attainments in scholarship.

4. Perhaps the Institute has done its best work if it has led to what may be called the *intel-*

lectual conversion of its members; that is, if it has induced a love for the vocation of the scholar.

The Teachers' Institute is subject to serious limitations, such as the shortness of its term, the method by which the instruction must be given, and the too often aimless nature of the attendance; but despite these drawbacks, there is probably no agency now at work, which is so efficient in disseminating improved methods, and in raising the general tone of educational thought.

I ought not to leave this subject without a word or two of *caution*.

1. *Be honest.* In all your intercourse with your fellow-teachers, be careful to use the words of "truth and soberness." In stating your experience, never allow your fancy to embellish your facts. Of this there is great danger. The young are sometimes *tempted* to tell a good story; but a deviation from the truth—always perilous and always wrong—may be peculiarly disastrous here. Experience overstated, may egregiously mislead the unwary inquirer after truth. Never overcolor the picture; it is better to err on the other side.

So, likewise, in exhibiting your school to fellow-teachers, be *strictly honest*. They come to learn from your every-day practice, and not from a counterfeit; and whenever you dress your school in a showy garb, to win the applause of a fellow-teacher, you do him a great injustice. You may not please your friend so much by your ordinary mode, as by something assumed for the occasion; but you may profit him far more; and in the end, you lose nothing by pursuing the line of duty.

I well remember, that a somewhat distinguished teacher once visited my own school, who, on going away, expressed himself somewhat disappointed, because he did not see any thing "*extraordinary*," as he said, in my mode of procedure. The truth was, nothing *extraordinary* was attempted. He saw what I wished to show him, an *ordinary* day's work; for I had before that time imbibed the opinion, that a man's reputation will be more firmly established, by sustaining *every day* a fair mediocrity, than it ever can be by an attempt to outdo himself on a few special occasions. As the value of biographical writing is often very much diminished, because the writer has endeavored to paint his character *too perfect to be human*,—so these visitations will lose their utility, whenever, by substituting hollow pretension for sober reality, the teacher endeavors to *exhibit* such a school as he *does not daily keep*.

2. *Avoid servile imitation of any model.* It is often remarked, that every man's plan is the best for him; and that many besides David can never fight in Saul's armor. This is generally true. All experience, then, should be considered, in connection with the circumstances under which it was tried, never forgetting the character and genius of the person who relates it. What might succeed

Adapt rather than *adopt* another's plans.—Avoid self-sufficiency.

in his hand, may fail in yours; particularly, as you will lack the interest of an original inventor.

The true secret lies in listening to the views of all, and then in making a judicious combination to meet your own character, and your own circumstances. It is often better to adjust and *adapt* the plan of another, than to *adopt* it. Servile imitation precludes thought in the teacher, and reduces him to a mere machine. The most successful teachers I have ever known, were those who would listen attentively to the plans and experience of others, and then strike out a course for themselves, attempting that, and that only, which they were confident they could successfully execute.

3. *Avoid undue self-sufficiency.* Men usually cease to learn, when they *think* they are wise enough. The teacher is in danger of falling into this error. Moving for the most part among children, where his decisions are seldom questioned, he is very apt to attach undue importance to his own opinions. Such a man meets his fellows with much self-complacency, and is but poorly prepared to be profited by the views of others. But the teacher should never cease to be *teachable.* There are very few men too old, or too wise, to learn something; and they are the wisest, if not the oldest, who are willing to welcome a real improvement, even though it should come from comparative "babes and sucklings," *out of whose mouths God has sometimes perfected praise.*

CHAPTER XV.

MISCELLANEOUS SUGGESTIONS.

ON looking over the notes which I have at various times made of my own experience and observation, during twenty years of practical teaching, I find there are several thoughts which may be of some service to the young teacher, and which have not been introduced under any of the general topics of this volume. I have therefore thought best to introduce a special chapter, with the above title, where I might lawfully bring together, without much regard to method, such varied hints as may convey to some reader a useful lesson. Some of these hints will refer to faults which should be carefully *avoided*, while others will point out some duties to be *performed*.

SECTION I.—THINGS TO BE AVOIDED.

1. *Guard against prejudice on entering a school.* It is not always safe to rely upon first impressions as to character. At the opening of a school, perhaps fifty individuals, for the first time, are brought before the teacher. Some of them are from humble life, and, perhaps, bear

Danger of prejudice.—Its injustice.—Why?

upon them the marks of parental neglect. Their persons and their clothing may present nothing to attract and gratify the eye of a stranger. Little accustomed to society, they exhibit an awkward bashfulness, or an impertinent forwardness, in their manner. Contrasted with these, others appear who have been the children of indulgence, and who have seen much more of the world. A more expensive garb attracts the eye; a more easy and familiar address, conforming to the artificial modes of society, is very likely to win the heart. The teacher is very prone to find his feelings committed in favor of the latter class, and against the former. But this is all wrong. A judgment thus hastily formed is extremely hazardous,—as a few days' acquaintance will usually show. The child of blunt or shy demeanor often has the truest heart,—a heart whose sentiments go out by the shortest course,—a heart that has never learned the artificial forms of the world, because it has never felt the need of them. And how unjust to the child is a prejudice founded on the circumstance of dress! Must the inability or neglect of his parent be doubly visited on him? Is it not enough that he daily feels the inward mortification of a contrast with his more favored school-fellows? Must he be painfully reminded of it by discovering that his teacher repels him on that account, and bestows his kindliest smiles upon those who are "the brightest and best clad"?

> Pupils not to direct their studies.—This the teacher's province.

And yet, such unjust prejudice is common; wrong and unfeeling as it is, it is too common. A fine dress, and a clean face, and a graceful manner, I know, are attractive; but the teacher has to do with the mind and the heart;—and he should never be deterred by any thing exterior, from making a diligent and patient search for good qualities which have their home behind the surface,—and he should ever possess a smile as cordial and a tone as parental for the neglected child of poverty and ignorance, as for the more favored son of wealth and ease.

2. *Do not allow your pupils to direct their own studies.* Whatever their age may be, they are seldom capable of doing this. It is the aim of the young to *get over* a long course of study. They are usually pleased to belong to higher classes, before they have mastered the branches taught in the lower. If children are suffered to direct their own studies, they usually make themselves very poor scholars. This is the bane of many of our select schools and academies, where the teacher yields this right in order to secure pupils and a salary. But no one, not even the parent, is as competent as the teacher ought to be, to direct in this matter. He has the best opportunity, daily, to fathom the pupil's attainments, and to understand his deficiencies. He may claim the right to direct. In case the pupil withstands his decision, the teacher should appeal to the parent, and endeavor there to sustain his

A mistake.—An egregious evil in all schools.—Illustrated.

point, a thing generally within his power, if, indeed, he is right. If the parent, too, is obstinate, and firmly insists upon the wrong course, the teacher may, perhaps, submit, though he can not submit without the consciousness that his province has been invaded.

It is too frequently the case that the teacher at the first yields all this ground voluntarily, by asking the children what they wish to study. When *he* has once made them a party in this question, he need not wonder if they claim to be heard. This he should not do. He should first be sure that he is qualified to direct aright, and then, as a matter of course, proceed to do it, just as the physician would prescribe for the physical malady of such a child. The latter is not more the rightful duty of the physician, than the former is of the school-teacher. Neither has the power to enforce his prescription against the parents' consent,—but that consent may be taken for granted by both, till informed that it is withheld.

I may here remark that in all my intercourse with the young, whether in the common or the higher school, I have found no greater evil than that of proceeding to the more difficult branches before the elementary studies have been mastered. It is no uncommon thing to find those who have "attended" to the higher mathematics—algebra, geometry, and the like—whose reading and writing are wretched in the extreme, and whose spelling is absolutely intolerable! They have been pursuing quadratics, but are unable to explain why they "carry one for every ten"; they have wandered among the stars in search of other worlds, by the science of astronomy, without knowing the most simple points in the geography of our own; they have studied logarithms and infinite series, but can not be safely trusted to add a column of figures or to compute the simple interest upon a common note! In short, they have *studied every thing*, except what is most useful to be known in practical life, and have really *learned—nothing!*

Now if this evil—grievous and extensive as it is at present—is destined ever to be abated, it is to be accomplished by the instrumentality of the teacher, acting in his appropriate sphere, in the capacity of a director as to the course of study for the young. He must not be a man who can merely *teach*, but one who understands the high import of a true education, and knows how to prescribe the order of its progress; one, in short, who will never attempt to erect a showy superstructure upon an insufficient foundation.

3. *Do not attempt to teach too many things.* There is a tendency at present to introduce too many things into all our schools. Nothing is more common than to hear our public lecturers declare, as they become a little enthusiastic in any given department, that "this branch should at once be made a study in our common schools."

Make no ambiguous mark upon mind.—"Mind your business."

This is heard of almost the whole round of the natural sciences. But it seems to me to be dictated by over-wrought enthusiasm. *Every thing can not be well taught in our schools;* nor should too much be attempted. It is the province of our schools—particularly our common schools—to afford *thorough instruction in a few things*, and to awaken a *desire* for more extended attainment. The instruction given should, as far as possible, be complete in itself,—while it should afford the means of making further advancement; but that instruction which being merely superficial, neither itself informs the mind nor imparts the desire and the means of future self-improvement, is worse than useless; it is positively injurious. A few branches thoroughly *possessed* are worth more than a thousand merely glanced at,—and the idea of changing our common schools to universities, where our children, before they pass from the years of their babyhood, are to grasp the whole range of the sciences, is one of the most preposterous that has grown up even in this age of follies. The teacher, then, should not undertake too much; he should be sure that he can accomplish what he undertakes. *The mark he makes upon the young should be no uncertain sign.*

4. *Never attend to extraneous business in school hours.* This is a common fault. Many teachers neglect their duties in school to write letters, or transact such other business as should

be done at home. This is always wrong. There is no time for it in any school; for a diligent teacher can always find full employment even with a small number. Besides, he has *engaged* to devote himself to the school; and any departure from this is a violation of his contract. The children will so view it, and thus lose much of their respect for the teacher. Moreover, if they see him neglect his business for some other, they will be very likely to neglect theirs, and thus disorder will be introduced. I hold that the teacher is bound to devote *every moment of school hours to active labor for the school.*

5. *Avoid making excuses to visitors for the defects of your school.* Franklin, I think, said that "a man who is good for making excuses, is good for nothing else." I have often thought of this as I have visited the schools of persons given to this failing. It is sometimes quite amusing to hear such a teacher keep up a sort of *running* apology for the various pupils. A class is called to read. The teacher remarks, "This class have but just commenced reading in this book." Stephen finishes the first paragraph, and the teacher adds, "Stephen has not attended school very regularly lately." William reads the second. "This boy," says the teacher, "was very backward when I came here—he has but just joined this class." Charles executes the third. "That boy has an impediment in his speech." Reuben follows. "It is almost impossible to make a good reader of

Pity excited.—"When *I came here.*"

Reuben; he never seems to pay the least attention. I have bestowed unwearied pains upon him." Mary takes her turn. "This girl has lost her book, and her father refuses to buy her another." Mary here blushes to the eyes,— for though she could bear his reproof, she still has some sense of family pride; she bursts into tears, while Martha reads the next paragraph. "I have tried all along," says the teacher, "to make this girl raise her voice, but still she will almost stifle her words." Martha looks dejected, and the next in order makes an attempt.

Now, the teacher in all this has no malicious design to wound the feelings of every child in the class,—and yet he as effectually accomplishes that result as if he had premeditated it. Every scholar is interested to read as well as possible in the presence of strangers; every one makes the effort to do so; yet every one is practically pronounced to have failed. The visitors pity the poor pupils for the pain they are made thus needlessly to suffer, and they *pity also the weakness of the poor teacher*, whose love of approbation has so blinded his own perception that he is regardless of the feelings of others, and thinks of nothing but his own.

This over-anxiety for the good opinion of others shows itself in a still less amiable light, when the teacher frequently makes unfavorable allusions to his predecessor. "When *I came here*," says the teacher, significantly, "I found them all poor readers." Or, if a little disorder occurs in school, he takes care to add, "I *found* the school in perfect confusion,"—or, "the former teacher, as near as I can learn, used to allow the children to talk and play as much as they pleased." Now, whatever view we take of such a course, it is impossible to pronounce it any thing better than *despicable meanness*. For if the charge is true, it is by no means magnanimous to publish the faults of another; and if it is untrue in whole or in part, as most likely it is, none but a contemptible person would magnify another's failings to mitigate his own.

There is still another way in which this love of personal applause exhibits itself. I have seen teachers call upon their brightest scholars to recite, and then ask them to *tell their age*, in order to remind the visitor that they were very young to do so well; and then insinuate that their older pupils could of course do much better.

All these arts, however, recoil upon the teacher who uses them. A visitor of any discernment sees through them at once, and immediately suspects the teacher of conscious incompetency or willful deception. The pupils lose their respect for a man whom they all perceive to be acting a dishonorable part. I repeat, then, *never attempt to cover the defects of your schools by making ridiculous excuses*.

6. *Never compare one child with another.* It is a poor way of stimulating a dull pupil to com-

pare him with a better scholar. It is the direct way to engender hatred in the mind of the one, and the most consummate self-complacency in the other. Not one child in a thousand can be publicly held up to the school as a pattern of excellence, without becoming excessively vain; at the same time, all the other scholars will be more or less excited to envy. Such a course is always unsafe; almost always injurious.

7. *Avoid wounding the sensibilities of a dull child.* There will always be those in every school who are slow to comprehend. After their classmates have grasped an idea during the teacher's explanation, they still have the vacant stare, the unintelligent expression. This may be so after a second or a third explanation. The teacher is now strongly tempted to indulge in expressions of impatience, if not of opprobrium. This temptation he should resist. Such children are to be pitied for their dullness; but never to be censured for it. It is an unfeeling thing to sting the soul that is already benighted. He should cheer and encourage such a slow mind to greater effort, by the sunshine of kind looks and the warm breath of sympathy, rather than freeze up the feeble current of vivacity which yet remains there by a forbidding frown or a blast of reproach. A dull child is almost always affectionate; and it is through the medium of kindness and patience that such a one is most effectually stimulated.

8. *Never lose your patience when parents*

unreasonably interfere with your plans. It must be expected that some of the parents will wish to dictate to the teacher what course he shall pursue, at least in relation to their own children. This will sometimes bring them to the school-room, perhaps in a tone of complaint, to set the teacher right. Whenever a parent thus steps beyond the bounds of propriety, the teacher should never lose his self-possession. He should always speak the language of courtesy, in frankness, but in firmness. He should reason with the parent, and if possible convince him,—but he should never insult nor abuse him. It may be well to propose to see him at his own house, in order to talk over the matter more at his leisure. I recollect once a parent sent a hasty refusal to purchase a necessary book for his son,—a refusal clothed in no very respectful language. I gave the lad a courteous note directed to his father, in which I intimated my desire to have an interview with him at his house at such time as he might appoint. In half an hour the boy came bounding back with the desired book, informing me that his father said, "he guessed he might as well get the book, and done with it." My intercourse with that parent was ever afterward of the most pleasant kind. A supercilious parent can never gain an advantage over a teacher, unless he can first provoke him to impatience or anger. As long as the teacher is perfectly self-possessed he is impregnable.

The study of the Bible.—Ride no hobbies in teaching.

9. *Never make the study of the Bible a punishment.* I have known a teacher to assign sundry passages of the Bible, condemnatory of a particular sin, to be committed to memory as a punishment. I have also known the idle scholar to be detained after school to study passages of Scripture, because he had failed to learn his other lessons in due time. I believe this to be bad policy, as well as doubtful religion. The lessons that a child thus learns are always connected, in his mind, with unpleasant associations. His heart is not made better by truths thus learned. The Bible, indeed, should be studied by the young; but they should be *attracted* to it by the spirit of love, rather than *driven* to it by the spirit of vindictiveness. They who suppose that children can be made to love the Bible by being thus driven to the study of it, have sadly mistaken the human heart.

10. *Ride no "hobbies" in teaching.* Almost every man, in whatever vocation, has some *hobby*, some "*one idea*," which he pushes forward on all occasions, no matter what may be the consequences. It is not strange that it is often thus with the teacher. If the teacher has any independence of mind, any originality, he will, at some period in life, naturally incline to try some experiments in teaching. Partly on account of the novelty of the plan, and partly on account of the teacher's interest in the success of his own measure, he finds it works well in the class

A discovery becomes a hobby.—Oral instruction.

where it was first tried; and he rejoices that he has made a *discovery*. Teaching now possesses a new interest for him, and he very likely becomes enthusiastic. He applies his new measure to other classes and loudly recommends it to other teachers. For a time it succeeds, and it becomes his *hobby*. Whenever a stranger visits his school, he shows off his new measure. Whenever he attends a teachers' meeting, he describes it, and perhaps presents a class of his pupils to verify its excellence. He abandons his old and long-tried plans, and persists in the new one. By and by the novelty has worn away, and his pupils become dull under its operation, and reason suggests that a return to the former methods would be advisable. Still, because it is *his invention*, he persists. Others try the experiment. Some succeed; some fail. Some of them by a public speech commit themselves to it, and then persist in it to preserve their consistency. In this way a great many objectionable modes of teaching have gained currency and still hold their sway in many of our schools.

Among these I might mention *concert recitation*, and *oral instruction* when made a substitute for study. Of the origin and tendency of the former, I have spoken more at length in the chapter on "Conducting Recitations." Of the latter, a word or two may be said in this place.

It was found years ago, in the earlier attempts to teach the blind, that they made very

MISCELLANEOUS SUGGESTIONS. 357

Origin of the *oral mania*.—Baby-talk!—Great learning!

rapid strides in acquiring knowledge through the sole medium of oral instruction. As might have been foreseen, they became intensely interested in hearing about things which had surrounded them all their days, but which they had never seen. Shut in as they were from the privilege of sight, there was nothing to distract their attention from whatever was communicated to them through the sense of hearing; and as they had been blind from their birth, this discipline of attention had been going on from infancy. Under these circumstances, their progress in knowledge by mere oral teaching was astonishing. This was all well. But soon, some one conceived the idea of substituting oral instruction for study among *seeing* children. Immediately there was an *oral mania*. Infant schools grew up in every village,—infant school manuals were prepared, filled with *scientific baby-talk*, for the use of the worthy dames who were to drive the *hobby*, and the nineteenth century bade fair to do more toward lighting up the fires of science than all time before had accomplished! It was truly wonderful, for a time, to listen to the learned volubility of these same infant schools. The wonders of astronomy, chemistry, botany, and zoology, with the terms of Cuvier's classification, and a thousand other things, were all detailed with astonishing familiarity by *pupils* under five years of age! Some eminent teachers sagely took the hint and adopted the oral system with their older classes. The sciences were taught by lectures. The pupils of this happy day had nothing to do but to *sit* and *receive*. To be sure, sometimes, they would become inattentive, and it would be discovered by their teachers that they did not retain *quite all* that was told to them. This, however, was no fault of the system, it was urged; the system was well enough, but unfortunately, the pupils had eyes, and their attention was frequently diverted by the unlucky use of these worthless organs. A royal road, sure enough, was found to the temple of science, too long beyond mortal reach, by reason of the rugged footpath over which the student was compelled to climb. Happy, glorious day! No more must toil and thought be the price of success! No more must the midnight oil be consumed, and the brain be puzzled, in search of the wisdom of ages! No more must the eyes be pained—(they are hereafter to be considered encumbrances)—in searching the classic page; the ear is to be the easy inlet to the soul. * * *

Such was the *hobby* of 1829 to 1831 in our own country. During sixteen years past, those babes of the infant schools have grown into "young men and maidens," in no way distinguished, after all, unless they have since achieved distinction by actual study. The pupils of those

God wiser than men.—Other hobbies.—Patent methods.

higher schools have obtained whatever they now value in their education, mainly by the *use of their eyes*, notwithstanding at one time their worthy guides would have almost deemed it a blessing to have had their eyes put out. It has been found that God was indeed wise in the bestowment of sight,—and some, at least, have acknowledged that a method that is well suited to the instruction of those who are blind, because it is the only possible one for them, may not be the best for those who can see. At the present time, the sentiment begins to prevail, that oral instruction can never supply the place of study; that the lecturing, or "pouring-in process," can not long secure the attention; that the mind, by merely *receiving*, gains no vigor of its own; and that scholars must be made, if made at all, mainly by their own exertions in the use of books.

It would be easy to mention other examples of *hobbies* which have been ridden by teachers very much to the injury of their schools. Those already given may, however, suffice for the purpose of illustration. Let it be remembered, then, that no one method of instruction comprises all the excellences and avoids all the defects of good teaching; and that he is the wisest teacher who introduces a judicious variety into his modes of instruction, profiting by the suggestions of others, but relying mainly upon his own careful observation, eschewing all "patent methods," and *never losing his* COMMON SENSE.

Higher branches.—Things to be done.—The scholars' friend.

Under the head of *hobbies*, I may add one other remark. Many teachers have some *favorite branch of study*, in which, because they excel, they take special delight. One man is a good mathematician, another an expert accountant, a third a skillful grammarian. Now the danger is, that the favorite branch of study may become the *hobby*,—and that the other branches will be neglected. This is, indeed, not unfrequently the case.

Again, some teachers are more interested in the *higher branches* generally, because they were the last pursued in their college course, or for some other reason. They therefore neglect the lower studies, to the great detriment of the youth under their charge. Against all such partial views, the teacher should take great pains to guard himself. He may fall unconsciously and almost imperceptibly into some of these errors. Let me add the caution, then,—*never allow your partiality for one study, or a class of studies, to divert your attention from all those other branches which are necessary to constitute a good education.*

It is surely to the discredit of teachers that they are so readily "tossed to and fro, and carried about with every wind of doctrine, by the slight of men, and cunning craftiness." Growth or evolution is entirely consistent with moderation and stability. To know what we should grow into, we must trace our route into the

Spasmodic efforts at reform.—Their results.

future by the light of educational science, and that there may be perfect continuity of growth, we must know the past and the present of education. We will gain sureness and stability in the formation of our opinions by recollecting that a course of practice that has had the long sanction of the wise and the good is likely to have a large measure of truth in it; and that "the suppression of every error is commonly followed by a temporary ascendency of the contrary one." (*Spencer.*) Every decade has its educational epidemic made possible by shallow thinking and a chronic discontent with things as they are. These spasmodic efforts at reform are the source of some good and much evil. They call attention to imperfections; but by a gross exaggeration of defects they destroy public faith in what is good, and by the show of false lights betray the cause of substantial progress. "Progress," says the *Dictionnaire de Pédagogie*, "is not a force that acts spasmodically, but is a logical and graduated evolution, in which the idea of to-day is connected with that of yesterday, as the latter is to a still more remote past."

SECTION II.—THINGS TO BE PERFORMED.

I. *Convince your scholars by your conduct that you are their friend.* It is all-important that you should gain complete ascendency over the minds of your pupils. In no way is this point so successfully gained as by leading them to feel that you are their true friend. When they feel this, all their sentiments of generosity, gratitude, and love, conspire to lead them to render cheerful obedience to your wishes. Government then becomes easy; instruction is no longer irksome; and you can most cordially respond to the poet, in that beautiful sentiment too seldom fully realized:—

> "Delightful task! to rear the tender thought,
> And teach the young idea how to shoot,
> To pour the fresh instruction o'er the mind,
> To breathe the enlivening spirit, and to fix
> The generous purpose in the glowing breast."

But effectually to convince them that you are thus their friend, is not the work of a moment. Words alone can never do it. You may make professions of interest in them, but it is all to no purpose. Your actions, your looks, your whole spirit must show it. In order thus to exhibit it, you must *feel* a deep, an all-pervading interest in the welfare of every child. You must love your profession, and you must love—sincerely love—those whom you are called to teach. If you do not love the work of teaching, and can not bring yourself to love the children of your charge, you may not expect success. It was long ago declared that

> "Love only is the loan for love,"—

and this is specially true with the love of children. Their souls spontaneously go out after those who love them. Strive, then, to gain this point with them, not by empty pretensions, always quickly read and as quickly despised by the young; but by that full, frank, cordial expression of kindness in your manner toward them, which, being based upon deep principle in yourself, is sure at once to win their affection, and their ready compliance with all your reasonable requisitions.

II. *Take special care that the school-house and its appendages are kept in good order.* This is a part of every teacher's duty. He should have an eye that is constantly on the alert to perceive the smallest beginnings of injury to any part of the premises. It is often painful to see a new school-house, that has with much care and expense been put in perfect order, very soon cut and otherwise disfigured by the pupils,—the glass broken, the ceiling soiled, the desks and floors stained with ink, and every thing bearing the marks of youthful destructiveness. The teacher should be held accountable for such results, for he can by proper vigilance prevent them.

Some of his first lessons to his pupils should be upon the subject of practical neatness, in regard to every thing that pertains to the school. They should be impressed with the belief that he holds neatness as a cardinal virtue. Daily should he watch to discover the first violation of propriety upon the premises. This first violation should be promptly met. There is great wisdom in the adage which enjoins us to "*resist the beginnings.*"

So, too, he should exercise an oversight of the books belonging to the pupils. Many books are speedily destroyed by children for the want of a little care of the teacher,—probably more than are worn out by use. He should also occasionally inspect the desks, with a view to promote a commendable neatness there. The teacher has an undoubted right to inspect any part of the premises,—but by a little adroitness he can interest the children in a reform of this kind, and then they will *desire* that he should witness their carefulness.

I may add further, that the children should not only be required to respect the school-house and its appendages, but they should also be taught to regard the sacredness of all property, either public or private. The neighboring garden or orchard should be held to be inviolable. The teacher may not have the authority to *compel* compliance with his direction or advice beyond school-hours; but he should endeavor to exercise a moral influence in the school which will be more powerful even than compulsion. So in regard to public buildings, such as churches and court-houses; and all public grounds,—as parks, commons, and cemeteries,—the teacher should inculcate not only the duty to abstain from injuring them, but a commendable desire to see them improved and beautified. In America, it is

American destructiveness.—General reformation.—Illustration.

remarked by foreigners, there is a strange tendency to destructiveness. In our public buildings the walls are usually disfigured by names and drawings; and even our cemeteries do not escape the violence of the knives of visitors, the trees being cut and marked with names, and the flowers plucked off and carried away. It is to be hoped that our teachers will so exercise a reforming influence, that the next generation shall exercise a higher principle, as well as a better taste, in all these matters, which, small as they are, make up no mean part of the manners and morals of a people.

III. *When scholars do wrong, it is sometimes best to withhold immediate reproof, but to describe a similar case in general instruction.* This is one of the most effectual modes of curing the evil in the wrong-doer himself. It, moreover, gives the teacher a valuable text for a lesson on morals before the whole school. Care should generally be taken not to lead the school to suspect the individual in your mind, while at the same time the parable should so fit the case, as to preclude the necessity of saying to the offender, as Nathan did to David: "Thou art the man."

A case will illustrate this. I recollect once to have found, among a large number of compositions presented by a class, one that I knew to have been copied. No notice was taken of it at the time; but some days afterward, a *case* was described to the class, resembling the one that

A confession.—Accuracy.

had actually occurred. After exciting considerable interest in the case, they were told that such a thing had happened among their own number: that I did not choose to expose the individual; but, if any of them thought it would be honorable for them to confess such an offense to me in case they had committed it, they might seek a private opportunity to do so. In less than twenty-four hours no less than four made such a confession, detailing freely the extent and the circumstances of their offending. In this way four were reformed, where by direct reproof only one could have been reached. It was a frank, not a forced confession; and I was thus easily made to know the extent of this sin in the school. By this simple expedient, I have reason to believe, plagiarism was effectually eradicated, for that term at least, in the whole class, and that too without the loss of any pupil's good-will.

It is generally wiser to endeavor to reach the evil in its whole extent, than to expend one's strength upon a single instance of wrong-doing. The conscience of the whole school may sometimes be profitably aroused, while the particular individual is quite as effectively corrected as he would be by a direct reproof.

IV. *Be accurate.* This is necessary in order to secure the respect of your pupils. What the teacher professes to know he should be sure of. Approximations to the truth are not enough to satisfy the young mind. Whenever a teacher

Certain knowledge.—Prof. Olmsted.

makes a blunder by stating what is not true in regard to any fact or principle in science, any event in history, or any item of statistics, he lowers himself very much in the estimation of all those who are capable of detecting his error. If he *does not know*, he may frankly say so, and incur no just censure, provided the point be one about which he has not had the opportunity to gain the requisite information. But when he attempts to speak with the authority of a teacher, he "should know that whereof he affirms." "The character of the teacher," says Professor Olmsted, "is sullied by frequent mistakes, like that of a book-keeper or banker. It is surprising to see how soon even the youngest learner will lose his confidence and respect for his teacher, when he has detected in him occasional mistakes. At every such discovery he rises in his own estimation, and the teacher proportionally sinks. The very character of the pupil is injured by such an incident. He rapidly loses the docility and modesty so essential to the scholar, and becomes uplifted with pride and self-importance." The superciliousness thus induced in the pupils, becomes a sore vexation to the teacher. He finds that his pupils are watching for his halting,—and he frequently fails, from this very circumstance, to do as well as he might. I know of no more pitiable condition on earth than that of a teacher, who is attempting to teach what he does not fully understand, while he is conscious that his pupils doubt his ability, from a frequent detection of his mistakes.

V. *Cultivate a pleasant countenance.* Frowns and scowls always sit with ill grace upon the teacher's brow. I know that the trials and perplexities incident to his daily life are eminently fitted "to chafe his mood" and to provoke his impatience. I know, too, that protracted confinement from the pure air and the bright sunlight, will almost necessarily render the nervous system morbidly sensitive, and the temper of course extremely irritable. The outward exponent of all this is a dejected, and perhaps an angry, countenance. The eyebrows are drawn up so that the forehead is deeply and prematurely furrowed, while the angles of the mouth are suffered to drop downward, as if in token of utter despair. By and by the roguishness of some unlucky urchin disturbs the current of his thoughts,—and suddenly the brow is firmly knitted with transverse channels, the nostrils are distended, the jaws are firmly closed, the lips are compressed, the cheeks are flushed, and the eyes almost emit sparks from the pent-up fire within him. For the next half-hour he frowns on all about him. The children, at first, are awed by such a threatening aspect,— but soon they become accustomed to it, and the terrible very naturally gives place to the ridiculous.

No man has a moral right to render those uncomfortable who surround him, by habitually

Sympathy between the heart and the countenance.

covering his face with the looks of discontent and moroseness. It is peculiarly *wrong* for the teacher to do it. It is for him to present an example of self-government under all circumstances, so that he can consistently enforce the duty of self-control upon the young. It is for him to show himself a man of principle, of benevolence, of cheerful devotion to his duty, however full of trials that duty may be; and in no way can he do this more effectually than by an amiable and engaging countenance. A peevish, frowning teacher is very likely to produce petulance and sullenness in his pupils; while a cordial smile, like the genial beam of the spring-day sun, not only sheds a welcome light on all around, but it imparts a blessed heat, which penetrates the frigidity of the heart, dissipates the cheerless mists that hover there, and warms the generous affections into life and beauty.

We are so constituted that the inward and the outward sympathize with each other. Solomon says, "a merry heart maketh a cheerful countenance,"—and I may venture to add, and with almost as much truth, *a cheerful countenance maketh a merry heart*. An honest attempt to bless others with the sight of a countenance that is expressive of content and patience, is an act so praiseworthy in itself, that it will never go unrewarded. The gratifying response which such a countenance is sure to call forth from others, brings with it a rich revenue of inward enjoy-

A question.—Yes.—Carlyle.—Means recommended.

ment. He, therefore, who habitually bears about with him a sad or an angry countenance, while he constantly impairs the happiness of others, lacks at the same time an important instrumentality for securing his own.

But the question will arise,—can a man gain such ascendency over himself as to control the expression of his countenance? I answer, without hesitation, YES. "Whatever ought to be done, can be done." It is not perfectly easy to do it, especially for the teacher. Still, self-control—full, complete self-control—is his appropriate duty as well as privilege. He must, as Carlyle quaintly enjoins, "learn to devour the chagrins of his lot." He must calculate beforehand that every day will bring its cares and its trials; but he should daily resolve that they shall never take him by surprise, nor betray him into sudden impatience. Each morning, as he walks to the scene of his labors, he should fortify himself against sudden anger or habitual moroseness on this wise: "No doubt this day some untoward occurrence will transpire, calculated to try my patience and to provoke me to fretful words and angry looks. All my past experience leads me to expect this. But this day I will try to resist the temptation to this weakness. I will try to be self-possessed. If any child is vicious, or fretful, or dull, or even impudent, I will endeavor to show that I can command myself. If I feel some angry passion enkindling within me, I will stop and *think*, and I will *en-*

deavor to *smile* before I speak. If I can to-day gain the victory over impatience, and can maintain an even and cheerful temper, and express it constantly in my countenance, it will be easier to do it to-morrow. *At all events, I'll try.*"

Taking hold thus in earnest, any man may soon be his own master. *He can gain the victory.* If he *can* do it, he ought to do it. Hence I urge it as a duty. Nor is it merely a duty. It is a high privilege. A complete victory for a single day will bring its own reward. A man who feels that he has risen above his temptation, can return to his rest with a light and happy heart. Sleep to him will be sweet, and he will arise on the morrow with renewed strength for the fresh conflict,—and in the moral as well as in the literal warfare, every contest which ends in victory gives additional strength to the victor, while it weakens and disheartens his enemy.

VI. *Study to acquire the art of aptly illustrating a difficult subject.* Some teachers content themselves with answering in the precise language of the book, whenever a question for information is propounded. This, however, is by no means sufficient, even when the language of the book is strictly accurate; much less, when the language is so vague as to convey no definite idea to the mind, either of the learner or the teacher. On the other hand, a man who is apt to teach, will devise some ingenious method of enlightening the mind of his pupil, so that he shall lay hold of the idea as with a manly grasp, and make it his own forever.

This point will, perhaps, be best illustrated by an example. A young man was employed to take charge of a school for a few days during a temporary illness of the regular instructor. He was a good scholar, as the world would say, and was really desirous to answer the expectation of his employers. After the regular teacher had so far recovered his health as to be able to leave his room, he walked one pleasant day to the school, to see what success attended the labors of the new incumbent. A class was reciting in natural philosophy. The subject under consideration was—the obstacles which impede the motion of machinery. The *attraction of gravity*, as one of these, was pretty easily disposed of; for the class had before been instructed on that point. *Friction* came next. Here, too, the pupils, having had some practical experience of their own, in dragging their sleds, in skating, or perhaps in turning a grindstone, found no great difficulty. The book spoke a language sufficiently clear to be understood. Next came the "resistance of the various media," to use the language of the text-book. "Yes," said the teacher, as one of the pupils gravely quoted this language, "that has no inconsiderable effect."

"The '*resistance of the various* media'?"—repeated one of the boys inquiringly, "I do not know as I understand what *media* means."

A puzzle.—Further doubts.—An interposition.

"A medium is that in which a body moves," was the ready reply which the teacher read from the book.

Pupil. A *medium?*

Teacher. Yes; we say *medium* when we mean but one, and *media* when we mean more than one.

Pupil. When we mean but one?

Teacher. Yes; *medium* is singular—*media* is plural.

After this discussion, which began in philosophy but ended in grammar, the teacher was about to proceed to the next question of the book. But the scholar was not yet satisfied, and he ventured to press his inquiries a little further.

Pupil. Is this room a medium?

Teacher. This room?

Pupil. Yes, sir; you said that a medium was "that in which anybody moves," and we all move in this room.

Teacher. Yes, but medium does not mean a room; it is the *substance* in which a body moves.

Here the lad looked perplexed and unsatisfied. He had no clear idea of the meaning of this new term. The teacher looked at his watch, and then glanced at the remaining pages of the lesson, and seemed impatient to proceed,—so the pupil forbore to inquire further.

The regular teacher, who had listened to the discussion with no ordinary interest, both because

A smile.—Light breaks in.

he admired the inquisitiveness of the boy, and because he was curious to discover how far the new incumbent possessed the power of illustration, here interposed.

"John,"—taking his watch in his hand—"would this watch continue to go, if I should drop it into a pail of water?"

"I should think it would not long," said John, after a little reflection.

"Why not?" said his teacher, as he opened his watch.

"Because the water would get around the wheels of the watch and stop it, I should think," said John.

"How would it be if I should drop it into a quart of molasses?"

The boys laughed.

"Or into a barrel of tar?"

The boys still smiled.

"Suppose I should force it, while open, into a quantity of lard."

Here the boys laughed heartily, while John said, "the watch would not go in any of these articles."

"*Articles?*" said his teacher, "why not say *media?*"

John's eye glistened as he caught the idea. "O, I understand it now."

His teacher then said, that many machines worked in air,—then the air was the medium. A fish swims in water,—water is his medium.

A fish could hardly swim in molasses or tar. 'Now,' inquired he, "why not?"

"Because of the resistance of the medium," said John, with a look of satisfaction.

"Now why will the watch go in air and not in water?"

"Because the water is more dense," said John promptly.

"Then upon what does the resistance of a medium depend?"

Here the new teacher interposed, and said that was the next question in the book, and he was just going to ask it himself. The regular teacher put his watch into his pocket and became a spectator again, and the lesson proceeded with unwonted vivacity. The difference between these two teachers mainly consisted in the fact, that one had the ingenuity to devise an expedient to meet a difficulty whenever occasion required,— the other had not.

Now in order to teach well, a man should diligently seek for expedients. He should endeavor to foresee the very points where the learner will stumble, and provide himself with the means of rendering timely aid. If an object can not be described in words, let it be compared with what it resembles, or with what it contrasts. If it be an object of sense, and words and comparisons fail to describe it,—in the absence of apparatus to represent it, let the teacher spring to the blackboard and execute a hasty drawing

A moral impression.—Set lessons not useful.—The fit occasion.

of it. In this way the construction or the working of a machine, the form of a bone or the action of a joint, the shape of a town or the plan of a building,—in short, almost every subject that involves the relation of form, size, proportion, quantity, or number, will admit of visible illustration. He, then, is the successful teacher who is able at the moment to seize upon the best expedient, and render it subservient to his purpose.

VII. *Take advantage of unusual occurrences to make a moral or religious impression.* In a former chapter I have urged it as a part of the teacher's work, to cultivate and strengthen both the moral sentiments and the religious feelings of the members of his school. This is not most effectually done by a formal mode of speaking to them on these subjects. If a particular hour is set apart for formal lectures on their duty to their fellow-men and their obligations to God, they are very apt to fortify their sensibilities against the most faithful appeals, and thus render them powerless. The wise teacher will watch for the fit opportunity, and, just at the moment when the heart is prepared by some suitable occurrence,—when by some exhibition of the Creator's power it is awed into reverence, or softened into submission; or by some display of his goodness it is warmed into gratitude, or animated with delight,—with a few words, seasonably and "fitly spoken," he fixes the impression

Example I.—A thunder-storm.

forever. Speaking at the right time, every ear listens, and every heart feels.

Perhaps many of my readers can revert to some season in their childhood, endeared to them by a precious recollection of golden words thus opportunely uttered,—words fraught with truth which in after-life has had an unspeakable influence in the formation of their character. One or two examples connected with my own experience may be presented, more fully to illustrate my meaning; while at the same time they may afford, it is hoped, some valuable hints for the encouragement and guidance of such young teachers, as desire in this way to make themselves the instruments of lasting benefit to the young.

EXAMPLE I. I can never forget—nor would I if I could—a lesson impressed upon my own youthful mind, conveying the truth that we are constantly dependent upon our Heavenly Father for protection. In a plain country school-house, some twenty-five children, including myself, were assembled with our teacher on the afternoon of a summer's day. We had been as happy and as thoughtless as the sportive lambs that cropped the clover of the neighboring hill-side. Engrossed with study or play,—for at this distance of time it is impossible to tell which,—we had not noticed the low rumbling of the distant thunder, till a sudden flash of lightning arrested our attention. Immediately the sun was veiled by the cloud,

Confusion.—Alarm.—Teacher's self-possession.

and a corresponding gloom settled upon every face within. The elder girls, with the characteristic thoughtfulness of woman, hastily inquired whether they should not make the attempt to lead their younger brothers and sisters to the paternal roof before the bursting of the storm. For a moment our little community was thrown into utter confusion. The teacher stepped hastily to the door, to survey more perfectly the aspect of the western heavens. Immediately returning, he signified to the children that there would not be time for them to reach their homes before the tempest would be upon them. Oppressed with dread,—for it is no uncommon thing for children in the country to be terrified by lightning,—some of the youngest of us clung to our older brothers or sisters, while others, being the sole representatives of their family in the school, for the first time felt their utter loneliness in the midst of strangers, and gave utterance to their feelings in audible sighs or unequivocal sobs.

The teacher, meanwhile, with an exemplary calmness and self-possession, closed the windows and the doors, and then seated himself quite near the younger pupils, to await the result. The thick darkness gathered about us, as if to make the glare of the lightning, by contrast, more startling to our vision; while the loud thunder almost instantly followed, as it were the voice of God. The wind howled through the branches of a venerable tree near by, bending its sturdy trunk, and

A fearful tempest.—Awful pause.—Teacher's words.

threatening to break asunder the cords which bound it to its mother earth. An angry gust assailed the humble building where we were sheltered; it roared down the capacious chimney, violently closed a shutter that lacked a fastening, breaking the glass by its concussion, and almost forced in the frail window-sashes on the westerly side of the room. Quicker and more wild the lightnings glared—flash after flash—as if the heavens were on fire; louder and nearer the thunder broke above our heads, while the inmates of the room, save the teacher, were pale with terror.

At this moment there was a sudden cessation of the war of elements,—a hush—almost a *prophetic* pause! It was that brief interval which precedes the falling torrent. A dread stillness reigned within the room. Every heart beat hurriedly, and every countenance told the consternation that was reigning within. It was an awful moment!

With a calm voice, breathing a subdued and confiding spirit, the teacher improved this opportunity to impress upon our young minds a great truth. "Fear not, children," said he, "it is your Heavenly Father that sends the storm as well as the sunshine and the gentle breeze. You have been just as much in his power all day, as you are at this moment. He has been as near you, supporting you, supplying you with breath, with life, all through the pleasant morning; but then you did not see him. He is just as able to protect you now, for 'not a sparrow falls to the ground without his notice,'—and he ruleth the storm and 'rideth upon the wings of the wind.' We should ever feel willing to trust him; for he is ever able to grant us deliverance from all dangers which threaten us. God is here now to protect us."

Just as he had finished these words the rain began to fall. First the drops were few and scattered; but soon the windows of heaven were opened, and the thirsty ground was abundantly satisfied. The sound of the thunder became fainter and fainter as the cloud passed away; the sun burst out again in renewed splendor; the full drops glittered in his beams upon the grass; the birds began their songs; the rainbow spanned the eastern hills; and our hearts, taught by the timely instructions of a good man, began to expand with eager gratitude for our preservation by the hand of our Heavenly Father.

The remainder of the afternoon passed happily away; and when our books were laid aside, and we were ready to burst out of the room to enjoy the refreshing air and participate in the general joy, the teacher, taking the Bible from the desk, asked us to remain quiet a moment, while he would read a few words that he hoped we should never forget.

The passage was the following, from the 65th Psalm :—

MISCELLANEOUS SUGGESTIONS.

The Bible speaks.—Words fitly spoken.—The effect.

By terrible things in righteousness wilt thou answer us, O God of our salvation; who art the confidence of all the ends of the earth, and of them that are afar off upon the sea. Which by his strength setteth fast the mountains; being girded with power: which stilleth the noise of the seas, the noise of their waves, and the tumult of the people.

They also that dwell in the uttermost parts are afraid at thy tokens: thou makest the outgoings of the morning and evening to rejoice.

Thou visitest the earth and waterest it: thou greatly enrichest it with the river of God, which is full of water: thou preparest them corn, when thou hast so provided for it.

Thou waterest the ridges thereof abundantly: thou settlest the furrows thereof: thou makest it soft with showers: thou blessest the springing thereof.

Thou crownest the year with thy goodness; and thy paths drop fatness. They drop upon the pastures of the wilderness: and the little hills rejoice on every side.

The pastures are clothed with flocks; the valleys also are covered over with corn; they shout for joy, they also sing.

After closing the book, the teacher said, "Go out now, children, and witness how perfectly these words have been fulfilled toward us this afternoon,—and from this day's mercies, learn hereafter to trust God as confidently in the storm, when he displays his power by his outward 'tokens,' as when he kindly smiles upon you in the beams of the glorious sun, or gently breathes upon you in the morning breeze."

We went forth bounding in gladness and gratitude, and saw the "outgoings of the evening to rejoice,"—"the pastures clothed with flocks,"—"the valleys covered over with corn,"—"the little hills rejoicing on every side";—we heard also the general shout for joy,—and we felt as we never before had felt, a deep, thorough, abiding conviction of the truth that God is our father and our friend; the GOD OF OUR SAL-VATION.

I know not how soon these impressions faded from the minds of the other children,—but for myself I can say, that from that time to the present, whenever I have been exposed to apparent danger from the impending tempest, the warring elements, or the ravages of disease, the teachings of that hour have always revived in my mind to soothe my troubled spirit, and to re-assure my faith and confidence in the presence of an all-sufficient and merciful Preserver. A thousand times have I devoutly blessed the memory of that faithful teacher, for having so early and so happily turned my thoughts upward to HIM, in whom "we live, and move, and have our being."

EXAMPLE II. It was in the afternoon of a gloomy day in the latter part of November, when the pupils, consisting of some fifty boys, belonging to a school in a pleasant sea-port town in New England, were told by their teacher, a few minutes before the usual hour, that they might lay aside their studies, and prepare for dismission. During the early part of the day there had been one of those violent south-east rain storms, so common upon the sea-coast at that season of the year. It is well known to the observing mariner, that a storm from the south-east never continues beyond twelve or fifteen

Lull of the storm.—Change of wind.—Early dismission.

hours; and when the violence of the storm abates, it is a common remark of the sailor, that "the north-wester is not long *in debt* to the south-easter." Previous to this change of wind, however, there is what is expressively termed the "*lull of the storm*,"—a period when the rain ceases to fall, the wind dies away to a perfect calm, the barometer is suddenly depressed, the clouds hover almost upon the face of the earth, shutting out the light of the sun, and causing a cheerless damp to settle upon every thing terrestrial, and a dreary gloom to enshroud the mind itself. When the wind changes, these clouds are not gradually dissolved and broken up, so that the eye can catch transient glimpses of the blue sky beyond, as after a snow-storm in winter; but the dark drapery is suddenly lifted up, as if by an unseen hand, and the western sky, from the horizon upward, is left more bright and more charming than ever, to refresh the eye and reanimate the soul.

It was such a day, as before remarked, when the pupils of this school—partly because of the darkness in the school-room, and partly because of their protracted confinement within a close apartment during a gloomy afternoon—were, a little earlier than usual, about to be dismissed. The pupils all seemed to welcome the happy release that awaited them,—and in their eagerness to escape from confinement, they very naturally neglected to observe their accustomed regard

Impatience.—Light breaks in.—The "garment of praise."—Song.

for quiet and order in laying aside their books. It was, however, a fixed habit with the teacher, never to give the signal for leaving the room till all the pupils had taken the proper attitude for passing out with regularity, and then had composed themselves to perfect silence. On this occasion, perhaps two minutes passed away while the boys were gradually, almost impatiently, bringing themselves to a compliance with this rule of the teacher.

During this interval of waiting, the cloud, unperceived by the teacher, had been slowly raised up from the western horizon, just in time to allow the setting sun to bestow a farewell glance upon the sorrowing world at his leave-taking. Through the Venetian blinds that guarded the windows toward the west, the celestial light gleamed athwart the apartment, and painted the opposite wall, in front of the pupils, with streaks of burnished gold! In an instant every countenance was changed. A smile now joyously played, where before sadness and discontent had held their moody reign. The teacher was reminded, by all these circumstances, of the beautiful language of the prophet, which promised the gift of "the *garment of praise* for the *spirit of heaviness.*" What could be more appropriate on this occasion than a song of *praise?* Without speaking a single word, the teacher commenced one of the little songs already familiar to the whole school :—

Singing with the spirit.—An impression.—*God is good.*

> Lo, the heavens are breaking,
> Pure and bright above;
> Life and light awaking,
> Murmur—*God is love.*
> GOD IS LOVE.
>
> Round yon pine-clad mountain,
> Flows a golden flood;
> Hear the sparkling fountain
> Whisper—*God is good.*
> GOD IS GOOD.
>
> Wake, my heart, and springing,
> Spread thy wings above,—
> Soaring still and singing,
> *God is ever good.*
> GOD IS GOOD.

Instantly every voice that had ever sung, now uttered heartfelt praise. The attendant circumstances, taken at the happy moment, furnished such an impressive commentary upon the import of the words, that they were felt, as they never before had been felt, to be the words of precious truth. Every heart throbbed in unison with the sentiment. At the close of the song, there was profound silence in the room. After a moment's pause, during which the truth that *God is good* seemed to pervade each mind and hold it in silent reverence,—the signal for departure was given. One after another the boys passed from their seats with a light and careful step, as if noise and haste would be a desecration both of the time and place,—and when they reached the open air, refreshing and exhilarating as it was, there was no boisterous shout, no rude mirth; each took his homeward course, apparently with a new and lively conviction that GOD IS GOOD.

Other occasions.

It has always been a source of pleasure to that teacher to recall from the "buried past" the associations connected with that delightful hour and that charming song; and it has been among the most gratifying incidents of his experience as a teacher, to hear more than one of those pupils in later life recur to the memory of that day, and acknowledge with thankfulness the lasting impressions which then and there were made upon their minds.

It would be easy to furnish examples to almost any extent, of the manner in which this principle has been, or may be carried out in practice. The degradation of an intoxicated person who may pass the school,—the pitiable condition of the man who may wander through the streets bereft of his reason,—any instance of sudden death in the neighborhood, particularly of a young person,—the passing of a funeral procession,—in short, any occurrence that arrests the attention of the young and enlists their feeling, may be seized upon as the means of making upon their minds an impression for good. The facts developed in many of their lessons, too, afford opportunities for incidental moral instruction. The adaptation of means to ends,—the evidence of design and intelligence displayed in the works of creation,—the existence of constant and uniform laws as developed in the sciences,

Teacher's satisfaction.—Pleasant retrospection.

all furnish the means of leading the young mind to God.

That teacher will enjoy the richest satisfaction in the evening of life, who, in looking back upon his past experience, shall be conscious that he has improved every opportunity which God has given him, to turn the youthful affections away from the things of earth to seek a worthier object in things above.

CHAPTER XVI.

THE REWARDS OF THE TEACHER.

IT is proverbial that the *pecuniary* compensation of the teacher is, in most places, far below the proper standard. It is very much to be regretted that an employment so important in all its bearings, should be so poorly rewarded. In New England there are many young women who, having spent some time in teaching, have left that occupation to go into the large manufacturing establishments as laborers, simply because they could receive a higher compensation. I have known several instances in which young ladies, in humble circumstances, have left teaching to become domestics, thus performing the most ordinary manual labor, because they could receive better pay; that is, the farmers and mechanics of the district could afford to pay more liberally for washing and ironing, for making butter and cheese, for sweeping floors and cleaning paint, than they could for educating the immortal minds of their children!

Nor is this confined to the female sex. Young mechanics and farmers, as well as those employed in manufacturing, frequently receive higher wages than the common-school teacher in the same dis-

Driving pegs.—Injustice.—Extra expense.

trict. Many a young man who has only genius enough to drive the pegs of a shoe in a regular row, and skill enough to black the surface of the article when it is completed, having spent but a few weeks in learning his trade, receives more money for his work than he who, after having spent months, or even years, in gaining the requisite qualifications, labors to polish that nobler material, the human soul.

The injustice of this becomes more apparent when we bear in mind that public opinion demands, and justly too, that the teacher should be not only gentlemanly in his manners, but better clad than the mere laborer,—thus throwing upon him a greater burden without affording him the means of sustaining it. The female teacher of a district school, in order to be respectable, must be much more expensively dressed than the domestic in the family where she boards, and is thus compelled to consume most of her receipts upon her wardrobe,—while the domestic is able to place surplus money at interest in the Savings Bank. This injustice has so often been laid before the people, and yet has been so long continued, that many have given up in despair, and abandoned an employment that has yielded so little, choosing rather to engage in that lower service which is so much better paid.

This sufficiently explains why so many unqualified teachers have been found in our common schools. Men of talents and ability being

Living by wits.—Improvement.—Means of mental growth.

tempted to other employments, have left the field unoccupied; and those men who have failed to gain a comfortable living by their hands, have been allowed to try the experiment of supporting life *by their wits*,—that is, by becoming teachers!

Such has been the case for a long time past; and, though in many quarters the people are beginning to open their eyes to their true interest, and are gradually and commendably coming up to their duty, yet, for some time to come, the pecuniary compensation will not constitute the chief reward of the teacher. If he will go cheerfully to his work, and find his daily enjoyment in his daily toil, he must have a higher object, some more elevating, inspiring motive, than mere money-getting. The chief encouragements of the faithful teacher lie in another direction.

It is the object of the following paragraphs to point out some of these encouragements; for, having in the preceding pages required very much at his hands, I feel that it is but just that he should be invited to look at the brighter side of the picture, so that when he is ready to sink under the responsibilities of his position, or to yield to the obstacles that oppose his progress, he may have something to animate his soul, and to nerve him anew for the noble conflict.

I. *The teacher's employment affords the means of intellectual growth.* If a man teaches as he should teach, he must of necessity improve him-

Means of moral growth.—Illustrated.

self. Teaching, understandingly pursued, gives accuracy. I know it is possible for a man to be a mere school-master—a *pedagogue*, without any self-improvement. But I am speaking of the faithful, devoted teacher,—the man who studies, reflects, invents. Such a man learns more than his pupils. Every time he takes a class through any branch of study, he does it more skillfully, more thoroughly than before. He brings some fresh illustration of it, presents some new view of it, and hence takes a lively interest in it himself, and awakens a new zeal among his pupils. Measuring himself by his new success, he feels a *consciousness* of growth, of progress. This consciousness is a precious reward.

II. *The teacher's employment affords the means of moral growth.* Brought constantly in contact with those who need a careful guidance, he feels impelled to earnest effort in order to obtain the mastery over himself, as the best means of gaining complete influence over others. Studying the weak points in their character, he is constantly reminded of those in his own; and self-knowledge is the first step toward self-improvement. Beginning in the feebleness of inexperience, he bolsters up his authority at first by a frequent resort to force; but, as he goes on, he finds himself gradually gaining such ascendency over the vicious as to control them quite as effectually by milder means. At first, easily excited to anger or impatience, he frequently in-

Moral power.—Progress in the art of teaching.

dulged in severe language when it was unnecessary,—but, by careful discipline, he has learned to "set a watch before his mouth, and to keep the door of his lips." Encouraged by one victory over himself, he is prepared for another. Having learned by self-discipline to control his outward acts, he next attempts the mastery of his thoughts. He soon finds that his moral power over others is very much increased. Somehow—though perhaps he can not yet tell the reason why—he finds he can secure obedience with half the effort formerly required,—he gains the love of his pupils more readily,—and, with the exception, now and then, of an extreme case, he finds that he excites a deeper interest than ever before in the whole round of duty among the scholars. Why is this? he asks,—and the consciousness of increased *moral power* rising up within him, is a source of the highest satisfaction. Pecuniary emolument sinks into nothing considered as a reward, when compared with a conscious victory over himself.

III. *A consciousness of improvement in the art of teaching is another reward.* Such improvement will follow as a matter of course from his self-improvement in the particulars just named. As his own mind expands, he feels a new impulse to exert himself to interest others in the subjects he teaches. He soon comes to look upon the work of instruction, not as a mere mechanical business, to be done in a formal way, but as

Pupils' growth of mind.—Immediate results.

a noble art, based upon certain great principles that are capable of being understood and applied. He employs all his ingenuity to discover the natural order of presenting truth to the mind,—to ascertain the precise degree of aid the learner needs, and the point where the teacher should stop. He studies carefully the proper motives to be presented as incentives to exertion. Interested in his labor as a great work, looking upon his influence as telling upon all future time, he devotes himself daily with new zeal, and is *rewarded* with the *consciousness of new success*.

IV. *The teacher is permitted also to witness the constant growth of mind among his pupils*. I say *constant*, because the teacher is not obliged to labor without seeing *immediate* results. The minister of religion may sometimes sow the seed of the good word, while the fruit does not appear for a long season. Sometimes a spiritual apathy prevails, so that the most faithful warnings, and the most earnest appeals, seem to fall powerless upon the conscience; and he is led almost to despair of ever being able to break the deathlike slumber. It is not thus with the teacher. His labor tells immediately upon the young mind. Even *while he is yet speaking*, he is gratified with observing the soul's expansion, as it grasps and assimilates some new idea which he presents. From day to day, as he meets his classes, he *sees* how they go on from strength to strength,—at first, indeed, with the halting, tottering step of the feeble babe, but soon with the firm and confident tread of the vigorous youth.

A teacher who is for several years employed in his vocation, is often astonished at the rapidity with which the young, who come to him as mere children, grow into men and women, and take their places on the stage of life as prominent actors. Some of them distinguish themselves in the arts; some become noted for their attainments in science; some receive the honors of office and become leaders in civil affairs; some gain eminence as professional men; and very likely a large portion of them are engaged in the various departments of honorable industry. Wherever they are, and whatever they are, they are now exerting a powerful influence in the community. They have grown up under his eye, and have been essentially shaped by his plastic hand. He looks upon them almost with the interest and pride of a father. He counts them as his jewels; and when he hears of their success, their usefulness, and their honors, his heart leaps within him, as he thinks, "*they were my pupils.*" Even though he may have wasted the strength of his best days in the service, *what a reward is this for the teacher!*

V. *The teacher has the consciousness of being engaged in a useful and honorable calling.* What though he may not become rich in this world's goods? Who would not prefer above houses and lands,—infinitely above all the wealth

Professor Agnew.—Educates the mind.—Trains the affections.

of earth, the consciousness of being engaged in a work of usefulness? Man was made for usefulness,—and who would not desire to answer the design of his creation?

My pen is too feeble to attempt to portray the usefulness of the faithful teacher. *He educates the immortal mind,*—wakes it to thought,—trains it to discipline—self-discipline,—moves it to truth and virtue,—fills it with longings for a more perfect state, and sends it forth to exert its power for good through all coming time! "To this end," in the glowing language of Professor Agnew, "he communicates a knowledge of letters, opens out gradually before the child the book of nature and the literature of the world; he disciplines his mind and teaches him how to gather knowledge from every source; he endeavors to impart quickness and retentiveness of memory, to cultivate a refined and well-regulated imagination, to task, and thus to give vigor to his reasoning powers. He points out the appropriate objects of the several affections, and the proper exercise of the passions; he gives lessons to conscience, derived from the pure fountain of God's own revelation, and teaches him to subject his own will to the Highest Will. He instructs him in the various sciences, and thus displays before him worlds of wondrous interest, and invests him with the sources and means of pure enjoyment. He trains him for the sweet sympathies of social life; and unfolds

The infant becomes a man.—A transit.—No limits to usefulness.

before him the high behests of duty—duty to himself, his fellow-creatures, his family, his God.

"Under such a tuition, behold the helpless infant grown to manhood's prime,—a body well developed, strong, and active; a mind symmetrically unfolded, and powers of intellection closely allied to those of the spirits in celestial spheres. He becomes a husband and a father; in these, and in all the relations of life, he performs well his part. Above all, he is a Christian, with well-trained affections and a tender conscience, supremely loving God, maintaining a constant warfare with the world, the flesh, and the devil,— growing up into the stature of a perfect man in Christ, and anticipating the fullness of joy and pleasure for evermore which are at God's right hand. The time of his departure at length arrives; he has fought the good fight, he has finished his course, and he goes to obtain his crown and to attune his harp, and forever to dwell on the hills of light and love, where angels gather immortality. O, what a transit; from the dependent helplessness of infancy to the glory of a seraph; from mind scarcely manifested, to mind ranging over the immensity of Jehovah's empire, and rising in the loftiest exercises of reason and affection! *And how much has the faithful teacher had to do in fitting him for the blissful mansions of the skies!*"

If such be the teacher's work, where is the limit to his usefulness? Yet he may do this not

Honorable.—Why?—Our great men began as teachers.

for one merely, but for scores, or even hundreds. Eternity alone can display the immeasurable, inconceivable usefulness of one devoted teacher.

And is not the teacher's calling *honorable?* It is,—for its usefulness makes it honorable. To scatter the light of truth is always honorable. So some of the greatest and best men the world ever saw have believed, and have illustrated their faith by their practice. Confucius, Socrates, Seneca, Aristotle, and Plato were specimens of the teachers of ancient date. Roger Ascham, John Milton, Francke, Pestalozzi, Arnold, and a host of others, have adorned the profession in later times. Yet these are men who have taught the world to think. Their works live after them, —and will continue to live, when the proud fame of the mighty warriors, who have marked their course in blood, shall have perished from the earth.

If it were necessary and not invidious, how many distinguished men in our own country could be mentioned, who have been teachers of the young, or who are still engaged as such. Besides those who have made teaching the business of their lives, how many have been temporarily employed in this calling. Some of our presidents, many of our governors, most of our jurists and divines,—indeed, some of every profession, "*and of the chief, women not a few*"— have first distinguished themselves as schoolteachers. Well may teachers, then, regard their profession as an honorable one; always remembering, however, that "it is not the position which makes the man honorable, but the man the position."

VI. *The teacher enjoys the grateful remembrance of his pupils and of their friends.* When a distinguished writer said, "God be thanked for the gift of mothers and school-masters," he expressed but the common sentiment of the human heart. The name of parent justly enkindles the warmest emotions in the heart of him who has gone out from his native home to engage in the busy scenes of the work-day world; and when sometimes he retires from the companionship of new-made friends to recall the picture of the past and the loved of other days,—to think

> " Of childish joys when bounding boyhood knew
> No grief, but chased the gorgeous butterfly,
> And gambol'd with the breeze, that tossed about
> His silken curls—"

how sweetly do the gentle influences of home and childhood, with all their tender and hallowed associations, come stealing over the soul! The world is forgotten; care may not intrude upon this sacred hour; objects of sense are unheeded; the call to pleasure is disregarded;—while the rapt soul introverted—transported—dwells with unspeakable delight upon its consecrated recollection of all that is venerable, all that is sacred in the name of PARENT. At this favored hour, how the heart swells at the thought of a mother's

A devoted mother.—Teacher *next* to the parent.

love! The smiles, the kind words, the sympathy, the counsels, the prayers, the tears,—how fondly the memory treasures them all up, and claims them for its own! And though Death may have long since intruded, and consigned that gentle form to the cold earth, rudely sundering the cherished bonds of affection, and leaving the hearth-stone desolate,—though Change may have brought strangers to fell the favorite tree, to remove the ancient landmarks, to lay waste the pleasant places, and even to tread thoughtlessly by the humble mound that marks the revered spot where "departed worth is laid,"—though Time, "with his effacing fingers," may have been busy in obliterating the impressions of childhood from the mind, or in burying them deeply beneath the rubbish of perplexing cares,—still the true heart never tires with the thought of a fond parent, nor ever ceases to "thank God upon every remembrance" of *a pious, devoted mother!*

Thus it should ever be. Nothing on earth should be allowed to claim the gratitude which is justly due to judicious parents. But the faithful, devoted teacher, the former of youthful character and the guide of youthful study, will be sure to have the *next* place in the grateful heart. Whether the young man treads the deck of the noble ship, in his lonely watch, as she proudly walks the waters by night,—or journeys among strangers in foreign lands;—wherever he goes, or however employed,—as often as his thoughts re-

Gratitude of parents.—Example.

visit the scenes of his childhood, and dwell with interest upon the events that marked his youthful progress, he will recur to the old familiar school-house, call up its well-remembered incidents—its joys and its sorrows—its trials and its triumphs—its all-pervading and ever-abiding influences, and devoutly thank God for the gift of a *faithful, self-denying, patient teacher.*

But the teacher is rewarded also by the gratitude of parents and friends. Some of the sweetest moments a teacher ever experiences, are those when a parent takes him by the hand, and with cordial sincerity and deep emotion, thanks him for what he has done for his child. It may have been a wayward, thoughtless, perhaps a vicious boy, whom kind words and a warm heart, on the part of the teacher, have won back to the path of rectitude and virtue.

I have seen an old lady—and I shall never forget the sight—bending under the infirmities of age,—blind, and yet dependent mainly upon her labor for support, invoking the richest of heaven's blessings upon the head of a teacher, who, by kindness and perseverance, had won back her wayward grandson to obedience and duty. How her full soul labored as she described the change that had taken place! Her emotion—too deep for utterance in words—found expression only in tears that streamed from her sightless eyes! She felt that her boy was again a child of hope and promise, and that he might yet be

Widow's gratitude.—Approval of Heaven.—The Great Teacher.

a virtuous and a useful man. The world may raise its empty acclamation to honor the man of power and of fame,—it may applaud the statesman and weave the chaplet for the conqueror's brow;— but the teacher, humble and obscure though he may be, who is the object of the widow's gratitude for being the orphan's friend, with the consciousness of deserving it, is a happier, I had almost said a *greater* man. *Surely he receives a greater reward.*

VII. *The faithful teacher enjoys the approval of Heaven.* He is employed, if he has a right spirit, in a heavenly mission. He is doing his Heavenly Father's business. That man should be made wiser and happier, is the will of Heaven. To this end, the Son of God—The Great Teacher —came to bless our race. So far as the schoolmaster has the spirit of Jesus, he is engaged in the same great work. Heaven regards with complacency the humble efforts of the faithful teacher to raise his fellow-beings from the darkness of ignorance and the slavery of superstition; and if a more glorious crown is held in reserve for one rather than another, it is for him who, uncheered by worldly applause, and without the prospect of adequate reward from his fellowmen, cheerfully practices the self-denial of his master, spending his strength, and doing with diligence and patience "whatsoever his hand findeth to do," toward raising his fellow-beings to happiness and Heaven.

Lord Brougham.—An epitaph.—Cease repining.

It is such a teacher that the eloquent and gifted Lord Brougham describes in the following beautiful language:

"He meditates and prepares, in secret, the plans which are to bless mankind; he slowly gathers around him those who are to further their execution,—he quietly, though firmly, advances in his humble path, laboring steadily, but calmly, till he has opened to the light all the recesses of ignorance, and torn up by the roots the weeds of vice. His progress is not to be compared with any thing like the march of the conqueror,—but it leads to a far more brilliant triumph and to laurels more imperishable than the destroyer of his species, the scourge of the world, ever won. Each one of these great teachers of the world, possessing his soul in peace, performs his appointed course, awaits in patience the fulfillment of the promises, and resting from his labors, bequeaths his memory to the generation whom his works have blessed, and sleeps under the humble, but not inglorious epitaph, commemorating '*one in whom mankind lost a friend, and no man got rid of an enemy.*'"

In view of what has been said, let the teacher cease to repine at his hard lot. Let him cast an occasional glance at the bright prospect before him. He deserves, to be sure, a higher pecuniary reward than he receives; and he should never cease to press this truth upon the community, till talent in teaching is as well compensated as talent in any other calling. But whether he gains this or not, let him dwell upon the privileges and rewards to be found in the calling itself, and take fresh encouragement.

The apostle Paul exhibited great wisdom when he said, "*I magnify mine office.*" If the foregoing views respecting the importance of the teacher's calling are correct, he may safely follow the apostle's example. This is not, however, to be done merely by boastful words. No man can elevate himself, or magnify his office in public estimation, by indulging in empty declamation, or by passing inflated resolutions. He must *feel* the dignity of his profession, and show that he feels it by unremitted exertions to attain to the highest excellence of which he is capable,— animated, in the midst of his toil, chiefly by the great moral recompense which every faithful teacher may hope to receive.

Let every teacher, then, study to improve himself intellectually and morally; let him strive to advance in the art of teaching; let him watch the growth of mind under his culture and take the encouragement which that affords; let him consider the usefulness he may effect, and the circumstances which make his calling honorable; let him prize the gratitude of his pupils, and of their parents and friends; and above all, let him value the approval of Heaven, and set a proper estimate upon the rewards which another world

Final reward.

will unfold to him,—and thus be encouraged to toil on in faithfulness and in hope,—till, having finished his course, and being gathered to the home of the righteous, he shall meet multitudes instructed by his wise precept, and profited by his pure example, who "shall rise up and call him blessed."

CHAPTER XVII.

NOTES ON THE TEACHER'S AUTHORITY AND RIGHTS.*

TEACHERS are peculiarly exposed to criticism, censure, and to the annoyances and dangers of legal persecution. The relations of the teacher to school officers, pupils, parents, and the general public are so many, so delicate, so poorly defined, and so little understood, that danger from these sources is always imminent; and it should be a matter of first concern, for one so situated, to have some tolerably definite knowledge of his legal rights. What follows is a mere summary; but the references will enable any one to supplement this outline almost at will.

In public school administration, the downward distribution of rights, prerogatives, and duties is made as follows: By the election of the board of

---

* The references are to the following works by number and page:
1. The Lawyer in the School-room. By M. McN. Walsh. New York: 1867.
2. Common School Law. By C. W. Bardeen. Syracuse: 1878.
3. A Treatise on the Law of Public Schools. By Finley Burke. New York: 1880.
4. Recent School Law Decisions. Compiled by Lyndon A. Smith. Washington: 1883.
5. The Power and Authority of School Officers and Teachers. New York: 1885.

trustees or school committee, there passes from the hands of the people that part of their sovereign power which relates to the management of the school and its resources; and the power thus transferred to such officers can not be recalled at will, nor can the people interfere with their agents save in cases of gross maladministration, which would justify impeachment. In case of dissatisfaction, the people have their remedy in the opportunity for better selections when terms of office are about to expire.

The board of trustees may delegate certain duties to a superintendent or principal, and by this act they invest him with certain rights and prerogatives; and when this transfer has been made it is no more subject to recall than in the case just stated. Within his province the superintendent has just the same immunity from interference as the board has within its province.

In his turn, the superintendent delegates certain duties to his subordinates, and so invests them with certain rights and prerogatives; and within their province teachers should be as free from interference as their superior is in his.

A clear definition of these respective spheres of duty would relieve public school administration of many of its difficulties, and at the same time would promote a manly independence among teachers. It is a good thing to be charged with responsibilities, and at the same time allowed all proper freedom of action in working out required results. Noble natures are made better and stronger by being trusted. Without attempting an exact definition of the prerogatives of board, superintendent, and teacher, the following statements will indicate where the lines should be drawn.

Prerogatives of the board. The entire material support of the school; the employment of teachers; the adoption of courses of study; the selection of text-books; the making of general rules and regulations.

Prerogatives of the superintendent. The classification of pupils; general methods of instruction and government; the execution of the general rules of the board; the movements of pupils within the building and on the grounds; examinations and promotions.

Prerogatives of the teacher. The arrangement of the time-table; the seating of the pupils; the movements of pupils within the room; mode of recitation; methods of instruction and government within the general limits prescribed above. Where there is no superintendent or principal, the teacher's prerogatives will be considerably enlarged; and in isolated schools, as in the country, a wider jurisdiction should be allowed in the way of authority.

While the selection of subordinate teachers and of text-books is nominally a prerogative of the board, it should always be based on the judgment of the superintendent or principal; for the hearty co-operation of teachers can scarcely be secured unless they are conscious that their election and retention are somewhat dependent on the approval of their superior; and the relative merits of text-books can best be determined by those whose duties have given them special competence in such matters.

The State, as the patron of the public schools, may make certain studies compulsory; but beyond this, the board must prescribe what branches are to be taught. The teacher has no legal right whatever to introduce a study or a text-book on his own motion (**5**: 24, 33; **3**: 108, 111; **2**: 41).

It appears from recent decisions, that while the board may determine what subjects shall be taught, it may not compel pupils to pursue all the studies in the course; but must make exceptions on the demands of parents (**5**: 34, 41, 46; **3**: 112, 113; **2**: 42; **4**: 65, 78). If parents were generally to act in accord with these decisions it would be very difficult, if not impossible, to maintain a graded course of instruction; for in one case (**5**: 46) it would seem that a pupil who had not completed the studies of one grade might demand admission to a higher grade. Some check on these irregularities may be found in refusing graduation to those who have not completed the entire course of study.

The decisions of the courts uphold the right of boards to make regularity of attendance a

Suspension.—Expulsion.—Corporal punishment.

condition of membership, and to suspend pupils who have violated the attendance rule (**5**: 3, 10; **3**: 94; **4**: 74; **2**: 34). However, the law will not justify a teacher in barring the door against a tardy pupil, especially in inclement weather (**5**: 9). In case of absence, the teacher may require a written excuse from the parent (**5**: 22).

The power to expel lies with the board, and not with the teacher (**5**: 81, 84, 159; **2**: 56). The teacher may suspend pupils, even when there are no rules on the subject (**5**: 77; **3**: 117; **4**: 76).

The law will sustain the teacher in inflicting corporal punishment, provided it be reasonable and for sufficient cause (**1**: 71; **2**: 74; **3**: 119; **4**: 77; **5**: 105, 113, 114). The reasonable assumption is, that in respect of restraint and correction, the teacher is *in loco parentis*, and may exercise that degree of force that would be justifiable in a parent (**1**: 72, 73, 74, 109; **2**: 84; **3**: 119, 123; **4**: 77; **5**: 111).

The law regards the pupil as under the jurisdiction of his teacher, from the time he leaves his home till he returns there; and the pupil may be punished for offenses committed on his way to school and from school, if such offenses tend to injure the school, or bring the teacher or his authority into disrespect (**1**: 98, 110; **2**: 63; **3**: 129; **5**: 96). A pupil may be punished, even for offenses that he commits *at home*, if thereby the teacher suffers contempt (**3**: 129; **5**: 96).

Pupils over twenty-one years of age have no exemption from the rules of the school (5: 133; 3: 130). A pupil may be detained after school hours for discipline, or for learning a lesson (2: 72).

In general, the law leaves the question of religious exercise to the discretion of the board (3: 102; 2: 50; 1: Chapters II. and III.; 5: 68).

In all cases it is prudent for the teacher to have a written contract, in which should be specified the duration of the term of service, the time of beginning, the vacations and holidays that may be allowed, the length of the school month, and the amount and manner of payment (2: Part II.; 3: Chapter VIII.). Before a teacher can make a valid contract, he must have a license (3: 70). The teacher can collect pay for time lost while the school was closed by the board on account of an epidemic (3: 82).

What is known as "janitor's work," *i. e.*, sweeping, building fires, etc., can not be exacted of the teacher, unless there is an express agreement to this effect in the contract. It is the duty of the board to make provision for things of this kind, and the amount paid for such work can not be deducted from the teacher's wages. Very often such work is done by the teacher and older pupils, and this is well, where it is done voluntarily; but such service can not be *required* (2: 25). It would be unwise for a teacher at all times to insist on what he knows to be his rights; it is

The laws favor the teacher.

sometimes prudent to hold these in abeyance. There is sometimes a proneness, especially in the smaller communities, for those who are in authority to magnify their office unduly, and so to put a narrow construction on the jurisdiction of the teacher. The rule of safety is to keep clearly within the sphere of one's rights. In case these rights are assailed, it is both a public as well as a private duty to defend them. The law recognizes the difficulties incident to the teacher's office, and the necessity of upholding his authority; and the courts are ever disposed to put a generous construction on his acts and motives when engaged in the defense of decency and good order.

INDEX.

Abbott, Jacob, 188, 330; on "first day", 267.
Ability, 324.
Accuracy, 150, 366, 367, 391.
Acquisition, 180, 182.
Adaptation, 343, 386.
Addition, 92.
Additions to Text, 5, 6.
Admonition, 259.
Advancement, 176.
Affection, 194, 257, 395; freezing, 229.
Agnew, Professor, 395.
Agriculture, 81.
Aid, Mutual, 333-343.
Aim of education, 100-102, 184, 340.
Air, 306, 309.
Albany Normal School, 4, 6, 15, 16.
Alchohol, Physiological effects of, 83.
Algebra, 79.
Alphabet, 73.
Alternations, 275, 278.
Ambition, 159.
Analysis, 75.
Anger, 187, 250, 252.
Animation, 145.
Answers, 124, 125, 141.
Approbation, 175, 176, 194.
Aptness, 105, 137, 138, 380.
Aristocracy, 192, 266, 345, 346.
Aristotle, Science of Government, 86.
Arithmetic, 77, 78, 275; Colburn's Intellectual, 39; Mental, 39, 77; Written, 41.
Arnold, Matthew, 397.
Arrangements of schools, 262-295.

Art, 104; of illustration, 371-376; of teaching, 4, 22, 325, 327, 392.
Ascham, Roger, 396.
Assistant, 275.
Assumption, 188, 189, 341.
Astronomy, 88, 331, 357.
Attainments, 22, 71, 72, 73, 88, 103, 323, 340.
Attendance, Regularity of, 408, 409.
Attention, 119, 123, 127, 137, 138, 143, 146, 153.
Auburn Prison, 54-57.
Authority, 187, 188, 216, 217, 236, 237, 243, 405-411.

Baby-talk, 357.
Bacon, Francis, 21, 323.
Bain, Alexander, 135, 185, 330; on Text-books, 136.
Bardeen, C. W., 405.
Barnard, Henry, 11; Journal of Education, 11, 27.
Bartlett pear, 32.
Bathing, 61.
Belles-lettres, 90.
Bible, 50, 52, 178, 207, 249; study of, 355, 380; a means of torture, 223, 224, 355.
Blackguardism, 222.
Black marks, 209.
Blind, 181.
Boasting, 352.
Body, 396; punishment through, 218, 219, 234-249.
Book-keeping, 84, 85.
Books, Care of, 364; helps, 44, 45, 146; list of, 6, 330; use of, 40, 44, 135, 136.

INDEX.   413

Boorishness, 67.
Botany, 83, 331, 357.
Branch of study, 360.
Bronchitis, 317, 318.
Brougham, Lord, 96, 330, 402.
Burke, Finley, 330, 405, 408, 409, 410.
Business in school hours, 349, 350.

CALLING OF THE TEACHER, 319-343, 391, 394, 395, 396; honorable, 397.
Care of health, 304-318.
Care of school-room, 363, 410.
Carlyle, Thomas, 89, 370.
Catholicity, 52, 235, 236, 256, 260, 326.
Censure, 260.
Chagrin, 33, 229, 353, 370.
Change, 339; of program, 276; of work, 329.
Character, 60, 69, 95, 99, 177, 179, 260, 344, 345, 367.
Chart, Normal, 74.
Chastisement, 234, 249, 260.
Cheerfulness, 314, 315, 367-370.
Chemistry, 81, 331, 357.
Child, Capacity of, 27, 96, 97, 102, 180, 181; choice of studies, 346-348; danger of misguidance, 26, 94, 95, 106, 263, 347, 366; deformity of, 190; emulation in, 158; growth of, 180, 181, 393; health of, 36, 98, 180; home of, 238, 239; imitation of, 145; intellectual development of, 38, 95, 393; moral training of, 46, 96, 179, 217, 238, 395; neglect of, 34; obedience of, 181, 362; qualities in, 193, 194, 353.
Choice of studies, 347, 348.
Christianity, 51, 161, 176, 177, 396.
Classes, 278.
Classification, 271, 272, 273, 407; difficulty of, 276.
Cleanliness, 61, 62, 310.
Clock, 274.
Coarseness, 64, 145, 198, 222, 320.

Colburn, Warren, 309.
Colburn's Intellectual Arithmetic, 39, 77.
Comenius, S. S. Laurie's, 330.
"Comforter," The, 316.
Commonplace-book, 142, 143, 331, 332.
Common School Law, Bardeen's, 405, 408, 409, 410.
Comparisons, Invidious, 352, 353.
Compayre, G., 330.
Competence, 324, 325.
Competitors, 169, 170, 171, 172, 324, 325.
Composition, 41, 277, 332, 336.
Concert recitation, 151, 356.
Conduct, 260.
Conducting recitations, 137-153.
Confession, 368.
Confidence, 200; loss of, 227.
Confinement, 231, 232, 245, 246; of children, 286; futility of, 246.
Confucius, 397.
Confusion illustrated, 280-283.
Conscience, 47, 48, 97, 177, 178, 194, 229, 257, 368; a law, 203; a reward, 174, 391.
Consciousness of success, 391, 392, 393, 395.
Conservatism, 20, 321.
Contract, 410.
Contradictories, 157, 159, 160, 211, 213, 223, 235, 236, 260, 322, 373, 374.
Conversion, Intellectual, 341.
Convicts, Appearance of, 55, 56.
Corn, an object lesson, 119-125.
Corporal punishment, 235-240, 409; its abolition ideal, 241; limitations, 249-261, 409; Horace Mann on the necessity of, 237-241.
Countenance, 367-371.
Course of study, 330, 331, 348, 407, 408.
Courtesy, 64, 67, 198, 199.
Cousin, Victor, 96, 330.
Cramming, 46, 287, 290, 294.
Credits, 209.
Crime, 55.

Cruelty, 223, 224.
Culture, 23, 88, 89, 229, 325-333.
Curiosity, 180, 182, 183.
Cuvier, 357.
Cyclopædia of Education, Kiddle and Schem's, 330.

DAY-DREAMS OF A SCHOOL-MASTER, Thompson's, 330.
Deaf, 181.
Decimal notation, 148.
Decision, 194.
Declamation, 277.
Defining, 39.
Delay in punishment, 252.
Deliberation, 252, 253.
De Sacy, General Grammar, 79.
Description, 41.
Desires, 183; proper, 175-185.
Desks, 364.
Details of teaching, 4.
Detention, 410.
Development, 96, 361, 396; of the whole man, 98, 396.
Dictionnaire de Pedagogie, 361.
Diet, 305, 311, 312, 313.
Direction of pupils' study, 346, 347.
Disciplinary punishment, 253, 260.
Discipline, 97, 210, 395, 410.
Discovery, 116, 121, 130, 135, 183, 330.
Discretion, 203, 253.
Dismissing, 68, 383, 384.
Disrespect, 409.
District, Factions in, 241; state of, 205.
Divinity, 27.
Doing, 22; after knowing, 92, 119.
Do right, 177, 178, 202, 205, 229, 259, 323.
Drawing, 86, 274.
Drawing-out process, 109-114, 134.
Dress, 62, 306, 314, 345.
Drink, 313.
Driving, 308.
Dullness, 353.
Duty, 323.

EAR, 181, 219, 220, 221.
Education, 91, 100, 102, 330; aim of, 100-102, 184, 340; is development, 96, 98; discipline, 97, 184; history of, 19; not knowledge of facts, 97, liberal, 103; a life-work, 89; limitations of, 102; necessity of, 34; phases 22, 98, 102; professional, 21, 89, 93, 94, 104, 321, 330; right views of, 91-104.
Education, Spencer's, 330.
Educational epidemic, 361.
Educational library, 330.
Educational millennium, 321.
Education and School, Thring's, 330.
Education as a Science, Bain's, 330.
Effort, 169, 170, 171, 172.
Elementary sounds, 73, 74.
Elements of education, 38, 347, 348.
Elm, 126-129.
Elocution, 39.
Emerson, George B., 93, 94, 96, 305, 330.
Emile, Rousseau's, 330.
Employment, 200; of teachers, 320, 407.
Emulation, 155-162; in a good sense, 157-159; in a bad sense, 158, 159, 160.
Encouragements, 323, 324, 339, 340, 390, 401, 402.
Ends, 105, 258, 306, 386; of education, 5, 97, 100.
English grammar, 42, 79; bigotry in the study of, 79.
Enthusiasm, 138, 140, 143.
Envy, 158, 162, 165, 353.
Epidemic, 410.
Epping, 11.
Errors, 265, 266, 267, 268, 335, 337, 343, 366; in education, 99, 347.
Essays on Educational Reformers, Quick's, 330.
Ethics, 20, 84, 178, 179; professional, 333-343.
Evasion, 149.
Evolution, 102, 360, 361.

INDEX. 415

Examinations, 290-295, 407; objections to, 291; profitable, 294, 295.
Example, 47, 64, 66, 326; evil, 49; lost, 173.
Excitement, 145; artificial, 154, 182, 184; nervous, 36, 37, 219, 310.
Exciting interest in study, 154–185.
Exclusiveness, 334.
Excuses from parents, 409; to visitors, 350.
Exemplary punishment, 253, 260.
Exercises, 36, 305, 306; general, 118, 206; time for, 308, 309, 328.
Exercises, Religious, 410.
Exhibitions, 292, 294, 341, 342.
Expedients, 377.
Expenses, 389.
Experience, 21, 143, 255, 342.
Experiments, 22; upon children, 156, 163, 389, 390.
Explanations, 147; to parents, 299, 300.
Expulsion, 247; last resort, 259; 260; objection to, 247, 248; power of, 409.
"Extraordinary" to be avoided, 342.
Eye, 37, 38, 181; care of, 38.

Facts, 97; not fancy, 341.
Failure, 288; of teachers, 335.
Faith, 381, 382.
Family, The, 260, 315.
Fat, 313.
Favorite branch, 360.
Fear, 217, 259, 378, 379.
Feet, 314.
Few, The, 166, 167, 266.
Firmness, 194.
First-day, 263, 264, 267.
First impressions, 197, 198, 262, 268, 344.
Fitch, J. G., 330.
Fitness, grades of, 20, 325; for teaching, 19-24, 105, 138, 325.
Food, 306, 311, 312, 313; quantity of, 312.
Force, 215, 243, 244, 245, 409.

Form of thought, 39.
Fox, Mr., 98.
Francke, A. H., 397.
Franklin, Dr., 200; on excuses, 350.
Frankness, 367; to parents, 301. 302.
Friends, Personal, 265, 266, 267, 300, 301, 315, 339, 361, 362.
Friendship, 335.
Frowns, 368.
Fruit, 313.

Gardening, 307.
General Grammar, 79.
Genius, 171.
Geography, 40, 76, 271; anecdote in, 76; purpose of, 40.
Geology, 83, 331.
Geometry, 80.
Gifts, 138, 139, 172.
God, 27, 47, 50, 51, 52, 179, 370, 385; approval of, 29, 50, 177, 343, 379, 401, 402; kingdom of, 159, 179, 395, 396; our Protector, 380, 381, 382, 383; punishment from, 218, 219; rewards, 172, 179, 380, 382; teacher's need of, 53, 58, 59; wisdom of, 183, 217, 359, 379.
Goldsmith, Oliver, 222.
Government, 22, 191, 268, 407; equality in, 192, 193; a means, 210; of school, 186-261, 336, 340, 407; uniformity in, 192.
Graduation, 408.
Grammar, 41, 42, 43, 79, 144.
Great Teacher, The, 401.
Greek, 75.
Growth, 180, 326, 327, 329, 360, 390-394, 396.

Habits, Mechanical, 45; of study, 69, 146; of teacher, 60-70.
Hall, S. R., 147.
Hampton Academy, 11.
Head, 220, 253.
Health, Bodily, 36, 81, 82, 304, 305-318.
Heaven, 396, 401, 403.
Helping pupils, 114.
Higher branches, 360.

Hissing, 227, 228.
Histoire de la Pedagogie, Compayre's, 330.
History, 41, 76, 90; drawing out, 110, 111; of education, 19, 20, 23, 90; purpose of, 41.
Hitchcock, President, 307.
Hobbes, Thomas, 135.
"Hobbies" in teaching, 355, 356; of 1829 to 1831, 358, 359; cause of, 361.
"Holding a nail," 225.
Home, 315, 398, 399.
Home Education, Taylor's, 330.
Honesty, 54, 300, 341; in examinations, 293, 368.
Honor, 366.
Hope, 53, 54; disappointed, 33.
Household Education, Miss Martineau's, 330.
Howard, R. S., 13, 210.
Humiliation, 232, 366.
Hypocrisy, 232, 292, 293, 294, 300, 301, 342, 352, 363, 365.

IDEAL, 70, 91, 92, 95, 100, 101, 103, 104, 157, 184.
Ideas, 39; in child, 180, 181.
Ignorance, Inexcusable, 28.
Illustration, 76, 86, 329, 335, 371; of assumption, 189; the Auburn prison, 54; of immature choice of studies, 347; decimal notation, 148; of lack of discretion, 203, 204; drawing-out process, 109-114; of perfection in education, 100, 101; of relative and absolute in education, 102, 103; of effect of ridicule, 228, 229; of excuses to visitors, 350, 351; of lack of firmness, "the unjust judge," 195, 196; of parental gratitude, 400; of ignorance in science of government, 85; of interruption in district school, 280-282; that judges disagree, 168; the neglected pear-tree, 30-34; of "Order there!" and "teaching," 211-214; of lack of plan, 269, 270; of reformation, 365; of religious training, 377-387;

of scolding, 221; sculptor and spectator, 91, 92, 93; of self-control, 354; of lack of skill; 372-375; waking-up process, 117-129.
Imitation, 342, 343.
Immortality, 52, 396.
Impartiality, 193.
Impatience, 205, 221, 322, 392.
Impression, 197, 268, 365, 386.
Improvement, 143, 264, 270, 323, 325-333, 336, 337, 392, 403.
Impulse, 6.
Incentives, 155, 163, 167; proper, 175, 182.
Indifference, 53, 117, 141, 287; from the prize system, 165.
Inductions, 255.
Industry, 54, 210, 331.
Information, 326.
Injustice, 190, 219, 345, 388, 389.
In loco parentis, 217, 409.
Inquiry, 122, 265, 299, 300; time for, 264.
Institutes, Teachers', 16, 337, 338; benefit from, 340-343; definition of, 340; perversion of, 338.
Instruction, 20, 22, 96, 102, 182, 210, 258.
Instrument, 103, 104; in punishment, 253.
Intellectual growth, 390, 391.
Interest, 154-185.
Intermission, Duration of, 284, 285; hour for, 285; for each sex, 284.
Interruptions, 272, 279-283.
Intuition, 106, 138.

JANITOR'S WORK, 410.
Jokes, 222, 223.
Journal of Education, 11, 27.
Judges, 168; ignorant of conditions, 169, 345; ignorant of improper means employed, 170.
Judgment, 345, 370; of principal, 407.
Jug, Mind not a, 108.
Jurisdiction of teacher, 409.
Justice, 47, 109, 171, 187, 191, 192, 200, 203, 261.

INDEX. 417

KIDDLE, H., 330.
Knowing, 22; before doing, 91, 92, 93.
Knowledge, 102, 135, 181, 323, 324, 326, 395; certain, 362; desire for, 181, 183; not education, 97; not an end, 97; self, 391; important step to, 53, 54; unsafe, 95.

LALOR, 330.
Lancaster, his motto, 282.
Landon, Mr., 330.
Language, 64, 135, 144, 147, 180; how to study, 42, 43.
Language lessons, 42, 43.
Latin, 75.
Laughing, 223, 227.
Laurie, Simon S., 330.
Law, 20, 201, 203, 259; of conscience, 203; of physical health, 37, 82; of mind, 83.
Law of Public Schools, Burke's, 330, 405, 408, 409, 410.
Lawyer, 26.
Lawyer in the School-room, Walsh's, 405, 409.
Leading questions, 109, 134.
Lecturers, 338.
Lectures, 88, 107, 134, 340, 358, 359.
Lectures, Mann's, 330.
Lectures of the American Institute, 330.
Lectures on Teaching, Fitch's, 330.
Legal rights, 405.
Leonard and Gertrude, Pestalozzi's, 330.
Lessons, 274, 286-288, 410.
Letters, Silent, 73, 74.
Levana, Richter's, 261, 330.
Levity, 187.
Library, Teacher's, 330.
License to teach, 20, 410.
Life, Practical, 177; professional, 6, 332, 333; sedentary, 312; regular, 328.
Light, 309, 310.
Limitation of topics taught, 349.
Limitations and suggestions on corporal punishment, 241-261.
Lincoln, D. F., 37, 330.

Literary qualifications of the teacher, 71-90.
Literature, 77, 90; educational, 5, 330; purpose of, 41.
"Living by wits," 390.
Locke, John, 96, 330.
Logic, 84.
Love, 188, 194, 198, 227, 257; of scholars, 362, 392.
"Lull in the storm," 383.
Luther, Martin, 88, 207.

MAN, an instrument, 102, 103; prize, 166; strong, 167.
Management of school, 258, 340.
Mann, Horace, 13, 15, 72, 96, 145, 181, 330; on expulsion, 248; on quackery, 82; on corporal punishment, 237-241; on reading, 74, 75.
Manners, 66, 346, 365; of teacher, 60, 65, 145, 187, 188.
Many, The, 167, 266, 345, 346.
Map-drawing, 76.
Maps, 40.
Martineau, Miss, 330.
Mathematics, 80, 331; necessity of review in, 289.
Meanness, 266, 345, 351, 352.
Means, 105, 258, 386; of education, 96, 97, 98; improper, 170, 171; of moral growth, 391; to secure order, 197-215; of self-control, 370, 371, 391.
Meeting of teachers, 336, 337.
Memory, 44, 97, 99, 141, 167, 289, 332, 395; in examination, 291.
Mental arithmetic, 39, 40, 77, 271.
Methods, 19, 21, 23, 105-136, 139, 335, 336, 340, 373, 407; patent, 359.
Mill, J. S., 135.
Milton, John, 96, 397.
Mind, 102, 180; reached through the body, 218; development of, 102, 139, 140, 180; dignity of, 27, 50, 94, 179, 181, 395, 396; not like a jug, 108; crime of misleading, 29, 49, 50, 95, 100, 109, 182, 263.
Minimum of punishment, 258.

Miscellaneous suggestions, 344–387.
Misjudgment, 99, 106, 169, 170, 263.
Models, use of, 277; servile imitation of, 342.
Modern culture *trivium*, 41, 77.
Modes of teaching, 105-136.
Modesty, 302, 303, 345.
Morality, 33, 46, 48, 95, 97, 98, 175, 180; how developed, 48, 97, 365, 376-381, 386, 391, 393.
Moral suasion, 236.
Moroseness, 187, 315, 368, 370.
Mothers first, 300, 398, 399.
Motives, 154, 167, 172, 173, 178, 179, 180, 194, 293, 294, 393, 411; attractive, 259; classes of, 258, 259; in punishment, 216, 227, 257; repulsive, 259; of teaching, 25, 26, 95, 394-397.
Music, 86, 206, 207, 316.
Mutual aid, 333-343.
Myopia, 37, 38.

Nails, 62.
Napoleon, 159.
Natural Philosophy, 80, 290, 371-375.
Neatness, 61, 314, 363, 364.
Neck, 316, 317, 318.
Neglected pear-tree, 30.
Newbury, 12.
Newburyport, 15, 17.
Nibbling, Mental, 276.
Normal schools, 14, 16, 20, 321, 340.
Number, 39.
Nurslings, 106, 107, 112, 113, 114.

Obedience, 181, 202, 259, 362.
Object of the Author, 3, 4; of the Reviser, 5, 6; unworthy, 164.
Objections to prizes, 164-174.
Object lessons, 46, 119-129, 130.
Obligation, 177, 178.
Observation, 45, 122, 130, 131.
Offenses at home, 409.
Olmsted, Professor, 367.
Oral mania, 357, 358.

Oral teaching, 107, 134, 135, 356, 357.
Order, 63, 186, 197, 211, 213, 363, 384; of nature, 39, 139; of recitation, 153; of study, 38, 43.
Organization, 22, 258, 265, 405.
Orthography, 73.

Page, David Perkins, 4, 5, 6; age, 18; biographical sketch, 11-18; birth, 11; character, 18; death, 17; education, 12; experience, 344; lecturer, 13; methods, 13, 14; Principal of Normal School, 15; private school, 12; qualifications of, 15, 344.
Pain, Bodily, 218.
Parents, 217, 398, 405; acquaintance with, 265, 266, 297; benefited, 131, 132; not the teacher's confessional, 298; mutual duties with, 13, 208, 354; folly of, 246, 354; gratitude of, 399, 400; moral influence of, 47, 52, 242; teacher's relation to, 296-303; responsibility of, 35, 217, 238.
Partiality, 193, 360.
Passion, 187, 250, 370.
Patience, 279, 353, 354, 368.
Paul, The Apostle, 403.
Pay, 71, 72, 319, 320, 388, 402; in epidemic, 410; how to increase, 322, 323.
Pear-tree, 30.
Perfect manhood, 396.
Personal friends, 266, 268; of parents, 298, 299.
Personal habits of the teacher, 60-70.
Pestalozzi, 330, 397.
Philosophizing, 196.
Philosophy, 106, 138; the highest, 5, 24; of language, 79.
Phraseology, 43, 44.
Physician, 26, 28, 156, 347.
Physics, 80, 290; a lesson in, 371-375.
Physiology, 20, 81, 223, 224, 290.
Plagiarism, 366.
Plan, 201, 262, 264, 299, 331; of day's work, 269-278.

INDEX. 419

Plants, 125-129.
Plato, of culture, 23.
Pleasure, 181, 182; in learning, 184.
Politeness, 64, 65; value of, 67.
Potter, Dr., 14, 15, 96, 207, 330.
Pouring-in process, 107-109, 134, 357, 358.
Power and Authority of School Officers and Teachers, 405, 408, 409, 410.
Practice, 4, 22, 66, 177, 324, 325, 332, 338, 361; language lessons, 42; in morals, 48, 326.
Precept, 47, 64.
Precocity, 37.
Predecessor, 265, 266, 351.
Preface, Author's, 3, 4; Editor's 5, 6,
Prejudice, 344, 345.
Preparation, 22, 23, 28, 140, 262, 324; of lesson, 40, 140, 141, 142; neglect of, 27, 29, 141.
Prerogatives, 405, 406; of school board, 407; of superintendent, 407; of teacher, 407.
Press, The, 337.
Primary Instruction, Laurie's, 330.
Principle, 20, 44, 78, 139, 250, 340, 393; application of, 287, 393; caution in adopting, 255; of emulation, 158, 159, 161; moral, 47, 49, 177, 197.
Privileges, Loss of, 231, 259.
Prizes, 162-175, 179; difficulties of award, 168; improper motives, 173; objections to, 164, 165; reward what? 168.
Problem of the school, 5.
Profanity, 64.
Profession, The teacher's, 4, 22, 26, 71, 90 93, 319-343, 397, 398; dignity of, 403; protection of, 325; a stepping-stone, 28.
Professional feeling, 339.
Professional reading, 90, 329-331.
Proficiency, 291, 391.
Program of recitation and study, 273; remarks on, 274-278.

Promotions, 407, 408.
Promptness, 150.
Propagation, 129.
Proportion, 144.
Prosecution, Legal, 405-411.
Protection of the public, 325.
Prudence, 261.
Pruning, 31.
Psychology, 20, 83, 138, 139, 140.
Public examinations, 290-295; encourage deception, 292.
Public opinion, 251, 259, 322, 323; attempt to force, 256.
Punctuality, 68, 121, 267, 328.
Punishment, 203, 215, 216-261, 409; advertising, 244; classes of, 218; corporal, 235-249, 409; definition of, 216; improper, 219-230; in presence of the school, 251; proper, 230-235; right of, 218, 409.
Pupils, 399, 400, 405; bright, 275; detention of, 410; examination of, 291; laughing at "jokes," 223; regularity of, 409; self-respect of, 287, 288; studies of, 408; success of, 394; tardy, 410; treatment of, 189, 190; vicious, 239, 240, 247, 248.

Quacks, 22, 82, 321.
Qualifications, 95, 264; literary, 71-90.
Questioning, 120-129, 141, 153.
Questions, 44, 109, 144.
Quick, R. H., 330.

Ratio, 144.
Reading, 38, 39, 74, 275, 332; not elocution, 39, 74, 75; professional, 329-331.
Reading circles, 90.
Reasons, 139; in arithmetic, 77.
Recess, 272, 283-286.
Recipient, Passive, 108, 126, 128, 130.
Recitation, 44, 45, 137-153, 166, 271, 274, 407; length of, 277; time of, 278.
Recreation, 328, 329.
Reformation, 365, 366.
Register of credits, 200.

Religion, 51, 177, 178.
Religious exercises, 410.
Religious training, 50, 378.
Remembrance of pupils, 399.
Reproof, 230, 251, 259, 365, 366.
"Resolutions," 255, 338, 404.
Respect, 198, 259, 367.
Responsibility, 25, 34, 46; of the teacher, 30-59, 83, 167, 177, 178, 263, 390.
Restraint, 231.
Revenge, 216.
Reviews, 277, 288-290; frequency of, 289.
Rewards, 164; of God, 172, 403, 404; not necessary, 174; of teacher, 320, 388-404.
Rhetoric, 84.
Richter, J. P., 104, 260, 330.
Ridicule, 226, 227, 228.
Riding, Horseback, 307.
Righteousness, 177, 178, 205.
Right modes of teaching, 105-136.
Right to punish, 218.
Rights, 405-411.
Rights of property, 364.
Right views of education, 91-104.
Rivalry, 165.
Rod, The, 234, 235; a last resort, 244, 249, 250, 254; substitutes for, 245-248.
Roguery, 268.
Rousseau, J. J., 330.
Routine, 146.
Rowing, 308.
Rudeness, 67.
Rules, 23, 78, 201-205, 407; for teaching, 39; for constructing time-table, 277, 278.

SAWING WOOD, 308.
Schem, A. J., 330.
Scholars, 19, 46, 99; the best, 166, 167; classification of, 271; morals of, 48; politeness of, 65; recitations of, 287.
Scholarship, 19, 20, 98, 99, 287, 288; liberal, 21, 23, 138, 325, 340.
School, The Albany Normal, 4, 6; arrangements, 262-295; authority in, 236; dismissal of, 236;
government, 186-261; management, 258; model, 20; practice, 20; problem of, 5; punishment, 216-261; not a university, 340.
School and Industrial Hygiene, Lincoln's, 37, 330.
School Law Decisions, Smith's, 405, 408, 409.
School Management, Landon's, 330.
School officers, 320, 322, 323, 405, 406.
School-room, 327, 363; annoyances in, 279, 280, 281, 282; attractive, 46; hygiene of, 36, 37, 38; in institutes, 338.
School and School-master, Potter and Emerson's, 330.
Science, 349; of arithmetic, 78; of education, 22, 83, 100; of government, 85; of obedience, 202; of teaching, 4, 29, 90, 140, 156, 214, 325, 361.
Scientific baby-talk, 357.
Scolding, 221, 254.
Sectarianism, 51, 52.
Seeds, 125-129.
Self-control, 367-371, 378, 391, 392.
Self-government, 186, 187, 188, 189, 214, 250, 354, 368-370.
Self-improvement, 88, 89, 133, 143, 325-333, 391, 403.
Self-interest, 259.
Selfishness, 161, 191, 333, 334.
Self-reliance, 115, 116, 143, 151, 190, 191.
Self-righteousness, 229, 343, 367
Seneca, 397.
Shame, 217, 227, 229.
Silence, 214, 215.
Simultaneous recitation, 151, 152
Sincerity, 48.
Singing, 384, 385.
"Sitting on nothing," 225.
"Sitting on worse than nothing," 225.
Skating, 308.
Skepticism, 52.
Sketch, Biographical, 11-18.
Skill, 19, 29, 102, 103, 156, 324, 325.

INDEX. 421

Skimming, 287, 288.
Sleep, 306, 310, 313, 328.
Smiles, 222, 224, 346, 353, 367, 368, 399; a reward, 174, 371.
Smith, Lyndon A., 405.
Society, 315, 345.
Socrates, 397.
Solicitude, 32.
Sounds, 73.
Spelling, 39, 73.
Spencer, Herbert, 330, 361.
Spirit of the teacher, 25-29, 54, 70, 122, 266.
Stagnation, 320, 327, 329, 331.
State, The. 260, 406.
Stimulants, 183; abnormal, 182, 184; for a dull child, 353.
Studies, 21, 346, 347; compulsory, 408; sequence of, 22, 345, 346, 347; right to introduce, 408.
Study, 21, 88, 133, 141, 146, 201, 327, 331; agreeable, 185; collateral, 45, 69, 88, 89, 142, 307, 331; direction of, 346; interest in, 154-185; manner of, 43; order of, 38, 272; professional, 22, 69, 152, 327, 330; of school, 264.
Subject, Order of, 139, 140; study of, 44, 140, 146, 332, 348, 349.
Success, 171, 172.
Suggestions, Miscellaneous, 344-387.
Sums, 144.
Superintendent, 407.
Support of school, 407.
Surveying, 80.
Suspicion, 199.
Suspension, 409.
Symmetry, 184, 396.
System, 63, 262, 279, 282, 283, 328, 331.

Talent, 171, 292; how acquired, 139; condition of the highest, 26; in the teacher's profession, 319.
"Talk," 338.
Tasks, 233, 234.
Taylor, Isaac, 330.
Teacher, Accomplished, 138; attainments of, 22, 27, 72-87, 93, 138, 319, 336, 403; authority of, 405-411; benefited, 132, 133, 388-404; duty to community, 60, 93, 94, 208, 240, 323, 337; duty to pupils, 167, 189, 263, 350, 409; government in, 186, 240; health of, 304-318; honesty of, 293-295, 367; language of, 144; magnifying his profession, 398, 403; motives of, 26, 50, 94, 362, 390; of principle, 49, 197; pay of, 319-325, 388, 389, 390; purity of, 47; relation to his profession, 319-343, 362, 403; relation to parents, 296-303; relation to patrons, 208; responsibility of, 35-59, 83, 167, 177, 178, 263, 390; rights of, 405-411; social qualities of, 297, 315, 367; spirit of, 25, 145, 189, 208, 266, 333, 362; temptations of, 133, 327, 329, 333, 343, 350, 353, 370; time-table of, 277, 278, 407.
Teacher, The, 330.
Teachers' Associations, 13, 337.
Teachers' Meeting, 336.
Teaching, Art of, 4, 152, 392; Details of Teaching, 4; fitness for, 19, 25, 138, 191, 325; mechanical, 141; true medium of, 115, 116; modes of, 105-136; an occupation, 325; practical, 338, 344; a profession, 319-343; a science, 4, 20, 140; a secondary object, 28, 94, 320; works on, 330.
Teeth, 62.
Tests, 290-295; for reading, 39.
Text-books, 44, 117, 135, 136, 140, 407, 408; age for, 40; use of, 140, 141, 142.
Theology, 52; common ground of, 51.
Theory, 3, 4, 23, 66.
Theory and *Practice* of *Teaching*, 5, 18, 19, 71.
Theory and Practice of Teaching, Thring's, 330.
Thinking, 167, 289, 374.
Thompson, D'Arcy W., 330.
Thoroughness, 348, 391.

Thought, 102, 130, 230, 290, 332, 389; habits of, 102, 131, 392; not words, 44.
Thoughts on Education, Locke's, 330.
Threatening, 205, 221, 244.
Thring, E., 330.
Thunder-storm, its lesson, 377-382.
Time, 327, 328.
Tobacco, 63.
Topics, 146; of the day, 117; practical, 147.
Training, 103; mental, 38, 102, 103; moral, 46, 102, 179; physical, 36, 102, 103; religious, 50, 102, 103.
Training of Teachers, Laurie's, 330.
Translation of thought, 39.
Trigonometry, 86.
Truth, 48, 256, 257; how revealed, 45, 257.
Tyranny, 191.

UNIFORMITY, 192; of books, 278.
University, 20; study of education in, 20, 21.
Unusual occurrences, 376.
Usefulness, 177, 179, 394, 395.

VACATIONS, Mr. Page's, 16.
Vandalism, 363, 364, 365.
Vices, Inexcusable, 49, 320.
Victims of kindness, 108.
Victory, 371.
Views of education, 91-104.
Views of government, 191-193.
Views of the whole, 288, 289, 290.

Virgil, 190.
Visitation, Mutual, 334-336, 342.
Visits of patrons, 300, 335.
Vocal music, 86, 87, 206, 207, 385.
Vocation, of scholar, 341; of teacher, 391, 394, 395, 396, 397, 402.
Vulgarity, 64.

WAKING-UP PROCESS, 108, 117-129. 133, 134, 182, 205, 206.
Walking, 306.
Walsh, M. McN., 405.
Warren, Dr. J. C., 309.
Way, 104; of education, 5, 6; the more excellent, 114-117; mechanical, 44, 45.
Wayland, Dr., 96.
Webster, Dr., 158, 217.
Whipping, 235; thorough, 254.
Whittling, 365.
Wisdom, 326, 343.
Woodward, Dr., 82.
Word-analysis, 75.
Words, 38, 39, 135; without meaning, 44.
Worship, in prison, 56, 57.
Worth, 169-173.
Wright, Silas, 16.
Writer, 336.
Writing, 41, 76, 107, 271.
Written arithmetic, 41, 78.

YOUNG CHILDREN, 286.
Young, Col., 14, 15, 81.
Young, Dr., 335.
Youth, The dignity of, 29.

ZOOLOGY, 357.

Books for Teachers

FOR THE STUDY OF PEDAGOGY

Calkins's Manual of Object Teaching	$1.25
Hailmann's History of Pedagogy	.60
Hewett's Pedagogy for Young Teachers	.85
How to Teach (Kiddle, Harrison, and Calkins)	1.00
King's School Interests and Duties	1.00
Krüsi's Life and Work of Pestalozzi	1.20
Mann's School Recreations and Amusements	1.00
Page's Theory and Practice of Teaching	1.00
Palmer's Science of Education	1.00
Payne's School Supervision	1.00
Payne's Contributions to the Science of Education	1.25
Sheldon's Lessons on Objects	1.20
Shoup's History and Science of Education	1.00
Swett's Methods of Teaching	1.00
White's Elements of Pedagogy	1.00
White's School Management	1.00

FOR THE STUDY OF PSYCHOLOGY

Halleck's Psychology and Psychic Culture	1.25
Hewett's Psychology for Young Teachers	.85
Putnam's Elementary Psychology	.90
Roark's Psychology in Education	1.00

FOR THE TEACHER'S DESK

Schaeffer's Bible Readings for Schools	.35
Eclectic Manual of Methods	.60
Swett's Questions for Written Examination	.72
Appletons' How to Teach Writing	.50
Morris's Physical Education	1.00
Smart's Manual of School Gymnastics	.30
White's Oral Lessons in Number	.60
Dubbs's Arithmetical Problems. Teachers' Edition	1.00
Doerner's Treasury of General Knowledge. Part I.	.50
The Same. Part II.	.65
Webster's Academic Dictionary. New Edition.	1.50

Any of the above books sent, prepaid, on receipt of the price by the Publishers :

American Book Company

NEW YORK • CINCINNATI • CHICAGO

Practical Rhetoric

A Rational and Comprehensive Text-Book for the use of High Schools and Colleges. By JOHN DUNCAN QUACKENBOS, A.M., M.D., Emeritus Professor of Rhetoric in Columbia University.

Cloth, 12mo, 477 pages. Price, $1.00

THIS work differs materially from all other text-books of rhetoric both in plan and method of treatment. It first develops, in a perfectly natural manner, the laws and principles which underlie rhetorical art, and then shows their use and practical application in the different processes and kinds of composition. The book is clear, simple, and logical in its treatment, original in its departure from technical rules and traditions, copiously illustrated with examples, and calculated in every way to awaken interest and enthusiasm in the study. A large part of the book is devoted to instruction and practice in actual composition work in which the pupil is encouraged to follow and apply genuine laboratory methods.

The lessons are so arranged that the whole course, including the outside constructive work, may be satisfactorily completed in a single school year.

Copies of Quackenbos's Practical Rhetoric will be sent prepaid to any address, on receipt of the price, by the Publishers. Correspondence relating to terms for introduction is cordially invited.

American Book Company

New York   ♦   Cincinnati   ♦   Chicago

An Advanced English Grammar

FOR THE USE OF

HIGH SCHOOL, ACADEMY AND COLLEGE CLASSES

BY

W. M. BASKERVILL

Professor of the English Language and Literature in Vanderbilt University, Nashville, Tenn.

AND

J. W. SEWELL

Of the Fogg High School, Nashville, Tenn.

Cloth, 12mo, 349 pages . . 90 cents

This **new Grammar** is designed for advanced students who desire to extend their studies in English beyond the course ordinarily pursued in Common or **Grammar** Schools. In this work, grammar is treated as a science based on *facts and principles* derived from the actual use of the language and not from technical rules and traditions.

Its aim is to lead the pupil to deduce for himself grammatical rules from the best examples of construction and style to be found in English literature and to acquire skill in their use. For this purpose abundant and apposite quotations from standard authors are given to illustrate each grammatical relation and construction and to show the student that he is dealing with the *facts* of the language and not with the *theories* of the grammarians.

While the book represents original and advanced methods it is at the same time conservative in treatment, and aims to preserve what is good in the older methods.

Copies of Baskervill and Sewell's English Grammar will be sent prepaid to any address, on receipt of the price, by the Publishers:

American Book Company

New York   Cincinnati   Chicago

Psychology in Education

Roark's Psychology in Education

By RURIC N. ROARK, Dean of the Department of Pedagogy, Kentucky State College.

Cloth, 12mo, 312 pages $1.00

This new work is designed for use as a text-book in Secondary and Normal Schools, Teachers' Training Classes and Reading Circles. The general purpose of the book is to give teachers a logical and scientific basis for their daily work in the schoolroom. The teacher will gain from it knowledge for present needs, and stimulus and inspiration for further study of mind growth. While this is the special purpose of the book, it contains such a clear and accurate exposition of psychological facts and processes as to make it an interesting work for the general reader as well as for those who have to do with schools and education.

It is elementary in treatment, but every subject is presented in a most thorough, logical, and psychological manner. It makes a distinct departure from the methods heretofore in vogue in the treatment of Psychology and the application of its principles and processes to mind study and the philosophy of teaching. It is justly regarded as the most important contribution to pedagogical science and literature in recent years, and is the only work of its kind which brings the subject within the comprehension and practical application of teachers.

Copies of Roark's Psychology in Education will be sent prepaid to any address, on receipt of the price, by the Publishers:

American Book Company

New York • Cincinnati • Chicago

(38)

For Teachers and School Officers

King's School Interests and Duties

Developed from "Page's Mutual Duties of Parents and Teachers," from various Public Records and Documents, and from the Bulletins of the National Bureau of Education. By ROBERT M. KING.
Cloth, 12mo, 336 pages $1.00

This new work, original in its scope and plan, presents in one volume interesting and valuable expositions of the modern demands, best methods, and most important interests of our Public School Systems. Its central idea is to show the importance and value of co-operation in school work and the mutual duties of teachers, school officers, and parents. It also embodies synopses of the discussions on leading educational topics from the various fugitive reports and manuals issued, from time to time, by school officials and State Departments of Education. It will be found an invaluable manual and guide for school superintendents, officers, and patrons, and, indeed, for every one interested in educational work.

Mann's School Recreations and Amusements

By CHARLES W. MANN, A.M., Dean of the Chicago Academy. Cloth, 12mo, 352 pages . . . $1.00

This volume not only opens up a new field of much needed information and direction in the matter of physical training of pupils, but also furnishes suggestions for intellectual recreations which will greatly add to the interest and value of school work and lend a charm to school life in all its phases. Some of the subjects treated in this work are: Morning Exercises, Care and Equipment of Schoolrooms, Singing Games and Songs, Indoor Exercises and Outdoor Games, Experiments in Physics and Chemistry, Recreations in Latin, Outline for Reading Circles, etc.

Copies of the above books will be sent prepaid to any address, on receipt of the price, by the Publishers:

American Book Company

New York   •   Cincinnati   •   Chicago

Halleck's Psychology and Psychic Culture

By REUBEN POST HALLECK, M.A. (Yale)

Cloth, 12mo, 368 pages. Illustrated . . . . Price, $1.25

This new text-book in Psychology and Psychic Culture is suitable for use in High School, Academy and College classes, being simple and elementary enough for beginners and at the same time complete and comprehensive enough for advanced classes in the study. It is also well suited for private students and general readers, the subjects being treated in such an attractive manner and relieved by so many apt illustrations and examples as to fix the attention and deeply impress the mind.

The work includes a full statement and clear exposition of the coördinate branches of the study—physiological and introspective psychology. The physical basis of Psychology is fully recognized. Special attention is given to the cultivation of the mental faculties, making the work practically useful for self-improvement. The treatment throughout is singularly clear and plain and in harmony with its aims and purpose.

"Halleck's Psychology pleases me very much. It is short, clear, interesting, and full of common sense and originality of illustration. I can sincerely recommend it."
WILLIAM JAMES,
Professor of Psychology, Harvard University.

Copies of Halleck's Psychology will be sent prepaid to any address on receipt of the price by the Publishers:

American Book Company

New York • Cincinnati • Chicago

Handbook of Greek and Roman History

BY

GEORGES CASTEGNIER, B.S., B.L.

Flexible Cloth, 12mo, 110 pages. - Price, 50 cents

The purpose of this little handbook is to assist the student of Greek and Roman History in reviewing subjects already studied in the regular text-books and in preparing for examinations. It will also be found useful for general readers who wish to refresh their minds in regard to the leading persons and salient facts of ancient history.

It is in two parts, one devoted to Greek, and the other to Roman history. The names and titles have been selected with rare skill, and represent the whole range of classical history. They are arranged alphabetically, and are printed in full-face type, making them easy to find. The treatment of each is concise and gives just the information in regard to the important persons, places, and events of classical history which every scholar ought to know and remember, or have at ready command.

Its convenient form and systematic arrangement especially adapt it for use as an accessory and reference manual for students, or as a brief classical cyclopedia for general readers.

Copies of Castegnier's Handbook of Greek and Roman History will be sent prepaid to any address, on receipt of the price, by the Publishers:

American Book Company

New York • Cincinnati • Chicago

Fisher's Brief History of the Nations

AND OF THEIR PROGRESS IN CIVILIZATION

By GEORGE PARK FISHER, LL.D.
Professor in Yale University

Cloth, 12mo, 613 pages, with numerous Illustrations, Maps, Tables, and Reproductions of Bas-reliefs, Portraits, and Paintings. Price, $1.50

This is an entirely new work written expressly to meet the demand for a compact and acceptable text-book on General History for high schools, academies, and private schools. Some of the distinctive qualities which will commend this book to teachers and students are as follows:

It narrates in fresh, vigorous, and attractive style the most important facts of history in their due order and connection.

It explains the nature of historical evidence, and records only well established judgments respecting persons and events.

It delineates the progress of peoples and nations in civilization as well as the rise and succession of dynasties.

It connects, in a single chain of narration, events related to each other in the contemporary history of different nations and countries.

It gives special prominence to the history of the Mediæval and Modern Periods, — the eras of greatest import to modern students.

It is written from the standpoint of the present, and incorporates the latest discoveries of historical explorers and writers.

It is illustrated by numerous colored maps, genealogical tables, and artistic reproductions of architecture, sculpture, painting, and portraits of celebrated men, representing every period of the world's history.

Copies of Fisher's Brief History of the Nations will be sent prepaid to any address, on receipt of the price, by the Publishers:

American Book Company

New York • Cincinnati • Chicago

Eclectic English Classics

For School and Home Reading. Recommended for study and reading preparatory to admission to college. Uniform binding.

Arnold's (Matthew) Sohrab and Rustum	$0.20
Burke's Conciliation with the American Colonies	.20
Burns's Poems—Selections	.20
Byron's Poems—Selections	.25
Carlyle's Essay on Robert Burns	.20
Chaucer's Canterbury Tales—Prologue and Knighte's Tale	.25
Coleridge's Rime of the Ancient Mariner	.20
Defoe's History of the Plague in London	.40
DeQuincey's Revolt of the Tartars	.20
Dryden's Palamon and Arcite	.20
Emerson's American Scholar, Self-Reliance, and Compensation	.20
Franklin's Autobiography	.35
George Eliot's Silas Marner	.30
Goldsmith's Vicar of Wakefield	.35
Gray's Poems—Selections	.20
Irving's Sketch Book—Selections	.20
Tales of a Traveler	.50
Macaulay's Second Essay on Chatham	.20
Essay on Milton	.20
Essay on Addison	.20
Life of Samuel Johnson	.20
Milton's L'Allegro, Il Penseroso, Comus, and Lycidas	.20
Paradise Lost—Books I. and II.	.20
Pope's Homer's Iliad, Books I., VI., XXII. and XXIV.	.20
Rape of the Lock, and Essay on Man	.20
Scott's Ivanhoe	.50
Marmion	.40
Lady of the Lake	.30
The Abbot	.60
Woodstock	.60
Shakespeare's Julius Caesar	.20
Twelfth Night	.20
Merchant of Venice	.20
Midsummer-Night's Dream	.20
As You Like It	.20
Macbeth	.20
Hamlet	.25
Sir Roger de Coverley Papers (The Spectator)	.20
Southey's Life of Nelson	.40
Tennyson's Princess	.20
Webster's Bunker Hill Orations	.20
Wordsworth's Poems—Selections	.20

Copies sent, prepaid, to any address on receipt of the price.

American Book Company

NEW YORK   •   CINCINNATI   •   CHICAGO

An Introduction to the
Study of American Literature

BY

BRANDER MATTHEWS

Professor of Literature in Columbia University

Cloth, 12mo, 256 pages   -   -   -   Price, $1.00

A text-book of literature on an original plan, and conforming with the best methods of teaching.

Admirably designed to guide, to supplement, and to stimulate the student's reading of American authors.

Illustrated with a fine collection of facsimile manuscripts, portraits of authors, and views of their homes and birthplaces.

Bright, clear, and fascinating, it is itself a literary work of high rank.

The book consists mostly of delightfully readable and yet comprehensive little biographies of the fifteen greatest and most representative American writers. Each of the sketches contains a critical estimate of the author and his works, which is the more valuable coming, as it does, from one who is himself a master. The work is rounded out by four general chapters which take up other prominent authors and discuss the history and conditions of our literature as a whole; and there is at the end of the book a complete chronology of the best American literature from the beginning down to 1896.

Each of the fifteen biographical sketches is illustrated by a fine portrait of its subject and views of his birthplace or residence and in some cases of both. They are also accompanied by each author's facsimile manuscript covering one or two pages. The book contains excellent portraits of many other authors famous in American literature.

Copies of Brander Matthews' Introduction to the Study of American Literature will be sent prepaid to any address, on receipt of the price, by the Publishers:

American Book Company

New York   •   Cincinnati   •   Chicago

www.ingramcontent.com/pod-product-compliance
Lightning Source LLC
Chambersburg PA
CBHW051734300426
44115CB00007B/566